D0331386

The Literary History of Hamlet

The Literary History of Hamlet

The Early Tradition

by

Kemp Malone, Ph. D.
Assistant Professor of English in the University of Minnesota

HASKELL HOUSE
Publishers of Scholarly Books
NEW YORK
1964

published by

HASKELL HOUSE

Publishers of Scholarly Books

30 East 10th Street • New York, N. Y. 10003

Library of Congress Catalog Card Number: 65-15886

PRINTED IN UNITED STATES OF AMERICA

To

John Matthews Manly

Master and Friend

Preface.

The present work is an attempt to furnish a literary history of the hero Hamlet and the Hamlet saga. This history will be complete in three installments. The first of these treats of the origin of hero and tale and their development in early tradition. The second installment will deal with the later tradition and the period from Saxo to Shakspere; the third, with the post-Shaksperean period. The whole is designed to present the history of Hamlet in tradition, literature proper and criticism, from the earliest times to the present day.

Obviously the earliest period, the period to which the present installment is devoted, makes great difficulties for the historian. The facts definitely ascertainable are few in number and hard to put together. Our general knowledge of the period is meager. Our sources of information are often defective and untrustworthy. In sum, the difficulties are so formidable that the present writer seems to be the first to brave them! He therefore craves of the reader that indulgence which is always, and with justice, given to the pioneer and the pathfinder. And this all the more since he has felt it his duty to advance a clear-cut theory on every question at issue, or at any rate to give his opinion, even when the evidence available was too scanty to permit of well-fortified conclusions. A scientific theory is to be looked upon, not as a formulation of absolute truth, but as a working basis for further investigation. If the theory plausibly explains the known facts, even though these be few, it can be used as such a working basis. And in the absence of theory, of synthesis, of generalization, research has little value and leads nowhere. Of the numerous hypotheses brought forward in the following pages, then, even those that may seem little more than speculation will serve at least to raise definite issues, and to stimulate intelligent discussion, and in a pioneer treatise, at least, such hypotheses are in place and have a value of their own.

It follows that the present writer does not anticipate that his reconstruction of the period will stand for ever unaltered. Nevertheless, he believes that he has established his main thesis, and that the future definitive history of the period will differ from his own only in details. In any case, if his work proves a useful basis, on which future investigators may build, he will be content.

In conclusion, it is a pleasant duty to thank numerous friends and well-wishers: Professors A. S. Cook, C. N. Gould, G. L. Kittredge, F. Klaeber, J. M. Manly, J. B. Pike, F. N. Robinson, and J. D. Spaeth, who very kindly read and criticized various parts of the ms. in various stages of composition; the authorities of Princeton University, without whose generous financial support (during the school year 1920—21, when this book was written) and devotion to scholarship the writer would have been denied the leisure, the facilities and the atmosphere necessary to his undertaking; the general editor of the *Anglistische Forschungen,* who not only included this work in his series but also saw it through the press, since for reasons connected with the unsettled state of the times none of the proofs could be sent to America; Fräulein Else Hoops, who did most of the proof-reading; and, last but not least, the publishers, who in these troublous days had the idealism to undertake the publication of a work written primarily for learned circles.

Minneapolis, Nov. 1, 1922.

Kemp Malone.

Table of Contents.

Abbreviations.

A. = Amleth saga of Saxo.
AB. = Ambalessaga.
AfnF. = Arkiv för nordisk Filologi.
AS. = Arngrímr's synopsis of the Skjöldungasaga.
B. = Brjám tale.
Beowulf = Heyne-Schücking, 10th ed.
Björkman = Eigennamen im Beowulf, von Erik Björkman.
BR. = Bjarkarímur.
Chambers = Widsith, by R. W. Chambers.
DA. = Deutsche Altertumskunde, von Karl Müllenhoff.
Detlefsen = Entdeckung des germanischen Nordens, von D. Detlefsen.
Deutschbein = Studien zur Sagengeschichte Englands, von M. Deutschbein.
DH. = Danmarks Heltedigtning, af Axel Olrik.
EETS. = Early English Text Society.
ESt. = Englische Studien.
FAS. = Fornaldarsögur (ed. Rafn).
FG. = Folknamnet Geatas i den fornengelska dikten Beowulf, af Henrik Schück.
FMS. = Fornmannasögur.
Gollancz = Hamlet in Iceland, by Israel Gollancz.
H. = Helgasaga.
Heinzel = Über die Hervararsaga, von Richard Heinzel (WSB. 114. 417 ff.)
Helm = Altgermanische Religionsgeschichte, von K. Helm.
HEP. = Home of the Eddic Poems, by Sophus Bugge. Trans. by W. H. Schofield.
Herrmann = Nordische Mythologie, von Paul Herrmann.
HH. = Story of Harald and Haldan (Saxo VII, 216 ff.).
HZ. = Haupts Zeitschrift für deutsches Altertum.
JEGPh. = Journal of English and Germanic Philology.
Jónsson = Hrólfssaga kraka og Bjarkarímur, ed. Finnur Jónsson.
KG. = Vergleichende Grammatik der keltischen Sprachen, von Holger Pedersen.
KS. = Kilderne til Sakses Oldhistorie, af Axel Olrik.
Lawrence = Some disputed Questions in Beowulf Criticism, by W. W. Lawrence (PMLA. 24. 220 ff.).
Loewe = Die Reste der Germanen am Schwarzen Meere, von Richard Loewe.
Luick = Historische Grammatik der englischen Sprache, von Karl Luick.
ME. = Middle English.

MLN. = Modern Language Notes.
Mogk = Pauls Grundriß der germanischen Philologie (2d ed.), XI. Mythologie, von Eugen Mogk (vol. III, p. 230 ff.).
Naumann = Altnordische Namenstudien, von Hans Naumann.
OE. = Old English.
OEN. = Origin of the English Nation, by M. Chadwick.
Panzer = Studien zur germanischen Sagengeschichte, I, Beowulf, von F. Panzer.
PBB. = Paul und Braunes Beiträge.
PMLA. = Publications of the Modern Language Association of America.
Saxo = Saxonis Grammatici Gesta Danorum (ed. Holder).
Schmidt = Allgemeine Geschichte der germanischen Völker, von L. Schmidt.
SS. = Snorri's version of the Skjöldungasaga (fragments in Edda and Ynglinga).
Stjerna = Essays on Beowulf, by Knut Stjerna. Trans. by Clark Hall.
SY. = Studier i Ynglingatal, af Henrik Schück.
WSB. = Wiener Sitzungsberichte.
Zeuss = Die Deutschen und die Nachbarstämme, von Kaspar Zeuss.

Addenda and Corrigenda

p. 6 l. 17: *for* an *read* as
p. 9 l. 10: *for* mitissm *read* mitissimi
p. 11 l. 12: *for* Svaerike *read* Svearike
p. 14 l. 23: *before* Schmidt *insert* But
p. 27 bottom: *after* held *insert* presumably
p. 40 l. 11: *for* ý *read* ʒ
p. 40 l. 3 from bottom: *for* among other *read* among others
p. 42 l. 12: *for* 6th *read* 7th
p. 62 l. 23: *for* there *read* the
p. 91 l. 6: *for* 1173 *read* 1175
p. 92 l. 5: *for* Hjörvaðr *read* Hjörvarðr
p. 100 column 3 bottom: *for* Elfhere *read* Ælfhere
p. 100 l. 4 from bottom: *for* 28 *read* 29
p. 117 l. 2 from bottom: *for* Agantýr *read* Angantýr
p. 123 l. 18: *after* Áli *add* (perhaps because both had the same historical opponent, viz., Beowulf; see p. 84 above)
p. 133 l. 5: *after* Egill *add* (but see Schütte AfnF XXXVI 31)
p. 154 l. 2 from bottom: *after* Gylfaginning *insert* prologue
p. 159 l. 19: *for* at *read* a
p. 163 l. 5: *for* r-sound *read* r-sounds
p. 169 l. 14: *after the stop add* For the first notice of the Beowulf version as such, see Detter in PBB. XVIII 84 f.; and cf. B. Nerman in Edda III 1 ff.
p. 170 l. 2: *for* 503 *read* 509
p. 170 l. 7: *after* Kauffmann *insert* Frazer, Neckel
p. 196 l. 16: *for* for *read* form
p. 197 l. 7: *for* Halfdanr *read* Halfdanir
p. 199 l. 16: *for* Hrólfr *read* Hróarr
p. 203 l. 1: *for* untill *read* until
p. 265 l. 7 from bottom: *for* versoin *read* version
p. 266 l. 2 from bottom: *for* Kind *read* King

Chapter I.

The Germanic North in the Migration Period.

It is customary to divide the Germanic dialects into three groups, viz., East, North and West, on the basis of certain linguistic similarities and differences. West Germanic further falls into a northern division (Anglo-Frisian) and a southern (German). Essentially the same classification is made of the tribes themselves, with certain shiftings which it would be beside our purpose to discuss. Now the linguistic terminology, when carried over into the historical field, becomes highly objectionable in English, although acceptable enough in French and German. Our difficulties come chiefly from the ambiguity of the word *German*. Thus, when we speak of the West Germans, we may mean either the *Westgermanen* or the *Westdeutschen*. In the present treatise the name *German* will be used exclusively in the wider sense, in agreement with Latin, French and German usage and with the more customary terminology of historians of the early Middle Ages. For the southern division of the West Germanic group the name *Sundrian* 'southron' will be employed. Similarly, the Plinian term *Vandilian* will be used for the tribes of the East Germanic group; the term *Scandinavian* (or, for short, *Scandian*), for the tribes of the North Germanic group. The two latter terms are already in use, of course; *Sundrian*, however, is a coinage of my own; this coinage is justified, I think, by the need of having in English a word equivalent in meaning to *allemand* and *deutsch.* At any rate, the convenience of the new word will abundantly appear in the discussion which follows.

At the beginning of the Christian era the separation of the Germans into Scandians, Vandilians, Sundrians and Anglo-Frisians had not been wholly completed. The three former were already somewhat differentiated, it is true, presumably on account of their geographical position on the frontiers of Germania. Thus, the Vandilians held the Balto-Slavic frontier; the Sundrians, the line of the Rhine; the Scandians, the far North. The region centering around the Jutland peninsula, however, by virtue of its position in the middle of Germania, was exposed to Germanic influences from all sides. Hence the tribes inhabiting this region were the last of all to become sharply differentiated from their neighbors. As we shall see, this situation is reflected in various ways in the early monuments.

We are particularly interested in the two Northern divisions, the Anglo-Frisians and the Scandians. What information do the ancients give us about them? Tacitus in cap. 2 of his *Germania* (c. 100 A. D.) tells us that the Germans traced their descent from the god Tuisto and his son Mannus. The latter had three sons, apparently the eponymous ancestors of the three tribe-groups into which the Germans were divided, viz., Ingvaeones, Herminones and Istaevones. The first inhabited the coast, the second the interior. Tacitus does not tell us where the Istaevones lived, but from the *Historia Naturalis* of Pliny the Elder (d. 79 A. D.) we learn that their home was near the Rhine. The Ingvaeones seem to correspond roughly to our Anglo-Frisians and Scandians, while from other sources we know that the Herminones and Istaevones were subdivisions of the Sundrians. It is impossible to determine whether or not the more remote Vandilians were included in the classification; at any rate it was a classification which Tacitus made no practical use of. Pliny gives the East Germans a special name, that of Vandili (cf. the Vandilii of the Germania), whence our term Vandilian; he does not include the Bastarnae among these, however, but sets them apart as a fifth group.

We have seen that Tacitus does not distinguish Anglo-Frisians and Scandians, and that he locates the Ingvaeones only in the vaguest way, as living on the coast. Pliny gives us more definite information. He says (IV 96): incipit deinde clarior aperiri fama ab gente Ingvaeonum quae est prima in Germania. mons Saevo ibi, inmensus nec Riphaeis iugis minor inmanem ad Cimbrorum usque promunturium efficit sinum, qui Codanus vocatur, refertus insulis quarum clarissima est Scandinavia inconpertae magnitudinis, portionem tantum eius quod notum sit Hillevionum gente quingentis incolente pagis, quae alterum orbem terrarum eam appellat. The *Sinus Codanus* is usually identified with the waters between Denmark and the Scandinavian peninsula, and *mons Saevo* with the mountain range along the southern coast of Norway. This locates the Ingvaeones in the Jutland peninsula, the Danish islands, and the Scandinavian peninsula proper. Pliny, however, is apparently not certain whether the inhabitants of Scandinavia (i. e., the peninsula; the ancients thought it an island) were Ingvaeones or not. At least he gives

1*

them a special name, that of *Hilleviones,* which in form is parallel to and alliterates with the names of the sons of Mannus. For a discussion of the point see especially Helm I 336.

Tacitus does not tell us what tribes were included in the Ingvaeones group. Pliny, however, says (IV 99): alterum genus Ingvaeones quorum pars Cimbri Teutoni ac Chaucorum gentes. Ptolemy (c. 150 A. D.) locates the Cimbri at the northern end of Jutland, and the Jutland peninsula was known to the ancients as the Cimbric Chersonesus. This confirms the conclusions already reached as to the location of the Ingvaeones. It is doubtful, however, if in the time of Pliny, Tacitus and Ptolemy the Cimbri any longer existed except as a remnant. Certainly the bulk of the tribe, along with the Teutones (Teutoni), had been destroyed long before by the Romans. The Chauci lived on the North Sea coast, between the Elbe and the Ems. As this does not fit in with the general location of the group as given by Pliny we must suppose the Chauci to have been an outlying member.

Pliny evidently thought it sufficient to name those tribes of the Ingvaeones which were of special interest to the Romans; his words imply that there were other tribes in the group as well. These tribes must be sought in the North. Now we know from many sources that the old home of the Angles was in Slesvig; for an elaborate proof of this see Chadwick OEN 192 ff. In all probability, then, the Angles were Ingvaeones, if we accept at face value Pliny's and Tacitus's location of that group. But Tacitus mentions the Angles as one of seven tribes forming an amphictyony for the worship of the vegetation goddess Nerthus (cap. 40). It therefore becomes likely that all the members of the amphictyony were Ingvaeones; that they lived by the sea is made certain by the fact that their sanctuary was located on an island of the ocean. Let us examine the names of these tribes and see what we can make of them.

The tribes are named in the following order: Reudigni, Aviones, Angli, Varini, Eudoses, Svardones, Nuitones. If we apply Schütte's law to this list we find that the Reudigni (the tribe named first) had the greatest general importance and so were doubtless the custodians of the sanctuary, while the Nuitones (named last) were of the greatest special interest to Tacitus's informant, whoever he was. Müllenhoff (DA. IV 463 f.) by the etymological route comes to the same conclusions as to the Reudigni. All attempts to locate the tribes with reference to one another, however, have proved unsuccessful, because of the assumption, generally made but false, that Tacitus was naming the tribes from south to north. As a matter of fact he does nothing but give the location of the group, and even this only in the vaguest way, as somewhere north of the Langobards (deinde). We thus have no right to assume that he knew the geographical location of the individual tribes. He names them all together, and treats them consistently as a group, without giving us a single piece of information about any individual tribe. If he had had more precise information he would presumably have followed his usual method of locating each tribe in turn. This he does not do, and the only rational conclusion must be that his informant gave him the information substantially as we have it in the Germania. The order in which the tribes are named, then, was determined by the informant, not by Tacitus. In other words, the tribes are listed in accordance with Schütte's law. This law, though, applies only to the first and last names, strictly speaking. The order of some of the other names may well have been influenced (unconsciously, of course) by the geographical situation of the individual tribes. Thus, the chances are that the Aviones were neighbors of the Reudigni, and that the Angli were neighbors of the Aviones.

Where did the Reudigni live? If custodians of the sanctuary they must have occupied the island on which it was located. Many scholars suppose this island to have been Selund (Danish *Sjælland*); see especially Herrmann 201, and cf. Beowulf 175 ff. The word *Aviones* means 'islanders,' so the Aviones too must have lived on one or more islands; if neighbors of both Reudigni and Angli they can be located with some precision an living on the islands of Fyen and Laaland. The Angli held East Slesvig, as we have seen. We thus get a general direction of movement from east to west. It now becomes clear, though, that geographical considerations after all did not play an important part — it would be impossible to name the remaining tribes in the same order as that hitherto observed (which would take us into the North Sea!). We must find another guide. It is likely that among the Nuitones (whence, directly or indirectly, Tacitus's information was derived) the list of members of the amphictyony took a stereotyped form, and this form would presumably be in verse. If then we arrange the names to correspond we get the following:

Reudigni Aviones **Angli Varini**
Eudoses Svardones **Nuitones.**

Here the first line seems satisfactory, as it has the necessary alliteration, although it would be more effective if *Reudigni* too began with a vowel. There is something wrong with the second line, however, and the seat of the trouble clearly lies in the word *Nuitones*. Müllenhoff long ago pointed out that this name had suffered at the hands of the scribes, since *ui* is not a Germanic diphthong. I take the original reading to have been HEVTONES, with inorganic H. This might have been copied as HVITONES by anticipation of the V and consequent use of I (for E) because the copyist was accustomed to the order HVI from words like *huic, huius,* while the order HVE does not occur. Later the initial H might have been copied as N; confusion of these two letters is not infrequent in mss., and actually occurs in certain mss. of the Germania in this very word (cf. Much's comment in PBB. XVII 212). As all the extant mss. of the Germania are descended from a single ms. of the 8th or 9th cy., one may postulate with considerable plausibility such a series of changes as that supposed above. I therefore emend to *Heutones* = OE *Eotan* 'Jutes.' This emendation is supported by the fact that it gives us our needed alliteration in the second line and explains Tacitus's astounding omission of the Jutes.

Lappenberg was the first to connect the Svardones with the Sweordweras of Widsiđ 62. This would involve emending the name to *Sverdones,* of course. It is noteworthy that the Widsiđ gives the name of no king of the Sweordweras, while the word itself is identical in meaning with *Seaxe* 'swordsmen' Latin *Saxones.* The two names may thus well be synonyms for the same tribe, though if so the fact had been forgotten by the time the

Widsið was composed. The interpretation of *Svardones* here suggested enables us to account for what Chambers calls "the extraordinary omission of the Saxons by Tacitus" (Widsith 73).

Our list of tribes, as emended, reads as follows:

Reudigni Aviones Angli Varini
Eudoses Sverdones Heutones.

There are still some difficulties to be cleared up here. The Reudigni are otherwise unknown. Yet if the leading tribe of the Nerthus group and the possessors of Selund they must have played a prominent part in the events of the migration period. The silence of the records can be explained in only one way. The name *Reudigni* must have been a by-name of some sort. We know from the Beowulf that the Danes were also called Scyldings, while the Geats were sometimes referred to as Weders. Similarly, *Reudigni* was doubtless used as a special name for a tribe whose ordinary name was something else. The etymology of the name leads us to a similar conclusion. According to Müllenhoff (DA. IV 463) it means 'the people who redden with sacrificial blood,' and so was a name applied to the tribe in its religious capacity. The name would be particularly in place in the Germania, of course, where the cult holds the stage. What was the corresponding secular name? Before we can find it we must first determine who the successors of the Reudigni were. This is by no means a difficult task. Their successors were the Danes.

Our earliest trustworthy information about the Danes is to be found in Jordanes, who got his information (through Cassiodorus) from the Norwegian king Hroðwulf (see DA. II 57 ff.). Now Jordanes gives a long and systematic account of the political subdivisions of the Scandinavian peninsula. He mentions the Danes too, although only in an aside, as it were, but his statements concerning them are obscured by the corrupt condition of the text at that point and it will be necessary to examine the passage with some minuteness in order to determine its proper meaning. The passage in question reads as follows (I quote from Mommsen's edition, Getica 3, 23—4, pp. 59 f.): sunt et his exteriores Ostrogothae, Raumarici, Aeragnaricii, Finni mitissm, Scandzae cultoribus omnibus mitiores; nec non et pares eorum Vinoviloth; Svetidi, cogniti in hac gente reliquis corpore eminentiores: quamvis et Dani, ex ipsorum stirpe progressi, Herulos propriis sedibus expulerunt, qui inter omnes Scandiae nationes nomen sibi ob nimia proceritate affectant praecipuum. sunt quamquam et horum positura Granii, Augandzi, Eunixi, Taetel, Rugi, Arochi, Ranii . . . . Jordanes has been naming the tribes then living in the eastern part of the peninsula (now Sweden). He now (with *exteriores*) crosses the boundary into Norway. Here the Raumarici are readily indentified as the inhabitants of the district of that name located in Southeast Norway. Similarly, *Aeragnaricii* can be referred to the neighboring district *Ránríki*. Müllenhoff has therefore suggested that the extraordinary name *Vinoviloth* is a corruption of a name connected with *Vingulmörk*, a 'mark' or district located between Raumaríki and Ránríki. He offers no explanation for the ending *-oth*. Howevr, as Jordanes has just mentioned a branch of the Ostrogoths, settled in the same region, and since in the previous section he refers to the Gautigoths just across the border to the east, it is perfectly possible that we have here still another branch of the Gothic people. I therefore emend to *Vinguligoth* (parallel to Gautigoth, Ostrogothae and Vagoth). The reading *Vinoviloth* is easily derivable from an earlier form *Vinguligoth*; we need suppose only an interchange of *l* and *i*, and a misreading of *g* as *o* — the latter a particularly easy error, in majuscles at least.

Müllenhoff continues (DA. II 64): aber seltsam, wenn auch verständlich, und anstößig bei näherem Besehen ist doch 'Finni mitissimi, Scandzae cultoribus omnibus mitiores', da 'mitissimi Scandzae cultorum omnium' vollkommen genügt hätte. Ich vermute, daß Jordanes hier doch, wie an andern in den hss. feststehenden Fehlern seines Textes unschuldig ist und statt 'mitiores' vielmehr 'minores' schrieb. Dann konnte die Aufzählung ohne Anstoß von den Finnen noch einmal auf die Einwohner der zwischen Raumariki und Ranriki belegenen Landschaft Vingulmörk zurückgreifen, wenn diese als 'pares eorum', als gleich kleine Leute wie die Finnen . . . bezeichnet werden sollten . . . dann würde auch das Asyndeton des nächsten Satzes sofort verständlich durch den Gegensatz, weil hier die Suetidi . . . als 'cogniti in hac gente reliquis corpore eminentiores' hervorgehoben werden . . . .

We now come to the curious name *Suetidi*. This 'unform' (as Müllenhoff calls it) is usually taken as referring to the Swedes; cf. the Icelandic *Svíþjóð* 'Sweden.' But what are the Swedes doing in South Norway? Besides, they have already been mentioned (section 21) in their proper place and under their proper name *Suehans* (= Sueones OE Sweon). The form *Suetidi* therefore cannot with any plausibility be interpreted as a corrupt form of a name meaning 'Swedes'; for conjectures on the subject see v. Grienberger, HZ. 46, 139 and 47, 273 and compare Schück, FG. 12. The etymology of the name will probably be determined, if at all, by a study of place names or regional names in South Norway, and this task I shall have to leave to others. — The phrase 'in hac gente' apparently refers to the Vinguligoths; if so, the Suetidi and their kinsmen the Dani are to be derived from a branch of the Gothic people. This derivation is supported by both linguistic and archeological evidence, which connects the Danes emphatically with Götarike rather than with Svaerike. Important too as evidence on the point is the close friendship between Geats and Danes manifest in the Beowulf.

The next sentence, that beginning 'quamvis et Dani,' is clearly corrupt. Whatever the deficiences of Jordanes as a stylist, he could hardly have been guilty of so monstrous a confusion of ideas as that which the text offers us. He has just stated that the Suetidi have the reputation of being taller than the rest of their stock. He finds it necessary to qualify this, however, for he continues, "although the Danes likewise, come from the same stock," — lay claim to unusual greatness of stature? No, not at all! They "drove from their proper seats the Eruli!" This abrupt change of subject is followed by an ascription to the Eruli of the very tallness which one would expect the Danes to be credited with. I conceive the trouble to lie in the word 'qui' and I therefore read 'interque' for 'qui inter.' The copyist seems to have misread 'interque' as 'inter quos' (by a misinterpretation of the abbreviation) and so corrected to 'qui inter.' The sentence is still somewhat inconsequent. It would be improved, stylistically, if all reference to the Eruli were omitted. Nevertheless, it is well up to the standard of a Jordanes, and in this case at least we cannot blame him overmuch for his infelicity of expression, since to it we owe a piece of information of far greater importance than any amount of gossip about the relative tallness of Dani and Suetidi.

The last sentence in the passage tells us that the Granii etc. live "in their place" (horum positura). I take the *horum* to refer to *Dani*. If so, one would gather that the Danes originally lived in South Norway, but had emigrated from that region, driven the Eruli from their proper seats, and established themselves anew in the lands formerly held by their foes, leaving their former seats empty, to be occupied by the Granii etc. already mentioned. If so, they were not the first Northern tribe to migrate southward. Thus, the Charudes seem to have come to Jutland from Norway, while at a still earlier period other migrations took place, if we assume a connexion between the numerous Vandilian and Scandian tribes having similar or identical names.

Where were the new seats of the Danes located? Not anywhere in the Scandinavian peninsula, certainly, if Jordanes is any guide. For as we have seen he mentions the Danes as former inhabitants of South Norway, whose 'positura' was at that time in the possession of others. Furthermore, there is no evidence that any Eruli lived in the peninsula before c. 513, when, according to the well-known account in Procopius, a branch of the tribe found a home near the Gauts. This account, however, throws some light on the location of the Danes at that time, for it is stated that the Eruli, after passing the Danish tribes, proceeded by sea to Thule (i. e., the Scandinavian peninsula). From this it would seem that the Danes were at that time in possession of the islands. Whether they also held Jutland is more doubtful; the Eruli may have passed the Danes (without coming in contact with them) by using the land route as far as they could, viz., to the northern end of Jutland. Perhaps, however, Procopius need not be taken so literally as that. For the account see Procopius BG. II 15. As Schück (FG. 12) has shown, the Danes could not have conquered Skaane before c. 490, and to judge from Procopius they had not conquered it as late as c. 513. Yet they had evidently expelled the Eruli long before, probably as early as c. 400. The conclusion seems inevitable that the original seat of the Eruli was in Selund. Certainly the earliest known capital of the Danes, Hleiðr, was in Selund, and the hall Heorot of the Beowulf is generally located there.

This brings us back to our Reudigni, whom we may now plausibly identify with the Eruli. The history of the Eruli has certain features which go to confirm this identification. They were evidently a powerful and numerous tribe, and in close touch with the Vandilians, for from c. 250 to c. 500 they were active and successful in the attacks on the Empire and in the inter-tribal wars. They also appear in the West in the year 286, probably in conjunction with Angli and Varini (Schmidt 149). The constant stream of migration from the homeland must have left the stay-at-homes very weak from a military point of view, so that the attack of the Danes found them incapable of making effective resistance. Since in 409 we find the Eruli again active in the West, it seems plausible to suppose that the effect of their expulsion from Selund was to make vikings of them; we thus likewise get an approximate date for the Danish conquest. — If we substitute *Eruli* for *Reudigni* in our Tacitean list of tribes the alliteration in the first line simply becomes more pronounced. See above. — To judge from the Beowulf, the Danish conquerors assumed the religious functions of their opponents. To this we shall come back later on. In English tradition the Danes and the Reudigni or Eruli seem to have become identified, indeed. Thus, the Danish king Alewih mentioned in Widsið 35 as a contemporary of Offa has a name which reminds one strongly of the historical king Alaric of the Eruli (c. 350), but does not fit into either of the two early Danish lines, the Siklings and the Scyldings. Such an identification would be a natural development if in fact the Danes took the place of the Eruli both as to territory and as to religious hegemony.

The second tribe of the Nerthus amphictyony named in the Germania was the Aviones. We know very little about this tribe. It is referred to in the Widsið: Oswine weold Eowum (26a). Schmidt (149) identifies the Aviones with the Chaibones, who in company with the Eruli made a viking expedition into Gaul in 286. This identification, if correct, is of course a further support for my theory of the connexion between the Eruli and the worshippers of Nerthus. The desertion by the Aviones of their old seats in the Danish islands would indicate that they shared the fortunes of their neighbors the Reudigni.

The third tribe named by Tacitus was the Angli.

They lived in East Slesvig, but seem to have won the predominance over their neighbors on the peninsula at an early period. During the 5th and 6th centuries the bulk of the population migrated to Britain. A certain proportion of the tribe, however, took part in the Continental migration, invading the Netherlands (c. 300?) and penetrating deep into Germany. Even of these, however, most found their way to England eventually, settling in East Anglia (Schmidt 150). Our information about the Angles apart from their migrations is confined to a few scattered passages. The most important of these is the reference to king Offa (c. 350?) in Widsið 35 ff. He is pictured as a mighty hero who won "the greatest of kingdoms" and set the Eider river as the boundary between his kingdom and that of his neighbors to the south the Myrgings. The poet adds (43b f.):

heoldon forð siþþan
Engle ond Swæfe, swa hit Offa geslog.

The natural inference from this would be that the Myrgings migrated later on (as was the habit of the day) and that the Swæfe, who took their place, made no effort to shift the boundary. This interpretation, however, has never been advanced, so far as I know (see Chambers 205). On the contrary, the Myrgings are usually supposed to have been a branch of the Swæfe, and this in spite of Widsið 22 f.: Witta weold Swæfum, . . . Meaca Myrgingum, where the two peoples are clearly distinguished! They do seem to have been confused in late tradition, to judge from the story of Offa in Saxo (for a discussion of which see below, cap. VI), and this confusion would be natural enough, since the Swæfe took the territories vacated by the Myrgings and, after the migration of the main body of the Angles, invaded Slesvig, if the place-name Schwabsted on the Trene has any evidential value here. The Angles left in Slesvig would thus naturally come to regard the Swæfe rather than the Myrgings as their traditional enemies to the south, so that king Eadgils of the Myrgings in the continental Anglian (later the Jutish) tradition would become a king of the Swæfe, and the very name of the Myrgings be forgotten. There would be no occasion for such a development among the Angles of Britain, however, and in any case the testimony of the Widsið must be taken as authoritative in the matter. — The Beowulf has something to say about Offa's wife Þrýð; to what extent the story is historical it is impossible to determine.

The fourth tribe, the Varini, perhaps lived on the Warnow river (in Mecklenburg); cf. Bugge, HEP. 135 ff. The tribe is twice mentioned in the Widsið: Billing (weold) Wernum (25b); ic wæs . . . mid Wærnum (59a). The location of the tribal home in Mecklenburg is supported by the Procopian story of the return to the North of a branch of the Eruli (see above), who after crossing the territory of the Varini passed that of the Danish tribes by land (i. e., traversed Jutland from south to north). From an early date the Angli and Varini were closely associated, as appears especially from the history of their activities in Germany (for a sketch of which see Schmidt 148 ff.). More of the Varini than of the Angli seem to have been left behind in their old seats during the migration period; at least Procopius mentions the Varini (but not the Angli) in his tale just referred to. Pliny refers to the Varini as a branch of the Vandili, i. e., of the Vandilians. Pliny's classification obviously points to an easterly rather than to a peninsular location for the tribe, and to this extent supports the connexion with the Warnow river.

The Eudoses come next in our list. They are to be identified with the Sedusii of Caesar (BG. I 51), who appear as allies of Ariovistus. The initial *S* is to be explained as having been carried over, by some scribe, from the final *s* of the preceding word; that this was actually the case is made probable by the readings Eduses, Edures, Eudures in Orosius. The Eudoses are further to be equated with the Phundusioi of Ptolemy, where the *n* may be intrusive and the *Ph* due to a misreading as F of the E of Ptolemy's Latin source. See DA. IV 466, Zeuss 116 and 151 f. Finally, a tribe called Eudusianoi is mentioned in the anonymous *Periplus Ponti Euxini* (c. 480). They lived on the northeast coast of the Black Sea. See Loewe 19 ff. Judging from their appearance in Caesar one would conclude that portions of the tribe early followed the example of the Cimbri and Teutones and migrated southward. In this migration they were associated with the Charudes. That the two tribes were associated in some way at home as well seems therefore likely. The list in Tacitus tends to confirm this, for here no Charudes appear, and one may suppose that Tacitus's informant subordinated them to the Eudoses and so left them out. For we know from Ptolemy that the Charudes lived on the Jutland peninsula, and Olsen has proved that they were worshippers of Nerthus; see Helm I 317 and the references given there. The appearance of a branch of the Eudoses on the Black Sea indicates that they were associated with the migration southeastward of the Eruli

c. 250. This is further evidence of a connexion of the Eruli with the Nerthus group. The second migration of the Eudoses must have taken with it the bulk of the tribe. At any rate, after Ptolemy we hear nothing more of them in the West. The remnants of the tribe were probably absorbed by their neighbors and earlier subjects (?) the Charudes. These left their mark in the shape of the district name Hardsyssel in Jutland. No corresponding traces of the Eudoses have been found. Much (PBB. XVII 208) attempts to establish a connexion between the name *Eudoses* and the various forms of the name of the Jutes. He derives both words from a pre-Germanic root *eut-*. For a sounder etymology of the name *Jute* see Noreen in Schück, FG. 5 f. note.

The Sverdones we have already identified with the Saxones of Ptolemy (see above). Chadwick (OEN. 202 ff.) after a careful analysis of the evidence concludes (correctly, I think) that these Saxones lived in West Slesvig. Later on (296 ff.) he makes out a plausible case for the conquest of the Saxons by the Angles in the Continental period. He assumes that this conquest took place after the Saxon power in the homeland had been weakened by migrations, and in fact we know that from the year 286 the Saxons were active in Germany and along the Gallic coast. About this time the center of the Saxon power was clearly transferred from the peninsula to the German coast, while the Chauci, in earlier times located between Elbe and Ems, disappear completely. It looks as if the Saxon royal line, by marriage or by inheritance, had come to rule over the Chauci as well; otherwise it is hard to understand how a small tribe like the Saxons could so suddenly incorporate such an extensive area and impose its name on a people so much more numerous and powerful. For a discussion of the history of Germanic royal houses with special emphasis on just this sort of change see Chadwick, OEN cap. VII, where many parallels are given. With this shift in the center of gravity the original seat of the Saxon kings became an outlying province, and so would all the more easily fall a prey to the Angles (under Offa?). On the other hand, Chadwick does not make out his case for the membership of the Saxons in the Herminones group (227 ff.). The northern columns of Hercules belong on the island of Helgoland (Detlefsen 43 f.), and arguments drawn from the cult of the later Saxons of Germany proper cannot be extended to cover the small peninsular tribe of the times of Tacitus and Ptolemy. On the point see further Helm I 339. — For the early history of the Saxons in England see Chadwick, OEN cap. IV.

The last tribe mentioned by Tacitus as a member of the Nerthus amphictyony is the Nuitones, or, to follow my emendation, the Eutones. In this form the name is clearly identical with the Eotan or Eotenas of the Beowulf. These are generally and justly identified with the Jutes. They are mentioned in two of the stories told incidentally and all too briefly in that poem. Their part in the story of Heremod will be discussed below in another connexion. In the other story, that of Finnsburh, they appear as subjects of Finn, king of the Frisians. This is explicable only on the supposition that they had migrated from their original seats in Jutland, and this supposition is confirmed by the reference to them in a letter of the Frankish king Theodberht (c. 540) from which it appears that they at that time lived east of the lower Rhine. Linguistic evidence also points to a stay of the Jutes in the Netherlands or on the German coast for some time before the migration to Britain, which occurred c. 450. Enough Jutes must have remained in Jutland, however, to ensure the perpetuation of the name of the peninsula. We thus find the Jutes split up into three groups: the settlers in Britain (Kent and Isle of Wight with hinterland), the settlers on the German coast, of whom the settlers in Britain were a later offshoot, and finally the stay-at-homes, who eventually became Danicized as to speech and nationality but preserved their name and the name of the district, both of which the Danish settlers took over as a local rather than nationalistic designation. The Eotan who were subjects of Finn must have formed a part of the Jutish settlers on the German coast.

The leaders of the Jutes in their descent on Britain were Hengest and Hors. Now Hengest appears in the Beowulf and the Finnsburh fragment, but not as a Jute but rather as an opponent of Finn and thane of king Hnæf of the Healfdene (= Hocings; cf. Widsið 29a). Furthermore, Bede makes Hengest a grandson of Witta, who according to Widsið 22a ruled the Swæfe. Finally, according to Nennius Hengest and his followers came to Britain as a result of having been exiled from Germany. Evidently Hengest was an adventurer, and it is not altogether surprizing to find him functioning as leader of his former enemies the Jutes. The exact course of events nevertheless needs to be explained. Hengest was apparently a prince of the Swæfe who took service with king Hnæf of the Hocings and participated in that king's expedition to Finnsburh. Later he appears as leader of a band of Jutish fugitives. Now the Beowulf tells us how the Hocings overthrew Finn, and it is tempting to identify the fugitive Jutes of the Historia Brittonum with the fugitive Jutish subjects of Finn. But in that case Hengest must have changed sides during the course of the war between Finn and the Hocings. Our only information on the point is that given in the Finn episode of the Beowulf. Unfortunately enough, this episode is far from clear, especially as to the part played by Hengest. The following outline of events, however, seems fairly well established. Hnæf, while wintering with his brother-in-law Finn, falls victim to a treacherous attack made on him by Finn's Jutish subjects. Hnæf's followers, however, led by Hengest, hold out, and finally Finn and Hengest come to terms, apparently on the understanding that the Hocings are to be permitted to return home when spring has come and the seas are once more navigable. Certainly some of them, Guðlaf and Oslaf (Ordlaf) in particular, do succeed in getting away and the news they bring stirs up the Hocings to a thoroughly successful punitive expedition against Finn. There is no evidence that Hengest participated in this expedition. What became of him?

A careful reading of the Finn episode forces one to the conclusion that the Beowulf poet is an apologist for Hengest, whose behavior from beginning to end is presented in the most favorable light possible. This is to be expected of an English poet, of course. If then Hengest actually took part in the last fight with Finn one would certainly expect the poet to make much of the fact. His silence here, then, is indicative. Even more indicative is the poet's apology in the passage immediately preceding the account of the last fight and death of Finn. When winter was over, says the poet,

1137		fundode wrecca (Hengest),
	gist of geardum;	he to gyrn-wræce
	swiðor þohte	þonne to sæ-lade,
1140	gif he torn-gemot	þurhteon mihte,
	þæt he Eotena bearn	in ne-gemunde,
	swa he ne-forwyrnde	worold-rædende
	þonne him Hunlafing	hilde-leoman,
	billa selest,	on bearm dyde;
1145	þæs wæron mid Eotenum	ecge cuðe.

"Hengest did his best to leave (Finn's) court; he thought not so much of the voyage (i. e., of merely escaping) as of vengeance — whether he might bring on a battle, in which he would not be considerate of the Jutes, even as he had not failed his king (in that other battle) when he (Hnæf) laid in his lap Hunlafing, the battle-gleamer, best of bills; the edges of it were known among the Jutes." For the reading *worold-rædende* cf. Beowulf 51b; for its meaning 'earthly ruler, i. e., king' compare *rodera rædend* 'ruler of the heavens, i. e., God.' The sword Hunlafing was presumably so named from Hunlaf its former owner. From the passage as a whole one would conclude that 1) Hengest did not actually leave Finn's court, 2) he did not actually bring on the final battle, and 3) his conduct was such as to lay him open to the accusation that he had failed his lord — an accusation which the poet is not content simply to deny but seeks to make unreasonable by citing a previous deed of Hengest's inconsistent with the theory that he was or could have been a traitor. If Hengest had avenged on the Jutes the death of Hunlaf (using for the purpose Hunlaf's own sword) how could he, later, have made common cause with the Jutes against the Hocings, Hunlaf's own people? So the poet, who nevertheless is unable to dodge the fact that not Hengest but Guðlaf and Oslaf (Ordlaf) brought the Hocings down upon Finn.

What part, then, did Hengest actually play? Apparently, when spring came, Finn after all would not allow Hengest and his men to leave. This must have embittered Hengest's followers against their leader, who had himself made the pact with the slayer of their lord (not without opposition from the diehards, one may fancy) and who now had laid himself open to a charge of treachery, a charge which, however unjustified, would be strengthened by the fact that Hengest was no Hocing but a foreign warrior in Hnæf's service. The doubters carried the day; the Hocings planned and effected their escape, leaving Hengest behind and practically compelling him to take service with Finn in earnest. Nevertheless, when the Hocings returned to the attack, Guðlaf and Oslaf, who were under obligations to Hengest, the avenger of their brother, managed to give him a chance to escape. Hors (the Eaha of the fragment?) would naturally share his brother's fortunes. This reconstruction of the course of events, conjectural though it is, has at least the merit of accounting for all the facts.

Ptolemy locates on the Cimbric Chersonesus not only the Cimbri but also several tribes not mentioned at all by Tacitus. His location of the Charudes fits in well with the reference to that tribe in the Monumentum Ancyranum. We have therefore no reason to doubt his substantial accuracy in the other cases; the absence from Tacitus of the tribes in question may be accounted for in various ways, as on the assumption that they were subdivisions of tribes named, or late-comers into the amphictyony and so not included in the canonical list. Certainly, in as much as the Charudes were Nerthus worshippers, we may suppose that the other tribes under consideration likewise adhered to the Nerthus cult, in spite of the silence of Tacitus.

Of the various tribes associated in the worship of Nerthus the Angli, Sverdones, Eutones were Anglo-Frisians; the Varini, Vandilians; the Charudes, Scandians; the classification of the remaining tribes is doubtful. The cult of Nerthus therefore cannot be identified with the Anglo-Frisian group, which, as we have seen, was probably unformed in Tacitus's day, and which, when it did develop, included only a part of the amphictyony. One may suppose with greater probability that Nerthus was one of the chief deities of the Ingvaeones. There are certain difficulties even here, it is true. Thus, the Nerthus amphictyony does not seem to have included the Chauci. This difficulty is only apparent, however. The outlying Ingvaeonian tribes were too far removed from the Nerthus sanctuary to participate in the rites there, but they may well have worshipped Nerthus nevertheless. On the other hand, one may suppose that the Chauci, like the Cimbri and Teutones, once lived in the Jutland peninsula, and that they lost touch with the Nerthus cult (while dimly remembering their Ingvaeonian origin) in consequence of their migration. However, we have so little evidence here that the matter is perhaps not worth discussing. — The identification of Chauci and Hugas lacks a sound phonetic basis.

Who were the Ingvaeones, then? We shall not go far astray if we consider them to have been a group of Germanic tribes held together by a belief in descent from an eponymous ancestor Ing. The tribes in question seem to have lived on the North Sea and Baltic coasts, the Jutland peninsula, the Danish islands and the Scandinavian peninsula. The three sons of Mannus thus reflect an ancient subdivision of the Germans into one Northern and two Southern groups. By the time of Pliny and Tacitus, however, these groups had already broken down, as political or religious realities, and were remembered only in the mythical form taken by the historical tradition. Both the Scandians and the Vandilians (the Hilleviones and the Vandili of Pliny) are best taken as offshoots of the Ingvaeones. As to the Scandians, this is already a widely accepted theory. As to the Vandilians, the traditions and names of the historical tribes point to a Northern origin of the group; a specific connexion with Ing may possibly be indicated in l. 70 of the OE Runic Poem and in the Hadding saga of Saxo, if Müllenhoff is right in connecting the Hardings or Haddings with the Vandal royal line and the sanctuary of the Nahanarvali. It is important here to note that at least one Vandilian tribe, the Varini, was actually a member of the Nerthus group.

While the outlying tribes early became differentiated and developed new groups, the central tribes long maintained the old traditions and became the Ingvaeones proper. Eventually, however, with the differentiation and migration of the Anglo-Frisians, the migration of the Eruli and the conquests of the Danes, the central nucleus too was broken up and its remnants absorbed by Scandians and Sundrians respectively.

What was the connexion between Ing and the goddess Nerthus? Tacitus gives us no information on the point. His Nerthus is a vegetation goddess, Terra Mater, who dwells in a sacred grove on an island of the ocean. In the grove is kept the holy wain, the dwelling of the goddess. The wain is covered, and only the priest has access to it. Once a year the wain, drawn by two cows, makes the circuit of the island. During this time all weapons are locked up and peace prevails. The priest conducts the journey and brings the goddess back to her holy place. Thereupon the wain, its covering, and the deity herself, undergo a lavation in a sacred lake. The slaves who perform this duty are then put to death.

The ritual outlined above is generally interpreted as a fertility rite. It seems evident too that the priest acted as husband of the goddess or, rather, of her representative. The lavation, with the drowning of the slaves, is to be taken as a sacrificial act. Compare especially the OE Runic Poem 67 ff.:

Ing wæs ærest	mid East-Denum
gesewen secgun,	oþ he siððan est
ofer wæg gewat;	wæn æfter ran:
ðus Heardingas	ðone hæle nemdun.

The passage is far from preserving the story in anything like so primitive a form as that of Tacitus. Thus, Ing has usurped the place of Nerthus (for which see below) and in consequence there has been added the myth of the vegetation daemon or eponymous ancestor who, like the Scyld of the Beowulf, comes to Denmark by sea out of the unknown and later departs as he had come. Nevertheless, the departure certainly symbolizes the death of the god, who, *along with his wain,* apparently finds a watery grave, and this most peculiar finale one may well equate with the lavation of goddess *and wain* told of in the Germania. — In the last line the poet mentions the Heardingas (Icel. Haddingjar) as the source of his version of the story, thus implying that he knows another version in which the hero bears another name (presumably the name Nerthus). This is borne out by Saxo, according to whom (I 30) king Hadding introduced into Denmark the Freyr blót. From this one is tempted to conclude that the substitution of Ing for Nerthus first took place among the Vandals, and thence was imported into Denmark. Note in this connexion the word *est* of l. 68 above — if the god departed eastward when his work was done he probably came from the east as well. The evidence, however, is of course insufficient to admit of a definite conclusion, especially since *Heardingas* need not be taken as a proper name.

The further question now arises, what god was considered the husband of Nerthus? As it happens, we have definite information on the point. M. Olsen (Det gamle norske ønavn Njarðarlög) has shown that the god Týr was associated with Nerthus among the ?udes of Norway, who doubtless had taken over or inherited the cult from their kinsmen the Harudes of Jutland. See further Helm I 317. The priest attendant on Nerthus then acted as representative of Týr, who, as the old sky-god, was eminently in place in a fertility cult. His symbol the sword was also a phallic symbol, and the sword-dances held in his honor seem to have been rather fertility rites than martial rites, if one may judge from the nakedness of the participants.

The theriomorphic form of the goddess was obviously a cow. Her husband Týr, then, would presumably be a bull, and in fact bull-worship was a prominent feature of the religion of the Cimbri, as we learn both from Plutarch's Life of Marius and from archeological finds (in the Jutish district Himmerland). For the sky-god as a bull see especially A. B. Cook, Zeus I, 430 ff. The evidence as to Týr, however, is too meager to make us certain of our ground.

It is well known that not only the sky proper but also the heavenly bodies might be looked upon as manifestations of the sky-god. Association with the moon would seem more likely in Germanic lands, where the word for moon was masculine, while that for sun was feminine. And certainly the moon played an important part in war, agriculture and law — all matters pertaining especially to Týr. Cf. Helm I 257 f. and note 36 (with bibliography). There is a certain amount of further evidence. In Gylfaginning 12 Snorri tells of two wolves (sons and doubtless doublets of Fenrir) who are destined to swallow up, the one the sun, the other the moon. The moon-wolf, Hati by name, is particularly formidable (cf. Völuspá 40); he is known also by the kenning *Mánagarmr* 'moon-dog.' This beast can hardly be separated from the hell-hound Garmr who is the opponent of Týr at Ragnarök (Gylfaginning 51). Originally the two must have been distinct, it is true, and doubtless Hati, not Garmr, was the proper opponent of Týr at Ragnarök. By association with the kenning, however, and by an easy misinterpretation of Völuspá 44 (cf. Müllenhoff, DA. V 139), the bearers of the tradition eventually came to consider the hell-hound as Týr's opponent. Týr was also known by the kenning *úlfsfóstri* 'foster-father of the wolf.' The wolf in question, paradoxical as it may seem, was Hati. For the moon-wolf was looked upon as in some sort a member of the lunar household. In origin, of course, the wolves were merely theriomorphic explanations of such phenomena as false suns, moon phases and eclipses; they thus did double duty. The frequency and supposed importance of the moon phases caused the moon-wolf (who did the damage) to be considered more formidable than the rarely dangerous sun-wolf; but see DA. V 125. If the sky-god also served as a moon-god we have an explanation for the rather peculiar fact that the m-rune is not named for the moon.

Not only the sun and moon but also the stars might be looked upon as manifestations of the sky-god. Cf. A. B. Cook, Zeus I, 740 ff. and 777. There is a certain amount of evidence that Týr, like Zeus, was on occasion associated with stars. In the OE Runic Poem, against the T-rune (which properly belongs to Týr), are placed the following verses (48 ff.):

Tir biþ tacna sum, healdeð trywa wel
wiþ æþelingas; a biþ on færylde
ofer nihta genipu. næfre swiceþ.

Here the use of *Tir* for *Tiw* is generally explained as a euphemism. The verses themselves are best explained as referring to the morning star, which, however dark the night, never fails to bring the day. The reference may however be to the dawn, which likewise is a never-failing precursor of day. To refer the verses to a circumpolar constellation is to ignore the 'næfre swiceþ' of the poem — if the night were sufficiently cloudy even the pole-star would fail the 'æþeling' whereas the morning star or the dawn would not fail him under any circumstances whatsoever.

If now we go on to l. 90 of the Runic Poem we find a rune which bears two names, *Ear* and *Tir*. The verses attached are in explanation of the name *Ear*, which the poet takes to mean 'the grave,' and *Ear* is undoubtedly the proper name of the rune. Why, then, was the rune given the alternative name, and that a name already used for another rune? The name *Tir* as applied to the EA-rune may have come from Codex Cotton Dom. A 9, it is true, but this does n't help us much, for we have still to explain why that codex names the rune *Tir*, and why the Vatican codex names it *Ziu*. The explanation in reality is not very difficult. So far as its form is concerned the EA-rune seems to be simply a derivative of the T-rune, made from it by adding a couple of upstrokes. Its name too is probably derived from that of the T-rune; or, more accurately, *Ear* is nothing more or less than a Týsheiti, probably derived from an IE root meaning 'burn' and so applicable enough to the sky-god. *Ear* occurs otherwise as the first element of the name *ear-endel* 'jubar,' Icel. *Aurvandill*, German *Orendel*. According to Snorri's story (Skaldskaparmál 17) one of the stars (the morning star?) was known as 'Aurvandill's toe.' It would seem, then, that the English poet misinterpreted the meaning of *Ear*, and that the verses which he attached to the T-rune more properly go with the EA-rune.

There is additional indication that *Ear* was in truth a Týsheiti. Bavarian names for Tuesday are *Ertag*,

Erchtag, and many scholars, from Grimm to Mogk, have drawn the inference that *Er* was a by-name of Týr. No satisfactory explanation of the name however has as yet been offered. In my opinion the Bavarian forms are simply borrowings from the Anglo-Frisian, the Saxons acting as transmitters. Among the Anglo-Frisians the T-rune, in addition to its true name *Tiw*, seems to have boasted of at least one additional name, viz., **Æor* (from **Aur-*), the heiti discussed above. The form of the rune may also have given it the name **Ærh* 'arrow.' For the vocalization see Luick I 127 ff. Now the continental Saxons (or the Sundrian tribes which later became known under that name) were for a time very much under Anglo-Frisian influences — a well established historical fact. I conceive, then, that during this period they borrowed the names **Æor* and **Ærh* and transmitted these southward, where they took root among the Bavarians as alternative names for the god Tiw, eventually driving out the god's true name. In such case the foreign diphthong would be smoothed and the foreign words imitated as *Er-*, *Erh (Erch-)*. This explanation involves no phonetic difficulties — imitation of foreign sounds is rarely perfect, and here we need suppose only that the adjustment to the native sound-system proceeded on obvious lines. The method of transmission assumed involves considerable difficulties, however: not in theory so much as in the fact that only the Bavarians, the very people furthest removed from the Anglo-Frisian territory, seem to have preserved the forms in question. This kind of survival is of course by no means unexampled, but the necessity of assuming it makes my explanation uncertain. — As to the method of compounding. *Ertäg* seems to be a formation parallel to *Earendel* etc., and *Erchtag* was doubtless formed on the same model.

On the present theory, then, Earendel or Aurvandill, like Heimdall, is simply a hypostasis of Týr, and, again like Heimdall, is especially connected with the dawn. Note in this connexion that Aurvandill in the Fjölsvinsmál goes by the name Sólbjartr — evidently a sky epithet; that his wife is Gróa — a fertility deity; that his son is Svipdagr; and that, like the Týr of the Hymiskviða, he is of the race of giants and is the companion and follower of Þórr.

Returning now to the Ing passage of the Runic Poem, we find other interesting features. The sacral function of the Danes is strongly emphasized, as in the Beowulf, where the Danes are called Ingwine and their capital is a cult center. Noteworthy also is the fact that the Danes appear no less than three times in the Widsið. One may infer that they took over the functions of the Reudigni at an early period, a period so early that the Angles before their migration had become accustomed to the new regime and looked upon the Danes as their religious leaders. We can therefore hardly set a date later than c. 400 for the Danish conquest of Selund. On the other hand, we can hardly set an earlier date than this, as king Hroðwulf's references to historical facts would not carry us much further back than the beginning of the 5th century. We are therefore able to date the conquest of Selund with some assurance at c. 400 A. D.

Again, as already noted, the position of Ing in the passage shows that he had superseded Nerthus as the central deity of the cult. This is confirmed by the Beowulf and the Scandian monuments. The change seems to have come about somewhat as follows. First, the word Nerthus, as an u-stem, tended to and finally did become masculine. During the transition period Nerthus was referred to, now as a god, now as a goddess, and this led to the development of a bi-sexual deity quite parallel to Tuisto, whence it was easy for the two to become identified. In this way (with the loss of the shadowy Mannus) Ing became the son of Nerthus and so obtained a place in the Nerthus cult. With Nerthus a bi-sexual deity Týr had no further function in the cult and so was eliminated from it and remembered only as a god of war. Ing now grew in importance at the expense of Nerthus until, in Sweden at least, he came to be known as Freyr, i. e., the Lord pure and simple, and as such was the chief popular deity. For bibliography see Chambers 70 note 4. Nerthus eventually became simply a male deity but his earlier bi-sexual nature finds its reflex not only in his replacement of Tuisto but also in his marriage with his sister (herself nameless).

The only Scandian tribe definitely located in the North by Tacitus was the Sviones, i. e., the Swedes (OE. Sweon). They are said to have had a fleet, but from the description given of the vessels and the method of rowing it would appear that the fleet was adapted better to inland waters than to the open sea. The Sviones were governed by a king, whose power was absolute, and who kept his people unarmed, weapons being kept under lock and key and in the custody of a slave! Schütte (AfnF. XXXIII 78) has called attention to the connexion between this disarming of the people and the similar practice prevailing among the Nerthus worshippers during the progress of the goddess. If the locking up of the weapons was a religious act among the Sviones as well, it would occur only at the time when the goddess was making her progress through the land. This explanation makes the passage in Tacitus much more intelligible; as it stands one must assume permanent disarmament of the people, a state of affairs hardly credible. Another extraordinary feature of the Tacitean account is the use of a slave as keeper of the weapons. This practice too is borne out by native tradition, however: Snorri in the Ynglingasaga (cap. 26) tells of a certain slave who was the royal treasurer, and as in those days the chief valuables were weapons we may assume that the slave was the custodian of the king's armory. As Schück (SY. 117) has pointed out, the custom of using slaves for such a purpose must have made easy a servile insurrection, and in fact such an insurrection took place, if the Ynglinga is to be trusted. The slaves doubtless rose while the Nerthus celebration was in progress and the people were thus disarmed.

Although the Sviones were probably worshippers of Nerthus, they must have had a sanctuary of their own, as their name does not appear in Tacitus's list; furthermore, they lived so far away from Selund that their participation in the rites there would hardly have been feasible in any case. The Scandinavian monuments bear this out. The Swedes were devoted to the worship of Freyr or Yngvi (Ing), the son of Njörðr (Nerthus), from the earliest times of which these monuments give record, but there is no evidence whatever that they had any part in the worship at the island sanctuary of Tacitus. For evidence that Týr in Sweden as well as in Norway and Denmark was associated with the vegetation rites see Karsten's Tiwaz (in Nordiska Ortnamn, the Noreen Hyllningsskrift, pp. 195 ff.).

So far the discussion has been based primarily on the Germania of Tacitus. Turning now to the Getica of Jordanes we find a comprehensive treatment of the tribes of the Scandinavian peninsula, though the islands and the Jutland peninsula are given no place in the scheme. I have already discussed the Norwegian part of this account (see above), so here I will confine myself to Sweden. The account in Jordanes describes conditions as they were c. 490. At that time the Svehans (Sveones, OE. Sweon) or Swedes proper lived in their historic seats in the Uppland district of the modern central Sweden. According to Jordanes they paid especial attention to horse-breeding, and to judge from Karsten (loc. cit.) their god Týr was particularly connected with this horse-breeding — i. e., like Zeus he was a fertility deity. South of the Swedes were a number of tribes: Vagoth in East Götland, Theustes in North Kalmar, Bergion on the Smaaland coast (with Öland and Bornholm), Liothida in Skaane and Hallin in South Halland. All these tribes lived in a level and fertile region, says Jordanes, and on this account suffered much from the attacks of less fortunately situated tribes. The next sentence in Jordanes reads: post hos Ahelmil (Chelmir?), Finnaithae, Fervir, Gautigoth, acre hominum genus et at bella prumtissimum. The Chelmir or Helmir, and the Fervir, lived in Halland, the Finnaithae in South Smaaland and the Gautigoth in West Götland and Bohus.

Specially important is the statement about the fighting qualities of the Gauts (Gautigoth). Procopius refers to the Gauts too, saying that they were one of the most numerous tribes of Thule (i. e., the Scandinavian peninsula). There is a reference to Goutoi as early as Ptolemy: this however probably means the Goths (the Vagoths of Jordanes?). Jordanes gives the name of no tribe which can be definitely located in Blekinge, although the Bergio may have lived there. That some region near the Gauts was actually empty is indicated by the fact that the returning Eruli of the Procopian story obtained land there without trouble, and Björkman 122 locates these Eruli in Blekinge. The assumption that the inhabitants of Blekinge were neighbors of the Gauts involves of course the further assumption that by c. 513 the Gauts were not confined to their historic seats in West Götland but had overrun most of what is now South Sweden, and this assumption finds support in the regional names East Götland and Götarike, names which could hardly have come into use had the Gauts not extended their rule across the peninsula. In this connexion should be noted the statements of Jordanes as to the troubles of the eastern tribes and the warlike qualities of the Gauts, together with the statements of Procopius as to the numbers of the Gauts.

We now come to the Beowulf. This poem has a good deal to say about Danes, Geats and Swedes, but gives us only incidental information about other tribes. Thus, in l. 461 the Wylfings are mentioned as a tribe which the Geats were evidently afraid of. The incident must then have taken place before the rise of the Geats to power. Jordanes mentions no tribe of

Wylfings, but he could hardly have omitted them, as they figure a good deal in Germanic saga. Here the Widsið helps us out. In l. 29 of that poem we find the statement: Helm (weold) Wulfingum. One may accordingly identify the Wylfings with the Helmir of Jordanes (if *Helmir* is accepted as the proper reading). The Helmir lived near the Gauts, and if the equation Geats = Gauts holds (as I think it does) the Geats' fear of their neighbors is easy to understand. If the Wylfings on the other hand are located in Blekinge (see Björkman loc. cit.) the Geatish trepidation becomes harder to explain. The name Wylfing, like so many other Scandian names, occurs also among the Vandilians, in this case in connexion with the story of Theodoric the Goth. There is no reason to doubt a connexion between the migrant Wylfings and those who stayed in Scandinavia. The history of the tribe however cannot be recovered.

The only other tribe about which the Beowulf gives us much incidental information is the Bards. To judge from their name these were related to the Langobards. In the Widsið (47b) the Bards are called *Wicinga cynn* (see also 59b). This would indicate that they were pirates, and the usual etymology of the name Wicing makes it mean 'the people who live in camps,' i. e., the people who devote themselves entirely to war, as contrasted with the more settled tribes who have houses to live in. This picture of the Bards, however, does not fit in well with the passage of the Beowulf (2032 ff.) which tells of the marital difficulties of Ingeld. Here the king of the Bards has a hall with all its appurtenances, and the houseless and migratory conditions assumed by the etymologists are not to be found. The evidence is thus neither full nor clear. We have a few definite supports, however. The most important of these is the name of the tribe. It is hard indeed to argue this out of existence, and such a proceeding is thoroughly unjustified. We may start, then, by assuming that the (Heaðo-)Bards were an offshoot of the Bardi bellicosissimi of Helmold. These were that portion of the Langobards who did not accompany the main body in the migration to the Danube. As the Widsið calls the Bards Vikings we are forced further to assume that they were pirates. This fits in well with our identification, as only through such an assumption could the Bardi and the Danes well be brought into contact. Even a band of pirates must have a base somewhere, though (witness Jómsborg); it is absurd to press an etymology so far as to deny the Wicingas the possession of houses! On the other hand, the poet's picture of the Bardish court is doubtless largely conventional, so we need not assume that the court of Ingeld was on a par with that of the Danish kings.

The determination of the location of the piratical base is a matter of great difficulty. Bugge has made it seem probable (HEP. 126 ff.) that the Helgakviður of the Elder Edda localized the Bards in Mecklenburg. This localization is doubtless a reminiscence of the seats of the Bards at the beginning of their piratical career. It by no means follows, however, that they remained in Mecklenburg indefinitely, or (granting that some of them did remain there) that they established no other bases or colonies. On the contrary, it is of the nature of pirates to wander far afield, and to set up new colonies as opportunity affords, without necessarily abandoning the old ones, of course. Now since the brothers Haki and Hagbarðr (or the hero Haki-Hagbarðr, if the brothers were originally the same person) were pretty clearly Bardish, not Danish heroes, and since the Hagbarðr story is localized in western Selund (Olrik, KS. II 232), it may well be that the Bards had a colony in that region, and that after the conquest of the colony by the Danes the conquered Bards were eventually absorbed and their traditions adopted by the conquerors. Furthermore, in view of the relations between Starkaðr and the Bardish royal house it is tempting to locate a colony (perhaps the chief colony) of the Bards in Skaane, which as we have seen was conquered by the Danes much later than was Selund. In any case some Bardish settlement was presumably within the boundaries of the later Danish kingdom, else the adoption of Fróði and Ingjaldr as Danish kings, and of Starkaðr, Haki and Hagbarðr as Danish heroes in popular tradition would be hard to account for.

There is moreover a certain amount of evidence pointing to a Bardish settlement further north. Bugge has shown (HEP. 160) that the mythical king Höðbroddr is best interpreted as the poetic representative of the tribe of Heaðobards. Now Saxo makes this king a Swede. According to the Helgakviður his father was Granmarr 'the beard-famous one' and this name is obviously appropriate to a mythical Bardish king. As Bugge has made clear (HEP. 151), the king Granmarr of the Helgakviður is to be identified with the king Granmarr of the Ynglinga and the Sögubrot. The Ynglinga locates Granmarr in Suðrmannaland; the Sögubrot, in East Gautland. According to the second Helgakviða he dwelt at Svarinshaugr, a hill which Bugge locates (HEP. 137) in Mecklenburg. The discrepancies in the various monuments are best explained on the theory of a Bardish settlement somewhere on the East Gautish or Swedish coast, where the memory of a mythical king Granmarr survived among the descendants of the Bardish settlers. Some such settlement may have taken place under the leadership of the Bardish hero Haki (for which see below). However, the question must rest unsettled, of course, for lack of sufficient evidence.

We get further references to Svarinshaugr. In the Völuspá (14, ý) it is called *salar steinn*, presumably because Granmarr's hall was built upon it or in it. If the latter, king Granmarr is to be looked upon as a euhemerized elf, much as the Danish king Fróði is a euhemerized corn daemon. From Svarinshaugr came moreover certain dwarfs, the race of Lofarr; among these dwarfs are mentioned Alfr and Yngvi (Völuspá 16, 1). As however *Alfr* means 'elf' and Yngvi-Freyr was lord of Alfheimr, the so-called dwarfs were doubtless in reality elves. See further below (cap. VI).

In general the geography of the Beowulf is so indefinite that even the location of the Geats rests uncertain. Here again the name Geatas, which is phonetically equivalent to Gautar, must be our basis, and all attempts to argue it away remain unconvincing. It cannot be denied, however, that there is a great deal of evidence connecting the Geats with Jutland. For this evidence see especially Bugge, PBB. XII 1 ff., Schütte, JEGPh. XI 575 ff., Weyhe, ESt. XXXIX 37 ff. For the other side see among other Stjerna 64 ff., Schück, FG. A compromise theory, which assumes a migration of Geats from Götland to Jutland, is advanced by Schütte,

AfnF. XXXIII 85 ff. This theory will be taken as a working basis in the present treatise. Without trying to restate the material presented in the discussions cited above, I will point out from time to time in the following various points the bearing of which on the question has in my opinion been overlooked or insufficiently emphasized.

The exact boundaries of the Denmark of Beowulf, although not so much a matter of dispute as the location of the Geatish kingdom, are nevertheless very hard if not impossible to determine. It is generally agreed (in spite of Stjerna) that Selund was the chief seat of the Danes. Beyond this we know extraordinarily little. Two passages in the poem have been cited to prove that Skaane was a part of the Danish realm, but, as we shall see, these passages prove nothing of the kind. The first of them (18 f.) reads:

Beowulf wæs breme, blæd wide sprang
Scyldes eafera Scedelandum in.

Here by *Scedelandum* is meant Scandia in the Ptolemaic sense, viz., the Danish islands and the Scandinavian peninsula. To confine the young king's fame to Skaane would be to make nonsense of the passage. The second passage (1684 ff.) reads:

on geweald gehwearf worold-cyninga
þæm selestan be sæm tweonum
þara-þe on Scedenigge sceattas dælde.

In other words, the hilt fell into the hands of Hroðgar. Here too *Scedenig* obviously refers to Scandinavia in its classical sense. In neither passage is there any reason whatever to confine the meaning to Denmark, much less Skaane; on the contrary, such a narrowing of the sense would do violence to the evident meaning of the text;

note particularly *worold-cyninga* and compare Pliny's quae (i. e., Hillevionum gens) alterum orbem terrarum eam (i. e. Scandinaviam) appellat (IV 96). There is, however, a Beowulfian usage which points to a wide extension of the Danish kingdom, viz., the names North-, South-, East- and West-Danes. Here we naturally think of Skaane, Slesvig, Selund and Jutland respectively. The nomenclature cannot be denied vagueness though and for that matter of course dates from the composition of the poem, not from the historical events which form its background. The geographical terminology may thus reflect late 6th century conditions.

As to Sweden, the poem gives us no indication at all of its location except that it was reached by water. This has been used as an argument for putting Geatland in Jutland, but the argument has absolutely no justification. To get to the Sweden of that day, i. e., Uppland, one would have to proceed by water whether one started from the mouth of the Götaelf or from some point on the Jutland peninsula (there were no railways or even highways in those days!). Schück has pointed out the possibility of using an inland water route from West Götland to Uppland, and since this route crosses lake Væni such an expression as 'ofer wid wæter' might well be applied to it. Compare ModE. *water* 'lake.' The important point here, however, is that in any case the journey would have to be made by water, so that from such expressions no conclusions can be drawn as to whether Geatland is to be identified with Gautland or Jutland.

If the Beowulf gives us little geographical information it makes up for it by supplying us with a clear outline of the political situation towards the close of the migration period (the earlier part of the 6th century). If we combine the Beowulfian account with the information obtainable from other sources, as the Widsið, Jordanes, Procopius, the Ynglinga etc., and above all the archeological records, we can get a pretty good general idea of the course of events. Stjerna (loc. cit.) has attempted to make this synthesis, but his attempt is not wholly successful, largely because of his neglect of Jordanes and Procopius. In the following, therefore, I will attempt an outline on my own account, using Stjerna pretty freely where I agree with him. I sketch the story briefly, and with as little argument as possible.

From the beginning of the migration period (c. 250) the North participated in the movement. The only tribes whom we know to have migrated as such were the Eruli and perhaps the Wylfings, but the former, in their western ventures at least, brought in their train a considerable proportion of their associates in the Nerthus amphictyony (see above), while from c. 300, as the archeological evidence shows, a steady decrease in population went on in Southeast Scandia in general; evidently great numbers of fighting-men from the North were streaming southward to share the spoils of the Roman Empire. These men for the most part joined forces with their kinsmen the Vandilians, who were of Northern origin. For such reinforcements the Vandilian kings paid in gold. Hence the mother country, as it became depleted of warriors, grew rapidly in wealth. The great wealth of the Southeast Scandians of the period is amply demonstrated by the archeological finds, especially those on the islands of Gotland, Öland and Bornholm.

The wealth and military weakness of Southeast

Scandia invited attack, and this was not slow in coming. The first invaders seem to have been the Danes, who c. 400 chased the Eruli from their seats in Selund and assumed the leadership of the Nerthus amphictyony. Their further expansion was facilitated by the migration of the Angles and Jutes; the latter had probably already begun to leave the peninsula by c. 400, whereas the Angles did not complete their migration before c. 550. Certainly at the time of Beowulf's visit to Hroðgar's court the Danes were in full possession of parts at least of Jutland (Beowulf 335 f., 348). On the other hand there is nothing in the English poem to indicate that by that time the Danes had conquered Skaane, and the conquest of that province is most plausibly connected with the Bardish wars, which were hardly concluded before c. 530.

Towards the end of the fifth or the beginning of the sixth century the Geats likewise built up a powerful kingdom, pushing their boundaries eastward to the Baltic and apparently overrunning the territories of the prosperous eastern tribes (Vagoth, Theustes, Bergio) mentioned in Jordanes. This expansion seems to have taken place under the Geatish king Hreðel, the founder of the Hreðling dynasty. Their enlarged kingdom once established, the Geatish kings in their turn became possessors, and so defenders, of great wealth. To put it differently, the erstwhile disturbers of the status quo became its most ardent champions. The new situation is well reflected in the Beowulf, where indeed three clear-cut phases may be distinguished. In the first phase the Geatish kings, though already on the defensive against their neighbors, defend themselves with vigor and success, answering raid with counter-raid and keeping a firm grip on their rich holdings. Thus, the forays of the Swedes lead to a counter-attack which results in the defeat and death of the Swedish king Ongenþeow. The old aggressive spirit survives sufficiently, indeed, to flare up for the last time in Hygelac's strictly offensive expedition to the Low Countries. The disastrous outcome of this expedition brings us to the second phase, in which the Geatish kings, unable to maintain themselves longer by sheer force of arms, resort to diplomacy to bolster up their power. Here they were extraordinarily aided by the political situation in the neighboring states (for which see below) and so succeeded in staving off the evil day for a long time. The third phase, viz., the final breakdown of the Geatish kingdom under the attacks of the Swedes, appears in the Beowulf in the shape of forebodings.

The Beowulf poet evidently looked upon the Geatish kingdom as a great power in the Scandinavian world, a power on equal terms with Denmark and Sweden. In the later Scandian tradition however (West) Gautland was remembered only as a petty kingdom. Accordingly the Geatish kings, so far as they survived in tradition, were given other realms to rule, realms better befitting a great king. Thus, Hygelac in Danish tradition became the Danish king Huglek (Saxo IV 117); in Norwegian tradition he became the Swedish king Huglek (Ynglinga cap. 22). In the Ynglinga he is described as unwarlike, very rich, avaricious and much given to luxury and magic. This description does not fit the historical Hygelac, of course, but it clearly does reflect, accurately enough, the tradition of decadence which must have become attached to the Geatish royal house as a result of the decline and fall of the Geatish kingdom. Similarly, the Swedish king Egill is represented in the Ynglinga (cap. 26) as unwarlike, and as we shall see this feature of Snorri's account, so flatly in contradiction to the Beowulf, is due to influence from the later Geatish tradition, which had made Egill into a Geatish king.

Let us now resume our narrative. The death of Hygelac (c. 525—30) left the Geatish kingdom greatly weakened. The Bards seem to have taken advantage of the situation to seize the eastern provinces, although their conquest was not effected without resistance, if we follow the story in the Ynglinga (cap. 22) and with Olrik (KS. II 58 note) consider Svipdagr to have been originally a Gautish champion (Beowulf?). In any case the Bardish conquest did not prove permanent. From the account in the Ynglinga (cap. 23) one would infer that the Swedes attacked Haki and his Bardish horde; that although he beat off the attack he was himself slain in the battle; and that his forces were so reduced by the struggle that the Bards could no longer maintain themselves in their new possessions. For a fuller discussion of the Bardish wars see below (cap. IV).

The period which now follows may be described as the period of family feuds. In Sweden the feud was between Onela (the son of Ongenþeow) and his brother Ohthere's sons Eanmund and Eadgils, the question at issue being the succession to the throne. In Denmark a similar feud arose between king Hroðgar and his son Hreðric on the one hand and Hroðulf (son of Hroðgar's younger brother Halga) on the other;

Heorogar, the elder brother of Hroðgar and his predecessor on the throne, likewise left a son, Heoroweard, and he, after the death of Hroðgar and Hreðric, became the leader of the faction opposed to Hroðulf. In both these feuds the Geats were involved, supporting among the Swedes the enemies of Onela, among the Danes the enemies of Hroðulf, and in both cases the faction supported by the Geats finally won the victory after having suffered a heavy initial defeat. The facts on which this sketch of events is based will be given below in the appropriate chapters.

After the death of Hroðulf his opponent Heoroweard became king of Denmark. From Beowulf 2160 ff. it is apparent that Heoroweard was not all he might be though the exact nature of his deficiencies is not made clear. Courage at any rate he did not lack (2161). According to the Scandian accounts his reign was short, and he came to a violent end. His death was seemingly followed by an interregnum, in which the Dano-Geatish alliance lapsed. After a period of uncertain length Haraldr hilditönn made himself king and restored, for a time, Danish power and prestige in the North. We have conflicting accounts of his origin; thus, the Sögubrot makes him the son of a Hrœrekr (Hreðric?), while according to Saxo he came of a Skaane family. The most important event in his life was his expedition to East Götland, where at Brávellir he fell in battle against king Hringr. For this expedition see especially Olrik in Nordiska Ortnamn 297 ff. Haraldr's opponent was doubtless a Gaut. Olrik supposes that Hringr was the king's true name, but it seems more natural to consider it a nickname of some sort — perhaps a name associated with a solar cult, in which case it would of course be a title borne by every king. Who was Hringr, then? I am inclined to identify him with Beowulf, whose dragon fight seems to have been substituted for an earlier historical last fight. Cf. Bugge, PBB. XII 45 ff. The omission of any account of Brávellir is of a piece with the poet's consistent practice of avoiding mention of Dano-Geatish conflicts. His hero had to die, however, and a dragon fight was a familiar device for concluding a hero's career. Wiglaf's exhortations and the forebodings are best explained as survivals of the suppressed historical account. In this connexion it is interesting to note that Saxo (VIII 259) mentions a certain Bjarki (Beowulf?) among the Geatish supporters of king Hringr. — Hringr survives the battle in the Scandian accounts, which thus in this circumstance offer no parallel to the death of Beowulf. The discrepancy, however, may be explained on the theory that Hringr was a cult name borne by Beowulf's successor as well. It may have some bearing here that Böðvarr Bjarki's grandfather was named Hringr.

After the death of Beowulf the power of the Geats rapidly declined (perhaps on account of their heavy losses in the battle of Brávellir), until at last the Geatish state was overthrown by the Swedes (cf. Beowulf 2999 ff., 3028 ff., 3150 ff.). We have no information as to the particulars of that event, but of its occurrence there can be no doubt. What became of the Geats? The bulk of them became Swedish subjects, of course. There is however a good deal of evidence pointing to an emigration of Geats to Jutland, where the emigrants would become Danish subjects. The linguistic evidence for such a settlement is presented briefly by Schütte

(AfnF. XXXIII 85 ff.). For further evidence see the references cited above. In addition the Geatish elements in the Jutish saga tradition of Saxo need to be emphasized. Thus, the Geatish king Hygelac appears in Saxo as a Danish king. That Saxo got this Hygelac from Jutish tradition has been pointed out by Olrik (KS. II 191). Similarly, king Hather of Jutland (Saxo VII 239, 247) may be a reminiscence of Hæðcyn, especially in view of his association with Røric (Hreðric). Another Danish king known to Danish but not to Icelandic tradition was Viglek, the father of Vermund and grandfather of Uffe. These kings were taken over from the Angles, as the Old English monuments show, and so first became Danicized in Jutland, though eventually adopted by all Denmark. The name Viglek, however, does not correspond accurately to the English Wihtlæg. One may therefore conjecture with some plausibility that the king Viglek of Saxo is a fusion product, owing his existence to the similarity in name between the Geatish king Viglef (OE. Wiglaf) and the Anglian king Wihtlæg. This supposition is strengthened by the statement in the Annales Ryenses that Viglek was a Norwegian king — a nationality easily attributed to a king of the then ignored Geats (whose former territories had been in part annexed to Norway) but inexplicable if the original was the Anglian king pure and simple.

Again, the story of the death of king Athisl of Sweden at the hands of Ket and Vig, the sons of Frøvin duke of Slesvig, is in origin a Geatish story, going back to the Beowulfian account of the death of Ongenþeow at the hands of Wulf and Eofor, the sons of Wonred. In Saxo the story forms part of the

Jutish (originally Anglian) saga of king Uffe. Weyhe (ESt. XXXIX 21 ff.) was the first to show in detail the identity of the two accounts.

Finally, it is the chief purpose of this treatise to show that the Amleth tale of Saxo was likewise a product of Geatish tradition as developed in Jutland. That Saxo derived the tale from Jutland is unquestioned; its Jutish timbre was established once for all by Olrik (KS. II 158 ff.). I purpose to demonstrate, however, that the roots of the story go back to Geatland, and that traces of it are to be found in its original home.

If for the moment this theory be accepted without proof, it follows that the so-called Jutish kings of Saxo without exception were originally aliens. Ørvendill, Feng, Amleth, Huglek and Hather (?) were of Geatish origin; Vermund and Uffe were Angles; Viglek represents a blending of the two streams of tradition. The adoption of the Anglian kings by the later Danish settlers in Jutland is generally explained as a result of the absorption by the newcomers of what was left of the old population. The traditions were absorbed with the people, and became a part of the common inheritance. In the same way we may account for the adoption of the traditions of the Geats. The Geatish refugees in time were absorbed into the Danish population of the peninsula, and their sagas with them.

Another conclusion which we are also able to draw concerns the political status of Jutland in the Danish monarchy. If all its traditional kings were in origin aliens, it follows that Jutland from the time it became Danish was an integral part of the Danish state; it of course had local kings of its own, but these were normally subject to the central authority, and an independent state of Jutland, felt by its people as distinct and separate from that of the Danes of the islands, at no time existed. This conclusion is fully borne out in the Beowulf, which clearly envisages the Danes, whether of the north, south, east or west, as one people.

Finally, the relations between the Danes of Jutland and the other eleme[illegible]opulation now become clear. The Danish conquest was evidently peaceable, and immigrants from Geatland at least were welcomed. Otherwise the adoption of the alien traditions would be harder to explain.

Chapter II.

In the Introduction of Gollancz's edition of the Icelandic Ambales Saga appears the following statement (p. liv): "As a Teutonic word *amlóði* stands absolutely isolated, and no etymology hitherto advanced by Teutonic philologists commends itself to serious consideration." Gollancz then goes on to advance some possible Celtic etymologies, but comes to no definite conclusions. Since the publication (in 1898) of Gollancz's volume no further etymologies of the word have been offered, and thus the matter stands at present — an unsolved riddle. It is therefore with some diffidence that I offer an analysis which seems to have escaped the attention of my numerous predecessors — overlooked, perhaps, because of its very obviousness. In brief, I interpret the word to mean simply "mad Ole." The first element is thus an original *Anale* or *Anule* (OE. *Onela*), a name frequent enough in Scandinavia from an early period, and frequently associated, as an affectionate or familiar form, with the compounded name *Anlaifr* > *Óláfr*. *Anale* (which etymologically is a diminutive) developed by syncope of the middle vowel to *Anle*, then by loss of the nasal (with compensatory lengthening of the preceding vowel) to *Ále*, later *Áli*. The alternative form *Anule* underwent a similar development, except that the syncopated *u* caused rounding of the vowel of the preceding syllable, so that the final product was *Óle* or *Óli*. By virtue of its character as a familiar name, *Anle* would of course be especially liable to modification by the attachment to it of an epithet. In the present case the epithet attached was *óð*- 'mad.' The use of this word as a suffix in the formation of proper names occurs in other Germanic dialects, e. g., OHG. Berinwuoto (Piper), OE. Eadwod (Searle). Its use as an adjective suffix is especially characteristic of Icelandic, where it is still formative. When originally attached to Anle it must have given a phrase in which the two elements were still felt as distinct: *Anle óðe* (compare *Ari fróði, Haraldr snjalli* etc.). This stage in the development seems to be preserved in the Danish word *amlingestikker,* for which see below. However, with the elision of the *e* of *Anle* before the strest vowel which immediately followed it a coalescence of the two words in pronunciation would be attained, and this phonetic unity must eventually have brought about a psychological unity as well, so that the phrase ceased to be felt as such and came to be a single word — the name of the man in question. At all events, we find no phrase, but a unified name, in historic times.

There remains the *m*. Why do we have *Amlóði* instead of *Anlóði*? The answer to this question must be sought in the Irish Annals, where many references are made to various Scandinavians named *Anlaifr*, and where the *n* of their names is invariably represented as *m* or *mh (Amlaibh, Amhlaibh).* The reason for this is clear enough. The *n* of *Anlaifr* was at that time in course of absorption by the preceding vowel. It had not, however, disappeared altogether (witness the contemporary OE. form *Anlaf*), but was a nasal spirant. Now the only nasal spirant in Irish was the lenited *m*. There had of course been a lenition of *n* as well, but the differentiation between the two forms (lenited and unlenited) of the consonant was not so great as to cause the lenited form to become a spirant. In the case of *m*, however, a much greater differentiation took place, so much so that the difference in pronunciation received orthographic expression (*mh* for the lenited form). It was natural enough, then, for the Irish to substitute their labial nasal spirant for the dental which they heard in Scandinavian mouths. The subsequent adventures of the Irish form of the Scandinavian name *Anlaifr* are of course familiar enough to students of the Havelok tale. Perhaps, however, it will not be otiose to point out that in this tale the Irish form of the name, as modified in Cymric lands, drove out the original Scandinavian form, although the tale itself centers about a historical Scandinavian chieftain and both originated and reached its final form among the Scandinavian settlers in the British Isles.

Did a parallel development take place in the tale with which we are here concerned? As to the name, we have again the evidence of the Irish Annals, where, under the year 917 (Four Masters), and 909 (Three Fragments), a Scandinavian warrior named *Amhlaidhe* is mentioned as slayer of king Niall Glundubh. The name also appears in the Four Masters under the year 904. For a full discussion of these entries see Gollancz pp. l—lii and Zenker Boeve-Amlethus 111 ff. Here we have the Irish form of the name *Anlóði*, with the same substitution of *m* for *n* which we have already observed in the case of Anlaifr, and for the same reasons. The reduction of the *o* to *a* is also regular; as to this Pedersen says (KG. I 265): „Die kurzen und langen Vokale und Diphthonge werden im Irischen in nachtoniger Silbe, sofern sie nicht schwinden — also besonders in Silben von mittlerer Stärke —, in der Regel zu -a- reduziert." The *ð* of the original appears in Irish orthography as *dh*; as it was followed by an *e*, it necessarily became palatalized in Irish pronunciation, and the palatalization is indicated by the *i* which precedes the *dh*; this *i* was not pronounced, but served merely as an orthographical sign to indicate the palatalization of the consonant which followed it. The palatalized *dh* early became a palatal spirant pure and simple (see Pedersen, KG. I 512).

Our knowledge of the warrior referred to in the Annals is limited to the fact that he was the slayer of king Niall. In any case he cannot have been the original of the Amleth of Saxo, the primitive tales concerning whom are localized in Jutland, as Olrik has proved (see KS. II 158 ff.). His name is not difficult to account for, however. The word *amlóði* in Scandinavia (except Denmark) early became a common noun, with the meaning 'fool' (derived from the saga, of course), and it is still so used in Norway and Iceland. This usage must have arisen from a practice of giving *Amlóði* as a nickname to men who were thought to resemble the Amleth of the saga. Our warrior mentioned in the Annals then becomes simply the first recorded case of this practice, and the record is a lucky accident, due to the fact that the Irish knew the warrior by his nickname rather than by his true name. — As the English monuments make Sitric (the father of Anlaf Cuaran) the slayer of Niall, Gollancz is inclined to assume his identity with the Amhlaidhe of the Annals. The evidence, however, seems hardly sufficient to establish the identification (see Gollancz lii f.).

Our case for Irish transmission by no means rests on the name Amhlaidhe alone, however. In the first place, the saga itself, as we have it in Saxo, contains elements distinctly Celtic, and one incident at least which is specifically Irish. These elements will be examined in Part II of this work. Again, Snæbjörn, the 10th century Icelandic poet, who refers to Amlóði in one of his poems in such a way that it is clear he knew him as a fool, was himself partly Irish in descent (see Gollancz xvii). The two earliest occurrences of the name thus both point to Ireland. Even more important is the fact that the name occurs in Middle English in a form derivable only from the Irish *Amlaidhe,* and with the same meaning of 'fool' which we find attached to it in Scandinavia. I refer to the word *amlaȝe*, where *ȝ* = *y*, the palatal spirant to which the Irish *dh* early developed. This word occurs in l. 3542 of the ME. metrical romance "The Wars of Alexander" (ed. Skeat EETS. 1886). Skeat in his glossary refers it to Icel. *Amlóði,* without comment. Gollancz lvii ff. recognizes the impossibility of deriving the word phonetically from *Amlóði* and correctly refers it rather to the Irish form *Amlaidhe,* but since he takes the *ȝ* to represent a velar spirant he is unable to account for the phonetic development.

The passage in which the ME. word occurs reads as follows:

I, Porrus, that as principall possessed am in Ynde, (3540)
To this michare out of Messedoine this mandment I write.
Thou, Alexander, thou ape, thou *amlaȝe* out of Grece,
Thou little thefe, thou losangere, thou lurkare in cites . . .
Madding marred has thi mode and thi mynd changid. (3545)

Here *amlaȝe* is clearly used as a term of reproach, and, if we take into consideration l. 3545, the word can hardly be interpreted otherwise than as equivalent to the *amlóði* 'mad fool' of Scandinavian usage. Its form, however, necessitates the assumption that Amlaidhe was known as a fool in Ireland, and the name could hardly have made its way into English except in connexion with an Amlaidhe story essentially the same as the story told in Scandinavia, since the linguistic results were identical.

Our theory, then, assumes that the Danish vikings brought the Hamlet story with them to Ireland, the hero of the tale being then known as Anlóðe; that under Irish influence the tale itself underwent modification and expansion, and spirant *m* replaced spirant *n* in the hero's name; and that both tale and name in the new form found acceptance at home. What happened to the spirant *m*? The existence of such a sound both in Old English and in Scandinavian is well known. It occurred only when immediately followed by a nasal stop, however. Compare Icelandic *safna* with Danish *samla* 'collect,' where the *-la* prevented that change of *m* to a spirant which the *-na* favored. In *Amlóðe* and *amlaȝe*, then, the Irish spirant *m* was imitated as a stop, giving the forms found in Icelandic and in English respectively. For the form *Amleth* see Olrik, KS. II 158.

In Denmark, where the Hamlet tale developed far beyond the primitive version known elsewhere, the common noun *amlóðe* 'fool' did not arise. We do, however, find an expression *at göre amlingestikker* 'to injure others by foolish tricks' which fits the Danish version of the story neatly enough. The form *aml-ing* 'like Amle (or Anle)' (?) is confirmatory of my analysis of *Amlóði* as *Amle* + *óðe*.

Chapter III.

Beowulf and Onela.

We have seen that the name *Amlóði* may be analyzed as *mad Ole.* Now the earliest Ole of whom we have much information is the Swedish king Onela of the Beowulf. Let us see what the poem says about him.

After the death of the Geatish king Hreðel war broke out between his sons Hæðcyn and Hygelac, on the one hand, and the Swedes on the other. This war was precipitated by Onela and Ohthere, the sons of the Swedish king Ongenþeow. By their forays into Geatish territory (2477) they roused the Geats to retaliation. Hæðcyn and Hygelac got together a powerful force and invaded Sweden itself. The Geatish forces were divided into two armies, led by Hæðcyn and Hygelac respectively. Hæðcyn had a considerable initial success, capturing Ongenþeow's wife with her valuables; one would conclude that he attacked the king's hall, and took the king by surprize. Ongenþeow, however, evidently succeeded in escaping, for he at once returned to the attack with fresh forces, rescued his wife, defeated and killed Hæðcyn (2930) and drove the remnants of the Geatish army into a wood, where only the coming of night saved them from utter annihilation. The next morning, however, before Ongenþeow could renew the attack, Hygelac came up with his comitatus, drove back the Swedes and pursued them all the way to the king's fæsten (2950), where Ongenþeow fell in a two-against-one fight with the brothers Wulf and Eofor. We are not told what Hygelac had been doing the preceding day; presumably he had been engaged with Onela and Ohthere.

Ohthere succeeded to the Swedish throne after the death of his father (Ynglinga; the Beowulf gives us no information on this point). He seems to have died early, however, and then Onela gained the throne, to the exclusion of Ohthere's sons Eanmund and Eadgils. These, however, did not acquiesce in the situation. Defeated at home, they fled to the Geats for protection and assistance. At that time the youthful Heardred, the son of Hygelac, was king of Geatland. He welcomed the refugees and thus drew upon himself the hostility of Onela, who invaded Geatland and defeated and killed Heardred. Eanmund also fell during the battle, killed by Weohstan, one of Onela's retainers. Eadgils, however, succeeded in making his escape. Onela now set Beowulf on the Geatish throne, presumably as a subject king, and returned to Sweden. That he chose Beowulf was doubtless largely due to the fact that his retainer Weohstan was a kinsman of Beowulf and must have exercised his influence with Onela in his kinsman's behalf. Here both Onela and Weohstan made a serious miscalculation, however, for Beowulf did not remain loyal to the man who had set him on his throne but, moved partly by a feeling of obligation to avenge the death of Heardred (2391) and partly by a desire to gain political independence, allied himself with Eadgils and aided him in overthrowing Onela (2392 ff.).

The Beowulf gives no details of the final battle in which Onela was defeated and killed, but the Scandian monuments throw some light on the matter. According to the Skjöldungasaga and the Skáldskaparmál (43) the battle between Áli (Onela) and Aðils (Eadgils) took place on the ice of lake Væni. This indicates that the expedition of Eadgils was proceeding northward by the inland water route, and so must have started from the west coast. Consequently — as the expedition must be presumed to have set out from a Geatish base — we have a clear confirmation of the theory that the chief seat of the Geats was in the west rather than in Öland (as Stjerna would have it), as in the latter case no such route would have been chosen and the decisive battle could hardly have been fought in so remote a spot. As regards the battle having taken place on the ice we have further a possible reference in the Beowulf itself (2396a) and a certain reference in the Kalfsvísa. The latter poem gives us further information of some interest. The second stanza quoted in the Snorra Edda gives the names of Áli and four of his retainers who rode "to the ice." Now of these retainers the first, Vésteinn, is evidently identical with the Weohstan of the Beowulf, whom we know to have been a retainer of Onela. The second retainer, Vifill, appears in Saxo as an associate of Ole (Áli inn frœkni, for whose identity with Onela see below). The other two retainers seem to be mythical. Here it is clear that the reference to Vésteinn gives us the important piece of information that Weohstan remained loyal to his lord to the end, in spite of his kinsman Beowulf's defection.

How does the author of the Beowulf deal with these

events? In the first place, he says as little about them as possible. The whole story of Beowulf's alliance with Eadgils and the campaign against Onela which follows is reduced to six lines (2391—6). Beowulf's part (whatever it was) in the war between Heardred and Onela is omitted entirely. If he lifted a hand to help the son of Hygelac in his extremity the poem gives no indication of it, and this in spite of the fact that throughout the poem great play is made of Beowulf's loyalty to Hygelac, which went so far as to lead him to refuse Hygd's offer of the Geatish throne (2373 ff.). Again, the praises of Onela are sung in a most extraordinary fashion — extraordinary if one remembers that the Geats were consistently Onela's enemies and his opponents' friends. Thus, the poet explains as follows the origin of the feud between Onela and his nephews (2381 ff.): "They (Eanmund and Eadgils) had rebelled against the helm of the Scylfings, the illustrious prince, the best sea-king that ever ruled Sweden." This clearly puts the brothers in the wrong, though it was they, not Onela, who were the allies of the Geats. Here the poet goes out of his way to be unfair to the young princes, who, as we have seen, were there proper heirs to the Swedish throne, while Onela was a usurper. What on earth possessed the poet to distort the facts in this fashion? The explanation is easy. It will be remembered that after the death of Beowulf his kinsman Wiglaf succeeded him on the throne. Now Wiglaf's father Weohstan was, as we know already, a retainer of Onela. He participated in the campaign against the Geats and killed Eanmund with his own hand. He remained with his lord to the very end, as we have seen, in spite of Beowulf's hostility to Onela. After the latter's defeat and death, however, Weohstan could of course no longer remain in Sweden, which was now ruled by Eadgils, his bitterest enemy. He therefore sought refuge with his kinsman Beowulf, who gave him protection and seems to have made him a Geatish noble (see 2607 ff.). This must have resulted in embroiling the Geats with their late ally Eadgils, who, however, was never able to avenge his brother's death on the murderer in person (2624 f.). Going back to Wiglaf, we find the poet calling him "prince of the Scylfings, kinsman of Ælfhere" (2603—4). The name Ælfhere with its vowel alliteration and its association with Yngvi-Freyr the lord of Alfheimr is eminently suitable for a member of the Swedish royal house (the Scylfings), and names in Alf- actually occur among the Swedish kings named in the Ynglinga and Saxo. Furthermore, Ælfhere may be one of the two hostile kinsmen of Eanmund referred to in l. 2614 (the other one was Onela, of course). It may then be conjectured that Weohstan was married to a Scylfing princess, a daughter, perhaps, of Ælfhere, and that from her Wiglaf inherited his title "prince of the Scylfings." If so, he was, on his mother's side, a blood-kinsman of Onela, and he must in any case have had a loyalty of his own to his father's lord. Furthermore, he had inherited his father's feud with Eadgils, as we know from ll. 2999 ff. Hence the reasons for the English poet's extravagant praise of Onela are clear enough, as also the reason for his prejudice against Eanmund and Eadgils. No Geatish skald singing before Wiglaf or his successors would have dared to present Onela unsympathetically or Eadgils other than unsympathetically. On the contrary, the tendency would be to identify Onela more and more with the new Geatish royal house, that of the Wægmundings, until finally he would become purely and simply a Geatish king. The beginnings of this tendency are clearly observable in the Beowulf, as we have seen. There is reason to believe that the tendency was worked out to its logical conclusion. On the other hand, the story of Beowulf's hostility to Onela would tend to be minimized more and more by the poets, until finally it was lost altogether. Here too the beginnings of the tendency are clearly observable in the English poem. — It is conceivable that Beowulf's failure to keep faith with Onela might result in his development into a villain. However, his role as kinsman and benefactor of Weohstan and Wiglaf would prevent any development in this direction. It would therefore be necessary to eliminate altogether his connexion with Onela, a connexion which historically was one of hostility and so poetically was irreconcilable with Weohstan's loyalty to the same king.

Turning now to the Icelandic material (including the tales in Saxo derived from Icelandic sources), what treatment of these same matters do we find? The first thing we notice is the fact that Áli (Onela) does not figure as a Swede at all, but as a Norwegian. Clearly his historical hostility to his kinsmen influenced everywhere the development of the traditions concerning him, and the same process which in Norway took from him his proper nationality must be assumed to have had its effect in Geatland as well. What was the link that gave the Norwegians an excuse for adopting him? The epithet "inn upplenzki" attached to his name gives us the clue.

This epithet, which in reality referred to Áli's seat in the Uppland district of Sweden, was evidently taken by the Norwegians as a reference to their own uplands, and this resulted in Áli becoming a Norwegian king in Norwegian tradition as preserved by the Icelanders. As to Beowulf's part in the struggle, that has been absorbed into the Hrólfr cycle, and will be discussed below in connexion with that cycle.

The Icelanders preserved the memory of another Áli, called "inn frœkni," who, as I shall show, goes back likewise to the historical Onela. This Áli was apparently a product of Skaane tradition (Olrik, DH. II 141f.), and so, appropriately enough, becomes a Dane. What was the link here? The Hyndluljóð, a poem from the latter part of the 10th century, has the following to say on the subject (14, 1—2): "Áli was earlier, the strongest of men; Halfdanr still earlier, the highest of the Scyldings." As this is a genealogical poem, we are justified in concluding 1) that Áli and Halfdanr were relatives, and 2) that Áli belonged to the younger generation of the two — apparently to the generation immediately following that of Halfdanr. Who was this Halfdanr, and just what was the relationship between the two men? As a Scylding, Halfdanr would be a Danish king. Now the Beowulf tells us of a Danish king Healfdene, a Scylding, and uses to describe him the same adjective "high" (57a) which we find used in the Hyndluljóð. It seems, then, a reasonably safe inference that the two poems have reference to the same man. This would be made practically certain if we found the Beowulf connecting Healfdene with an Onela in some such way as the Hyndluljóð connects Halfdanr with Áli. And this is just what we do find. After telling of the three sons of Healfdene the English poet gives us the following information about Healfdene's daughter (62—3):

hyrde ic þæt . . . . . elan cwen,
Heaðo-Scilfingas heals-gebedda.

Line 62 is unfortunately defective, but it is clear that the name of the husband ends in *-ela*, and that he is a Scylfing, i. e., a member of the Swedish royal house. Onela, and Onela alone, satisfies both these requirements. Accordingly, many scholars, from Grundtvig to Klaeber, have emended the *elan* of the ms. to *Onelan*. We now have the key to the relationship left unspecified in the Hyndluljóð: Áli was Halfdanr's son-in-law. It will be noted that the two passages give each other mutual support. The ljóð confirms our emendation: the English poem explains why Áli, although properly a Swede, became a Dane in Scandian tradition (as we shall soon see, his connexion with Sweden was by no means forgotten).

How do we know that the Áli of the Hyndluljóð and the Áli inn frœkni of the Skjöldunga and Saxo are the same? Here I can do no better than to quote Olrik (DH. II 139): Hvad digteren har kendt om ham, "den stærkeste af mænd," maa være tapre kampe; i æt og daad slutter han sig saaledes til sagaernes Ole den frøkne. . . . I samtidigt skjaldedigt, fra sidste tredjedel af 10de aarh., er *Áli* typisk navn for en krigerhövding; *ála él* en staaende kenning for kampen. Ja ifølge et digt af Brage den gamle skal Áli navnet allerede optræde et hundred aar tidligere. Denne skikkelse lader sig næppe skille fra Áli "den stærkeste af mænd" i Hyndluljóð og fra sagaernes Ole den frøkne, der øvede alskens stordaad og i fremtrædende grad betegnes som søkonge.

What other evidence is there for the identity of Áli inn frœkni and Onela? In the first place, there is his ancestry and native country. As a Dane Áli could hardly hail from Uppland, so the Skjöldunga gives him a grandfather named Áli, king of the uplands in Norway. Here, just as in the case of Áli inn upplenzki, we owe Norway (instead of Sweden) to the Norwegian (Icelandic) line of transmission. In Saxo, moreover, we find Olav (for whose identity with Áli inn frœkni see Olrik, DH. II 134) credited with a step-father Áni. Now the historical Onela had a grandfather named Áni (Ynglinga), and the Saxonian stepfather of that name seems to be a reminiscence of this grandfather.

In the second place, there is his history. Áli is credited with numerous exploits the historicity of which it is impossible to determine. His relations with king Aun of Sweden, however, are closely parallel to the relations of Onela with Eanmund in the Beowulf. The Skjöldunga makes Áli a usurping king of Sweden, who drives Aun, the rightful ruler, into exile. Aun takes refuge in West Gautland. Now, as we have seen, Onela was a usurping king of Sweden, who drove into exile Eanmund, the rightful king (as eldest son of Ohthere). Eanmund sought refuge in Geatland. The parallel has already been pointed out by Belden (MLN. XVIII 149 ff.). There is likewise a correspondence in name between the two exiles. The Scandian form of *Eanmund* would be *Aunmundr.* No such name occurs in the monuments, but in its familiar form *Aun* (for such formations see Naumann 150) it is identical with the name of Áli's antagonist in the Ynglinga and Skjöldunga.

There are important discrepancies between the two

accounts, however, and it will be necessary to examine these in detail. In the first place, the Aun of the Ynglinga is also called Áni, as we have already noted. One of his two names must obviously be a nickname. Which one? Now a peculiar feature of the story of Aun is the phenomenal longevity ascribed to him, a longevity on account of which he is called by Ari in his genealogy *Aun enn gamli*. Schagerström and Hellquist derive *Áni* plausibly enough from an adjective **ánn* 'old' (AfnF. III 139 and VII 3), and this evidently fits in beautifully with Ari's *gamli* and with the story of Aun as told in the Ynglinga. We therefore have a right to conclude that *Aun* was the true name, *Áni* the nickname, especially since *Aun* is probably derived from *Auðwin* (Noreen) and if so cannot be a nickname. Nor indeed could it well have been used appellatively even if actually an uncompounded name answering to the *Aun-* of Burgundian *Aunemund* etc.; in view of the extensive use of this *Aun-* in compounds it can hardly be explained as a nickname, whatever its meaning may have been.

Secondly, Aun and Eanmund are widely separated temporally, Aun being historically the great-grandfather of Eanmund. Furthermore, Aun, unlike Eanmund, is not represented as having been killed by Áli, but survives him. How could Aun and Eanmund have become identified? Obviously no identification could take place so long as the names of the two men were different. When, however, *Aunmundr* (Eanmund) had come to be remembered exclusively as *Aun* (the short form of his name), and when the name *Auðwin* by phonetic processes had likewise become *Aun*, an identification of the two kings became as inevitable as it hitherto had been impossible. We have here a neat explanation not only for Aun's relations with Áli inn frœkni, but also for his extraordinary length of life, a peculiarity of the saga hitherto unexplained. We can now also account for the displacement of Áli from his proper chronological position as contemporary of the children of Halfdanr (a position which in the Hyndluljóð he still retains). The historical Onela was an antagonist of Eanmund and Eadgils. The former he defeated and drove into exile. The latter defeated and killed him. When Eanmund became identified with his great-grandfather, one of the effects of the identification was to split up Onela into two persons, one to act as antagonist of the now composite Aun, the other to act as antagonist of Aðils. The two Áli's thus formed were widely separated, temporally, and so lost all connexion with each other. The antagonist of Eanmund was actually successful in driving that king from the throne, and so would continue to be represented as a Swedish king. The antagonist of Eadgils, remembered only for his own defeat and death, would lose all connexion with the Swedish throne. Finally, the phenomenal longevity ascribed to Aun would prevent Áli from doing more than drive him into exile, so the historical death of Eanmund would necessarily be eliminated from the tale.

In spite of his historical displacement Áli did not lose his connexion with the Danish royal house. It was of course necessary, however, to locate him among the kings of a traditionally older period. He therefore became a son of Friðleifr and a brother of Fróði in the Skjöldunga, which makes these kings pre-Halfdanian. This brought him into connexion with the historical kings of the Bards and into contact with Starkaðr, the hero of the cycle of stories dealing with those kings.

There remains the death of Onela. Can the death of Áli inn frœkni be derived from it? In the Scandian monuments Starkaðr regularly appears as Áli's slayer. The oldest account of the deed is that contained in Starkaðr's Death Song (Saxo VIII 272). The passage in question reads as follows:

> Hercule non tunc me ferro spoliare petebas,
> Quando ter Olonis summo discrimine nati
> Expugnator eram. Namque agmine prorsus in illo
> Aut gladium fregit manus aut obstantia fudit;
> Haec gravitas ferientis erat.

The proper meaning of this passage has been the subject of much learned debate, and still rests uncertain enough. In the following I venture a new interpretation, which, I think, resolves all the difficulties and makes Saxo's reference intelligible. The chief seat of the trouble is the second line. Here the appearance of the caesura in the fourth foot gives us a hint that *ter* is to be construed with *summo*. I take it, then, that *ter summo* translates the superlative of some such adjective as *allstórr* 'very great' — an adjective which in the original may well have alliterated with *Óli*. The use of *ter* with an adjective as a simple intensive meaning 'very' is of course familiar enough. The phrase *ter summo discrimine nati* is best interpreted as an Óli epithet meaning 'a born champion' and parallel to the Hyndluljóð's *Áli . . . öflgastr manna* and to the kenning *ála él* (cf. Olrik, DH. II 139 f.). I follow Müllenhoff (DA. V 310 note) in his renderings *expugnator* 'victor' and *agmen* 'expedition.' So interpreted, the passage might readily be put in the mouth of Beowulf and serve as a reference to his victory over Onela (Beowulf 2391—9). Note in this connexion the English poet's praise of Onela (2380 ff., 2390).

The Death Song version of Áli's overthrow departs from the Beowulfian account only in the substitution of Starkaðr for Beowulf. No treachery on Starkaðr's part is so much as hinted at. The version is thus very primitive; in fact, it has every appearance of being a mere relic or survival, a reference handed down in song long after it had ceased to be understood, preserved in its primitive form, doubtless, largely because it was only a reference and so escaped contamination from the saga itself, which had grown away from the original form of the tale to such an extent that the Óli of the Death Song became dissociated from the Óli of the saga. The incidental nature of the Death Song reference manifests itself likewise in a marked incompleteness, even when compared with the Beowulfian version, which itself is not notable for fullness. This incompleteness, however, is of a piece with that of the other references in the Song, of course.

When now we turn to the Skjöldungasaga, we find Áli still the victim, and Starkaðr still the slayer, but the slaying no longer takes place in battle, in the course of a military expedition. On the contrary, Starkaðr is represented as a retainer of Áli who treacherously assassinates his lord. He enters Áli's service, and slays him, at the instigation of Áli's halfbrother Fróði, it is true, but nevertheless the deed is distinctly a betrayal, and reflects anything but credit on its perpetrator. Olrik has made it clear (DH. II 131 ff.) that this deed did not originally belong to Starkaðr, and he conjectures (p. 145) that a similarity of name or something of the sort caused him to become identified with the actual perpetrator. Let us see.

From the Beowulf we learn that Beowulf broke faith with Onela, apparently at the instigation of Eadgils, and by supplying the latter with arms and men enabled him to overthrow his uncle. It is not clear from the account whether Beowulf led the expedition in person or not, but certainly he played an active part in the events which led to the defeat and death of Onela. For his disloyalty to his overlord a good deal of justification could be found in the ethics of the time, of course, according to which his supreme duty would be to avenge the death of Heardred. It is thus not surprizing that the English poet does not condemn Beowulf for breaking faith with the man who set him on his throne. That Onela and his supporters took the same view, however, is more than doubtful, and at the least estimate it cannot be denied that we have here a germ which under favorable conditions could easily develop into a treachery story. However, a certain difficulty remains. For Beowulf, though probably a tributary king, was no retainer of Onela, and yet the primitive form of the story must have been of the faithless-repentant retainer type, for otherwise Eadgils' loss of his active role in favor of that of a mere instigator would be hard to explain. As it happens, though, the historical complex contains elements which would make easy the development of the kind of retainer which we actually find. For Beowulf's kinsman Weohstan was a faithful retainer of Onela, and if we suppose a fusion of the two kinsmen we get just the combination we need. Weohstan's contribution is obvious; Beowulf furnished both the treachery and the repentance — as we saw above, he later broke with Eadgils by taking Weohstan under his protection. On this point see also the following chapter. With Áli's shift in chronological position Fróði replaced Eadgils as the kinsman responsible for the crime.

In what way did the faithless retainer become identified with Starkaðr? When Fróði replaced Eadgils, Fróði's retainer Starkaðr would naturally assume the role hitherto held by Eadgils' ally Beowulf, who had been reduced to retainer through his fusion with Weohstan. The change would be somewhat assisted by certain resemblances between the two heroes. Thus, both Beowulf and Starkaðr were men of a strength so extraordinary that it led to their development into half-giants. Again, both heroes were actually faithful retainers (Beowulf, of Hygelac; Starkaðr, of Fróði), and in each case the part was fundamental, not incidental. To these considerations may be added the following, derived from Olrik's analysis (DH. II 131—77), though he was far from having the present solution in mind. Both the Starkaðr cycle and the stories about Áli seem to have developed in Skaane, so that the latter group (decidedly the lesser) was within the range of influence of the former and so would tend to be swallowed up by it, as actually happened. The unusual feature, of course, is the absorption by Starkaðr of the villain rather than the hero of the lesser cycle. This development was due primarily to the relations I have already pointed out, but it may have been assisted by certain peculiarities of the Starkaðr cycle itself, for a discussion of which I must refer the reader to Olrik.

What relation does the Skjöldunga version bear to the Death Song version? The latter seems to represent the bare historical facts, as remembered in Norway, modified in one respect by influence from the Skaane story, viz., in that Starkaðr took the place of Beowulf as the victor. The two versions are independent, in other words, and go back to the traditions of separate parts of Scandinavia, although they came into contact with each other in the course of time.

All the historical features of the Skjöldungasaga version of the Álasaga are thus accounted for. There remain certain other features which merit brief consideration. Historically Áli was no true Scylding; this fact was not forgotten, but was accounted for by the poets in a decidedly unhistorical fashion — he was made a bastard son of Friðleifr. His half-brother Fróði's hostility to him derives from Eadgils, of course, but may likewise have been influenced by the part which Fróði played in the Hrólfr cycle. The details of the plot against Áli and his death go back partly to the Starkaðr cycle (Olrik) and partly, it would seem, to the saga of Hermóðr (Bugge). For a discussion of the influence of Hermóðr on the Álasaga see Bugge, PBB. XII 37 ff. I may add that the name Ármóðr seems to be a contamination product (Áli + Hermóðr). Bugge does not explain how the two sagas came to be confused. The key to the confusion is nevertheless to be found in the Beowulf, I think. In the first place, both of the passages which treat of Heremod (901 ff., 1709 ff.) contrast him with Beowulf. This gives evidence of being a part of the poet's regular stock-in-trade, and was probably a traditional formula, or became one. Nothing would be easier, then, than to transfer Heremod's attributes and final end to Beowulf's great historical enemy Onela (Áli). The contrast thus became an antagonism and a justification for Beowulf's conduct. Such an interpretation of Áli would naturally arise among the Geats, and the Geatish border of Skaane probably contributed this element to the saga. Secondly, we are told (902) that Heremod was betrayed among the Jutes. Now Onela was betrayed (in a sense) by the Geats, and in view of the early confusion of Jutes with Geats a similar confusion of Heremod with Onela might easily arise both in Skaane and elsewhere. — The Saxonian version is valuable for our purposes chiefly because its patriotic substitution of Skaane and Denmark for Sweden reveals to us the location of the poet's workshop (but see Bugge, loc. cit.).

We have seen that the Swede Onela became a Norwegian in Norway and a Dane in Skaane, and in the Beowulf we have noted the beginnings of the process which, if our thesis is correct, made him a Geat in Geatland. His consistent loss of his proper nationality was not accidental. It grew naturally out of his hostility to his kinsmen Eanmund and Eadgils and his final defeat at the hands of the latter. The neighbors of the Swedes, who were continually at war with the Uppsala monarchs, would easily identify with their own side a man who likewise was an enemy of those monarchs. This alone, however, would not account for Onela's ready adoption and great success (if you will) as a saga hero. His personality and his exploits must have been such as to make him an attractive and sympathetic figure, a good subject for poetical treatment, so that the skalds would pounce upon any link they might find which would give them an excuse for making him into a hero of their own people.

Chapter IV.

Beowulf and Hroðulf.

Before proceeding further with the saga history of Onela it will be necessary to examine the career of the Geatish hero Beowulf at the Danish court. According to the English poem, Beowulf made an expedition to the court of the Danish king Hroðgar for the purpose of slaying a monster which was infesting the king's hall. The monster story is of course unhistorical. It must have grown out of some historical complex, however, and the determination of this complex is a matter of great importance to us. If we begin by assuming that Beowulf actually was at Hroðgar's court for a time, we need to determine his motive in going thither. Now in the normal course of events a Germanic youth of noble birth would take temporary service with a friendly foreign king (cf. ll. 1836 ff.). Was there any reason why Beowulf should serve this apprenticeship in war and courtly life with Hroðgar in particular? Yes. There were special bonds of friendship between Hroðgar and Ecgþeow (Beowulf's father). The poet tells us (459 ff.) how Ecgþeow, after having killed a warrior of the Wylfings, fled to Hroðgar for protection, and how Hroðgar settled the quarrel for him by a money payment. It is added that Ecgþeow swore oaths to Hroðgar. These oaths must have been in effect promises on Ecgþeow's part to support Hroðgar in his wars and other difficulties. Furthermore we learn (372) that Beowulf had already lived for a time, as a boy, at Hroðgar's court. This must have been during his father's stay there, of course. There is thus every reason to suppose that the Danish court would be the natural place for Beowulf to go to when the time came for him to seek experience abroad.

Is there any evidence, apart from the English poem, that this court was the scene of an event which might have given rise to a monster story? Yes. Saxo tells us how the champion Bjarki won fresh laurels there by killing a huge bear which he met in a thicket, and in the Hrólfssaga this bear has become a winged monster. The postulation of a historical fight with a bear at or near the Danish court naturally involves no great strain on one's credulity. If the bear were sufficiently large and ferocious such a fight might well be remembered and handed down in story, and its development into what we find in the Beowulf, on the one hand, and in the Hrólfssaga, on the other, is quite in consonance with the general bent of the primitive mind. With this development I am here not primarily concerned, and refer the reader especially to O. L. Olson (Relation of Hrólfssaga . . . to Beowulf, Chicago dissertation, 1916), to Deutschbein 249 ff., to Lawrence and to Panzer. It is my present purpose to examine in some detail the careers of the two heroes Bjarki and Beowulf, however, and as it will be necessary to begin with their names the bear story will have to be considered, if only briefly and without much argument.

The names Beowulf 'bee-wolf,' i. e., 'bear,' and Bjarki 'little bear' look like appellatives rather than true names.

Whence did they come? From the bear-like characteristics of the heroes, one may say. But where did the heroes get these characteristics? On the basis of Saxo's sober account we may safely assume that Bjarki while at the Danish court won fame by killing a bear. I will venture a further assumption: after killing the beast he drank of its blood. Cf. Jónsson 62 and 135. This of course gave him of the bear's strength, habits and spiritual qualities. Hence the nickname Bjarki came to be applied to him. But once the hero was given bear-like qualities the bear he had slain came to be looked upon as his kinsman. The blood-drinking thus became offensive — impossible, indeed. Bjarki was therefore provided with a companion, Hjalti, who served to relieve Bjarki of his grewsome meal. But if Bjarki killed the bear, while Hjalti drank of its blood, the next step in the growth of the tale would obviously be to connect the two traits in some rational fashion; hence Bjarki was made to kill the bear to give Hjalti to drink of its blood. But why? There could be but one reason. Hjalti needed strength and courage. In this way Hjalti became a coward, taken under Bjarki's protection and made into a man of courage by the bear's blood which Bjarki forced him to drink. But although the hero's blood-drinking was the most objectionable feature of the primitive story, his slaying of his kinsman the bear was hardly less offensive. A strong tendency would inevitable arise to give him another beast, or a monster, to kill. And the victim chosen would of course be an opponent appropriate to the hero in his new aspect as a man with bear-like qualities. Hence he attracted to himself a story of the bear's son type, for which see

Panzer. Beowulf probably developed in essentially the same way. The English version lacks a Hjalti, however — the poets seem to have solved their problem by eliminating the blood-drinking altogether, rather than by transferring it to a companion. It is clear, then, that the two versions developed independently, but the evidence calls for a common historical basis.

At this point it will be convenient to summarize the more obvious points of resemblance between the two heroes. Each is a foreign adventurer at the court of the Danish king, come thither from Gautland (Geatland), where a near kinsman is ruler. Shortly after arriving, each has a dispute with one of the retainers at court; in each case the retainer tries to pick the quarrel, but is silenced (Beowulf 499 ff.) or vanquished (Saxo, Hrólfssaga). Each fights and kills a beast or monster, to all appearance originally a bear. Each bears a name best interpreted as a nickname meaning 'bear' or 'little bear' and each has bear-like attributes. The details of the monster fight as given in the Beowulf and the Hrólfssaga present remarkable similarities (see Panzer's discussion p. 369 ff.). We have by no means exhausted the parallels with this list, however. In the following the attempt will be made to examine the other activities ascribed to the two heroes, and to come to some conclusion as to the identity of the men by comparing their lives.

To begin with, Beowulf serves Hroðgar, while Bjarki serves Hrólfr. This is however only an apparent difference. As is well known, Hrólfr became the central figure of the Scylding line of kings and drew to himself even the story of the building of Heorot (Saxo II 58), the most famous and most characteristic of the tales concerning Hroðgar. It is not surprizing, then, to find Bjarki attracted within his orbit as well, but it would be eminently unsafe to assume that he originally belonged there. The determination of the original overlord must be left to the end of this discussion; if Beowulf and Bjarki prove to be in fact the same person, the proper overlord for the hero necessarily becomes Hroðgar, for the authority of the English poem here can not be challenged.

Coming now to specific events, from the English poem we learn that Beowulf aided Eadgils in his attack on Onela. The Icelandic versions of the Hrólfr cycle, however, represent Bjarki, together with other Danish champions, as giving this aid (sent by Hrólfr, it is true). Here we clearly have another link between Beowulf and Bjarki.

The chief event in Bjarki's life seems to have been his duel with Agnarr Ingjaldsson. In Beowulf's career there is nothing to correspond. On the other hand, the Widsið tells of the defeat and death of Ingeld at the hands of Hroðgar and Hroðwulf; the battle took place at Heorot. We find nothing of the sort in Danish tradition. Yet the two slayings seem to belong together. The nature of the development becomes clear when we consider the Beowulfian account, which pictures Ingeld as a young man, whose married life was short, being ended by a renewal of the feud with his wife's people the Danes and his own death. Ingeld thus in all likelihood had no son for Bjarki to kill, and Bjarki's deed more probably goes back to the historical slaying of Ingeld by Hroðulf. How did this slaying get attached to Bjarki, and why was Agnarr created and made to serve as victim? As the central figure of his cycle Hrólfr, like Arthur and Charlemagne, would tend to become simply a noble figurehead, his personal exploits being neglected or even transferred to others. Furthermore, as we shall see, Hrólfr was thoroughly unscrupulous and his deeds usually wanted apology; the skalds therefore naturally concentrated on his more attractive characteristics, as his generosity and his winning personality (cf. Beowulf 1181) and his rather dubious exploits were conveniently ignored. Again, Ingjaldr was himself the center of a heroic cycle of stories, and was eventually adopted by the Danes as one of their kings; under these conditions it would never do, obviously, for him to be slain either by Hrólfr or by Bjarki, and the tradition developed accordingly. Other factors involved will be taken up below, in another connexion.

Bjarki the slayer of Agnarr must go back to Bjarki the foremost champion in the fight against the Bards. Why should he be drawn into this fight? Was there any special reason for him to be hostile to them? If for the moment we assume his identity with Beowulf we are at liberty to search for some such reason in the English poem. And here we find very definite indication of an alliance between Geats and Danes, directed against the Bards. Beowulf in his farewell speech to Hroðgar says, among other things (1822 ff.): "If I . . . may in any wise gain greater favor in thy sight, O king, through deeds of war, than I yet have done, I stand ready. If I learn . . . that neighbors oppress thee with dread, as enemies at times have done, I will bring to thy help a thousand warriors. I know of Hygelac . . . that he will support me with word and deed that I may honor thee well and bear the spear-shaft to thy aid . . . when thou art in need of men." Note also l. 1864. The neighbors in question could hardly have been other than the Bards, who as we know from the Widsið later actually did attack Heorot. Did Beowulf keep his promise? The poet does not tell us, but the promise, recorded long after the event, would hardly have been mentioned by the poet had it gone unfulfilled. Moreover, there is some indication in the Scandian monuments that the Bards regarded Geats and Danes as allied enemies of theirs. Thus, the Skjöldungasaga mentions a jarl Svertingr of Sweden, whose sons kill king Fróði and whose daughter is the wife of Fróði's son Ingjaldr. Essentially the same situation meets us in Saxo, where, however, Sverting is supposed to be a German. Now in the Beowulf Swerting is the ancestor of the Geatish kings (1203), while the wife of Ingeld is a Danish princess. We have therefore in the Scandian Ingjaldr or Starkaðr cycle (which presents things from the point of view of the Bards) a significant confusion or rather fusion of the historical Danes and Geats, the fusion product being given a Geatish name (Svertingr) and located in Sweden or Germany — the former perhaps a reminiscence of the original home of the Geats, the latter an identification with the chief enemy of the Danes at the time when the saga took shape. Olrik (DH. II 41) offers a rather fantastic explanation of the use of the term Svertingr in the North. To me it seems much more plausible to refer this use to the political alliance between Hroðgar and the Geats told of in the Beowulf.

We are on more uncertain ground when we come to the war between Haki and Hugleikr (Ynglinga, cap. 22;

Saxo VI 185 f.). Haki was certainly a Bardish, not a Danish hero, and his war with Hugleikr, if it has any historical basis at all, must go back to a war between Bards and Geats. But the story as we have it is undoubtedly late (cf. Olrik, DH. II 115 ff.) and may be pure invention. Nevertheless I incline to the opinion that it has a historical germ, viz., Hygelac's fall abroad, followed by a temporary conquest of, say, East Gautland by a Bardish horde. The fusion of these two events may serve to explain the discrepancy as to localization in the Ynglinga and Saxo. My theory derives some support from the curious parallelism in the careers of Beowulf and Bjarki on the one hand and Svipdagr on the other. And if Haki's opponents were Geats, Svipdagr, their true leader (along with the certainly unhistorical Geigaðr), answers precisely to Beowulf, the regent of Geatland after the fall of Hygelac. I am unable to explain, however, the application to Beowulf of such a name as Svipdagr, and so long as this cannot be made clear the whole theory must rest uncertain enough.

However it may be with Svipdagr, our other evidence is enough to make it highly probable that Beowulf actually participated in the struggle with the Bards. This is not sufficient, however, to account for the transfer to him of deeds really performed by Hrólfr in that struggle. Before Beowulf can be identified with Bjarki we must have more information about both heroes. Let us first examine the story of Bjarki's marriage. His wife was Hrút, who in Saxo's account is a sister of Hrólfr. According to the same authority she was originally destined for Agnarr, but after his death at the hands of Bjarki she was given to the latter as the prize of victory. Here it is obvious that Agnarr represents the Ingeld of the Beowulf, while Hrút stands for the Beowulfian Freawaru. This would make Hrút the daughter of Hroðgar, not Halga, and so a cousin, not a sister, of Hrólfr. Such an interpretation does not conflict, as a matter of fact, with the text of the Bjarkamál — the word *mágr,* which Saxo translates by *gener,* may mean brother-in-law, son-in-law, or simply relative by marriage (the last, e. g., in the Hyndluljóð 20, 2), and Bjarki was doubtless originally referred to simply as Hrólfr's kinsman-in-law. The ambiguity of the word, however, must early have opened the way to interpreting the wife of Bjarki as a sister of Hrólfr (Saxo) or a daughter (Skjöldunga, Hrólfssaga), and one or the other of these was probably the interpretation of the poet himself. In this connexion it must be remembered that as Hrólfr became the central figure of the cycle all the other characters would tend to be defined in terms of their relationship to him, and this fact made the word *mágr* play the part it did in altering the historical connexions and character of Hrút. Furthermore, as Hroðulf was actually the foster-son of Hroðgar, Hrút would be his foster-sister, whence the transition to true sister is easy. As to the name, Hrút rather than Freawaru is probably the historical form, since it alliterates with the names of the other Scyldings, and since it actually occurs as a woman's name in the Scandian monuments (see Olrik, DH. I 67), whereas no such name as Freyvör (Freawaru) has ever been found.

How did the name Freawaru come into existence? It could hardly have been introduced in Scandinavia, where the lady's true name was well known. In England, however, no such name as *Hrut* occurs, and the word itself, which means 'she-goat,' must have been felt as singularly inappropriate for a king's daughter, who by virtue of her high station deserved a high-sounding name. Another strong objection to the name in England would be that the verb *hrutan* 'snore' might be associated with it. It is therefore not surprizing that the name Hrut did not survive long in England. The scop who made the change certainly succeeded in choosing a name high-sounding enough, at all events, and rare enough, to be a creation of his own. — The name Hrút was finally lost in the North as well, presumably for reasons similar to those which made it objectionable in England. — It is interesting to note that the one line in the Beowulf in which the name Freawaru appears (2022) need suffer no change in meaning with the substitution of the original name: as it stands, the line reads:

þa ic Freawaru flet-sittende

which, with the original name, would read:

þa ic Hrute heal-sittende.

Additional evidence that Hrút was originally the daughter of Hróarr is to be had from the Gram saga of Saxo (I 12 ff.), although there the lady goes unnamed. The Gram saga is not a traditional story, but a deliberate work of fiction, composed by a conscious literary artist for the entertainment of his audience. It remains true, however, that the author did not invent his story outright; on the contrary, he derived every trait from traditional stories known to him, as we shall see. By taking old situations (and, to some extent, old names) and putting them together in new ways, he hoped to make a tale which would interest his hearers by virtue of both its novelty and its familiarity. Now as he had many more, and much better, sources of information to draw on than have we (for much of the old saga material has since perished), there is reason to suppose that his tale may contain traditional material not otherwise preserved to us. Let us analyze the story, then, and see what we can make of it.

The story may be epitomized as follows: 1) the hero's name is Gram; 2) he is the son of Skjold; 3) he is fostered by Roarius; 4) he marries the daughter of Roarius but later divorces her; 5) she then marries his retainer Bessus; 6) who is just as good a fighter as is Gram himself; 7) Gram begins war on king Sigtrygg because he hears that the latter's daughter, Gro, has been betrothed to a giant; 8) he meets Gro; 9) and seduces her; 10) he kills two robbers, and props them up on stakes in order to frighten his enemies, who would naturally think the robbers still alive; 11) he kills king Sigtrygg with a gold weapon, the king being invulnerable to ordinary weapons; 12) he kills Svarinus, governor of Gautland, and his 16 brothers; 13) he becomes joint ruler of Denmark; 14) he overthrows his assailant Ringo; 15) he begins war on Sumblus; 16) he meets Signe, the daughter of Sumblus, and the two are betrothed, Gram divorcing Gro; 17) he kills Henricus, the rival suitor (and Sumblus also?); 18) he is killed by the Norwegian or Swedish king Svibdager.

Bugge has already pointed out (HEP. 153 ff.) the indebtedness of the Gram saga to the Helgakviður. He has further shown that Helgi's prototype was the Scylding prince Helgi (the Halga of the Beowulf). He failed, however, to note that those traits of the Gram saga which cannot be derived from Helgi can be derived from other Scyldings — in other words, that the author of the Gram saga has simply attached to his invention, the fictitious hero Gram, a number of traits traditionally belonging to various characters in the Scylding cycle of stories and has thus made a saga the component parts of which are traditional enough. More specifically, in trait 2) Gram as the son of Skjold plays the part of Fróði, the mythical father of Halfdanr; in trait 3) he represents Hroðulf, who according to the Beowulf was fostered by Hroðgar (Saxo's Roarius); in trait 4) he is Ingeld, who, like Gram, married and later divorced the daughter of Hroðgar. According to trait 5) Roarius's daughter, after her divorce, was given in marriage to Bessus, Gram's retainer. The name Bessus is simply an affectionate form of the word for 'bear' and the retainer, so far as his name is concerned, can thus be equated with Bjarki. The emphasis laid, in trait 6), on the fighting qualities of Bessus likewise fits Bjarki well. Trait 10) properly belongs to the Hamlet saga, but probably came into the Gram saga by way of the Helgasaga; for the contamination of the latter by the Hamlet saga see below (cap. X). In trait 11) Gram, in part at least, represents Halfdanr (see Hyndluljóð 15, 2). In trait 13) he stands for Hroðulf, who appears in the Beowulf as joint ruler of Denmark with his foster-father Hroðgar. For Ringo and Svarinus, and for Gram's love-affair with Gro, see Bugge loc. cit. His affair with Signe seems to be only a duplication of that with Gro. Finally, Gram's death is to be referred to the death of Helgi at the hands of Dagr, though Bugge does not point this out.

It would seem, then, that Gram is the hero of an

early metrical lygisaga based on the events of the Scylding, or, more narrowly, the Hrólfr cycle of tradition. The only non-Scylding utilized by the sagaman as a source was Ingeld, and even he, of course, emphatically belonged in the primitive cycle though later eliminated in favor of his fictitious son Agnarr. Whether Agnarr had already taken his father's place in the version known to our poet cannot be determined. In one respect, however, that version was certainly more primitive than any version now extant: in it Hrút was still the daughter of Hróarr.

Was Hrút (Freawaru) Beowulf's wife? As the Beowulf poet does not tell us his hero's wife's name we are left in the dark, and shall have to grope our way accordingly. The scanty evidence available is closely connected with the death of Bjarki, as told in the Bjarkamál. The story of this remarkable poem may be sketched as follows. Hjalti calls his comrades of Hrólfr's comitatus from bed and to arms, to repel a treacherous attack of Hrólfr's sworn vassal Hjörvarðr. Bjarki wakes, but thinking that guests have come to court he makes no move to get up and put on his armor. Hjalti continues, appealing to his comrades' loyalty to their king, and telling them how Hjörvarðr and his Geats are pressing to the attack. He calls on the retainers to die to the last if need be around Hrólfr. The king is now hard pressed. Hjalti summons Bjarki again, and then rushes back to urge on the fighters, telling them how generously their king has dealt by them, how he slew his rival the parsimonious Hrœrekr (Hreðric, son of Hroðgar) and distributed that king's treasures among the warriors. All this in vain, though, for soon he sees the king fall, and now nothing is left but to die fighting. He calls to Bjarki for the third time, and this time stirs him to action. Bjarki puts on his armor, seizes his weapons and rushes out into the conflict. As he fights he tells of his famous duel with Agnarr. Soon, however, both he and Hjalti are cut down, the battle ceases, and Bjarki, protesting that he was not to blame for his late arrival, and shouting defiance into the teeth of Óðinn, dies. His wife comes out to him after the battle and is with him when he dies.

What can be the reason for the extraordinary behavior of Bjarki? Why does n't he begin to fight until the king is dead? In my opinion only one explanation is possible. Historically Bjarki was no adherent of Hrólfr, but was a follower of Hróarr, Hrœrekr and Hjörvarðr. He therefore does n't belong in Hrólfr's comitatus at all but rather on the other side. This would indeed follow at once from the fact that his wife was a daughter of Hróarr. When to this we add the testimony of the Bjarkamál, the conclusion becomes irresistible. It is possible that the poem describes the course of the conflict accurately enough; Bjarki may conceivably have kept out of the fight deliberately, not wanting to stain his hands with the blood of his wife's kinsman. Such abstention becomes incredible, however, the moment we make him a member of Hrólfr's comitatus and oath-bound to defend him at all costs—unless, indeed, we consider him a traitor to his lord, in which case his place in the Hrólfr cycle as it finally developed becomes in its turn incredible. The author of the Bjarkamál, by the use of supernatural machinery, could avoid these difficulties; we must face them.

Turning now to the English poem, we find abundant evidence that Beowulf was a supporter of Hroðgar. We have already noted his father's relations with that king, and his own alliance with him against the Bards. There are other passages that give evidence of intimate personal relations. Thus Wealhþeow, speaking to Hroðgar, says (1173 f.): "I have been told that thou wouldst have the warrior (Beowulf) for a son." Compare ll. 946—949, where Hroðgar says: "Now I am minded to love thee at heart as a son, Beowulf, best of men; keep well the new kinship henceforth." The same affection is expressed in more general terms (1876 ff.) upon Beowulf's departure.

As to Beowulf's relations with Hreðric we likewise have some information. Wealhþeow, after giving Beowulf some extremely valuable presents, says to him (1219 f.): "Make thyself known by thy strength and be friendly in counsel to these boys (her sons). I will not fail to reward thee for it." A few lines further on she adds (1226 f.): "Be thou friendly in deeds to my son (Hreðric), upholding his well-being." Beowulf accepts the gifts. His answer to the queen is made indirectly, at the conclusion of the speech in which he offers Hroðgar assistance in war. Here he adds (1836 ff.): "Furthermore, if Hreðric, the king's son, becomes a retainer at the court of the Geats, he shall find there many friends." We hear nothing further of this matter, and from the Bjarkamál it would appear that Hrólfr overthrew his cousin without much difficulty. Probably the struggle was in the nature of a coup (as Olrik has suggested), so that all was over before the Geats knew what was going on. Or the defeat and death of Hygelac may have so weakened the Geats that they were unable to stand up against Hroðulf. It is clear, however, that they assisted Heoroweard (Hjörvarðr) when he, much later, attacked Hroðulf at Heorot (see Bjarkamál passim; there are also two certainly unhistorical references to Swedes as followers of Hjörvaðr, perhaps introduced into the poem by way of compliment to the Swede who at the time of the poem's composition — c. 900 — ruled Denmark; see Olrik, DH. I 114 f.).

In the Bjarkamál the Geatish aid lent to Hjörvarðr stands isolated and unexplained. If, however, we take into consideration the intimate relations between Beowulf and Hroðgar, and Beowulf's obligations to Hreðric, it becomes obvious that Hroðulf and Beowulf must have been enemies. Hence it is not surprizing that Heoroweard was able to attack his cousin with a force made up largely or wholly of Geats. — Noteworthy also is the English poet's irrepressible though strongly censored sympathy for the Hroðgar-Hreðric faction, and his condemnation of Hroðulf's conduct. The figure of Beowulf himself, indeed, seems to be drawn in conscious contrast to that of Hroðulf. Thus (2163 ff.) after telling how Beowulf in compliance with Germanic custom turns over to Hygelac the presents he received of the Danes, the poet adds: "So it is proper for a kinsman to do, not at all to weave a net of evil for the other, with treacherous skill to prepare death for the comrade. To Hygelac was . . . his nephew very true." This is a clear reference to the unscrupulous conduct of Hroðulf, a nephew who, as we shall see, was anything but true to his uncle. Cf. also 2741 ff. Again, Beowulf's declination of the Geatish throne after the death of Hygelac and his insistence on the rights of the youthful Heardred (2369 ff.) can hardly be historical. It makes, however, a very striking poetical contrast to the conduct of Hroðulf under similar conditions. For direct though somewhat disguised denunciation of Hroðulf see Wealhþeow's pathetic speech (1180 ff.).

The Beowulf says nothing about Heoroweard's attack on Heorot. There is, however, a reference to the Scyldings (i. e., Danes) which throws a great deal of light on the situation subsequent to Hroðulf's death. This reference is the much debated one in l. 3005. The messenger of Wiglaf, after telling the story of the death of king Ongenþeow of Sweden at the hands of the Geats, goes on to say: "This is the feud and the enmity, the deadly hostility of men, of which I have expectation, namely, that the Swedes seek us out, when they learn that our lord is dead, he who formerly protected hoard and kingdom against the enemy, (and protected) the bold Scyldings after the fall of heroes." These forebodings seem singularly out of place, in view of the fact that Ongenþeow's death had long since been avenged by Onela. Clearly the passage which I have quoted bears little logical relation to the tale that precedes it, and we must search elsewhere to find the reason for the messenger's trepidation. Nor do we have far to seek. At the death of Beowulf his kinsman Wiglaf apparently succeeded to the Geatish throne. Now as we have already seen Wiglaf's father Weohstan had been a retainer of Onela and had killed Eanmund, the brother of Eadgils, and this slaying had never been avenged. Wiglaf would naturally inherit his father's feud with Eadgils, and it is to this feud that the passage quoted above has reference. The feud with the Wægmundings would obviously give the ruling Scylfing king an excuse for attacking the Geats, who, if Beowulf's last fight actually goes back to the battle of Brávellir, were now weakened by the loss of their king and many of their warriors.

Eadgils had not been able to take vengeance on Weohstan himself, to whom Beowulf had granted protection. Did this action of Beowulf's cost him the friendship and alliance of Eadgils? It could hardly have failed to have this effect, and if *hettendum* (3004) refers to the Swedes, as the context would indicate, we have a specific reference to a conflict between Beowulf and Eadgils. This fits in well with the fact that Beowulf's doubles Bjarki and Svipdagr both break with Aðils after first supporting him for a time (Skáldskaparmál 43; Svipdagsþáttr of Hrólfssaga kraka). Compare also the conflict between Bjarki and Aðils mentioned in Saxo (II 56 f.): Ab Atislo lacessiti Roluonis ulcionem armis exegit, eumque uictum bello prostrauit. Why does n't the poet give us a full account of this conflict? Let us see.

Line 3005 furnishes us with the key to the whole situation. Eadgils in slaying Onela drew upon himself the enmity of Onela's kinsman-in-law Hroðulf, who as we shall see actually made an expedition against him to avenge Onela's death. Under these conditions Eadgils was obviously unable to press his feud with Weohstan or break with his sole ally Beowulf. However, by marrying Hroðulf's mother Yrsa he became Hroðulf's stepfather and eventually got on friendly terms with his stepson, who like him was an enemy of the Geats, so that the two kings had good political reasons for forming an alliance. Beowulf, however, got wind of what was forward and struck first. He supported Heoroweard in his successful attack on Heorot, and thus put a friend on the Danish throne and deprived Eadgils of his ally. Eadgils must thereupon have attacked the now allied Danes and Geats in an attempt to avenge his stepson's fall, but without success. This is the attack, taking place "after the fall of heroes" (i. e., the slaughter of Hroðulf and his comitatus), to which l. 3005 of the Beowulf refers. Saxo too preserves the memory of this defeat of the Swedes (II 67 f.), although in a form confused enough. Evidently the new Danish king, who owed his crown to Geatish swords, was the subordinate partner in the alliance, so that the use of the word *geheold* (3003) to denote Beowulf's relation to the Scyldings is quite justified. The silence of the poet is then of a piece with his general practice, already noted, of omitting from his story all Dano-Geatish conflicts. It would be well enough, when singing before a Danish or partly Danish audience, to tell of a Geatish hero's exploits in behalf of a Danish king, or unconnected with Denmark, but his hostile relations with the Danish national hero Hrólfr would obviously have to be omitted in toto.

The poet's failure to give the name of Beowulf's wife can, I think, be explained on the same basis. Let us consider the matter first from the Danish angle. Here we find a prominent feature of the tradition to be Skuld, the wife of Hjörvarðr, who is represented as egging him on to revolt against Hrólfr. She is taken to be a sister of Hrólfr, and her unnatural conduct is the subject of much reprobation in the monuments. In fact, however, as Olrik has pointed out, she could not have been the sister of Hrólfr, as in that case her marriage to Hjörvarðr would be in conflict with the consanguinity tabus of the day. That these tabus had no influence on tradition was due to the fact that the relationship of Hrólfr and Hjörvarðr had been forgotten. Why did Skuld become Hrólfr's sister, then? I can see only one explanation, but that an excellent one. There was a historical Hrút, the daughter of Hróarr. She was later made into a sister of Hrólfr, as we have seen. Now in real life she must have done a deal of egging on. But she was married to the popular champion Bjarki. It would n't do, of course, to have Bjarki's wife keep this part, so she lost it in favor of Skuld. The link here lay in the fact that Skuld (or whoever actually was the wife of Hjörvarðr) undoubtedly herself did a deal of egging on. But the memory lingered that a kinswoman of Hrólfr was guilty of egging on. This memory turned Skuld into a second sister of Hrólfr.

Let us now return to the Beowulf. What was the poet to do with Hrút? In the early days when he composed, her egging on would not have been forgotten. He handles the ticklish situation well. He eliminates all connexion between his hero and the lady by telling in great detail about the lady's unfortunate first marriage but saying nothing at all about her second. — If one does n't accept this explanation of the extraordinary fact that Beowulf's wife goes unnamed, one is driven to assume either that the poet actually did not know his hero's wife's name (and this seems almost incredible), or else that he left out the name through inadvertence (likewise a highly improbable hypothesis).

The argument here must be considered in connexion with another most striking peculiarity of the story we are examining. In the bear's son folk-tale the hero usually rescues and marries a princess. Now Beowulf undoubtedly became a hero of the bear's son type, and, to judge from the story of Bjarki (who was Beowulf's Danish counterpart), a princess, Hrút, actually belonged in the historical complex to which the folk-tale got attached. Yet, in spite of all this, only Saxo's prose account makes the hero rescue as well as marry Hrút, while none of the versions connects her with the monster fight. Why did the folk-tale fail so signally to utilize historical material so well suited to its inner economy? To my mind there can be but one answer. Hrút's hostility to Hrólfr made her inacceptable (to a Danish audience) as a heroine. The poets had to neglect her, and though as a result of this neglect her original hostility came to be forgotten, it was then too late to incorporate her into the folk-tale in the orthodox manner. Indeed, the neglect of Hrút seems to have prevented the Danes (though not the West Scandinavians) from utilizing the folk-tale at all, so that Saxo's Bjarki is remarkably primitive.

What was the development of Bjarki, then, in Danish tradition proper? The starting-point must have been the retainer of Hróarr who kills a bear and marries Hrút, Hróarr's daughter. Since Hrút's first husband, the king of the Bards, had treated his wife ill, Bjarki's participation in the final battle with the Bards would have been an almost inevitable development even if it had not been historical. The poet's instincts would demand that Bjarki fight the man who had flouted Hrút, but this was impossible, as Hrólfr himself had killed this man. Ingjaldr was therefore given a son, Agnarr, who took over the matrimonial part of his father's career and the feud with Bjarki which went with it. Ideal poetic requirements still remained unsatisfied, however, for Hrút's unfortunate experiences were derogatory to her dignity. She must therefore be prevented from actually marrying Agnarr. In the Bjarkamál (and the Icelandic accounts, which were greatly influenced by it) this is accomplished by the simple expedient of eliminating altogether the relation between Agnarr and Hrút, thus leaving only the fight (and Bjarki's marriage). In Saxo's prose account however Agnarr, though he never becomes a husband, does reach the bridegroom stage, and the duel which we know actually took place between retainers at the wedding of Ingeld (Beowulf 2032 ff.) is here replaced by the fight between Agnarr and Bjarki which earlier was part of the battle with the Bards. For a different analysis see Olrik, DH. I 136 f.

The subordination of Bjarki to Hrólfr, the central figure of the cycle, was of course inevitable. He might conceivably have developed into the villain of the tale, but the natural person for this part was Hjörvarðr. Besides, Bjarki's marriage to Hrút would necessarily involve him in the war with the Bards, where he would fight for Hrólfr (in the more primitive version, for Hróarr), and this would automatically place him among Hrólfr's retainers. His failure to support Hrólfr at the last was not forgotten, however, as we have seen. This failure was not ascribed to treachery, but, apparently, to supernatural intervention. Historically no treachery was involved, and to this extent tradition preserved the facts. There was, however, an enmity, as I have shown; this enmity could not be reconciled with Bjarki's position and loyal service as Hrólfr's (earlier Hróarr's) retainer and so was eliminated from the story.

As a faithful retainer of Hrólfr, Bjarki would of course have to die with the rest of the comitatus. His actual death, however, could not have occurred at that time. As we have already seen, Bugge has pointed out a connexion between the Bjarkamál and the Beowulfian version of the hero's last fight (PBB. XII 45 ff.) and it may be that some lay celebrating Beowulf's death in the battle of Brávellir served as source or model for parts of the Bjarkamál, especially since the latter deals with the death of Bjarki rather more than with that of the king himself. All this must remain uncertain, however.

It seems likely, then, that a Geatish hero known at home by the nickname Beowulf, among the Danes by the nickname Bjarki, was drawn into the Danish cycle of stories centering around Hrólfr. This serves to explain the absence in Selund of a specific Beowulf saga. Does it throw any light on the Onela story? It presents at least a striking parallel, in that here too an original alien enemy becomes a national hero. And as we proceed other bearings will appear.

Chapter V.

Ermuthrud.

It is obviously of the greatest importance to determine who was the wife of the historical Onela. Her name originally appeared in l. 62 of the Beowulf, as we have seen, but this line is defective in the only ms. of that poem extant. Can we nevertheless, by an examination of all the evidence, reconstruct the line and wrest the woman's name from the records? Before venturing upon the attempt, it is necessary to point out that in migration times the names of the various members of any given Scandinavian royal family alliterate. The evidence of the Beowulf may be tabulated as follows:

Swertings	Wægmundings	Scylfings	Scyldings
Hreðel	**Wægmund**	**Ongenþeow**	**Healfdene**
Herebeald	**Weohstan**	**Onela**	**Heorogar**
Hæðcyn	**Wiglaf**	**Ohthere**	**Heoroweard**
Hygelac		**Eanmund**	**Hroðgar**
Heardred	Hocings	**Eadgils**	**Hreðric**
	Hóc	**Elfhere**	**Hroðmund**
Hæreðings	**Hnæf**		**Hrut (Freawaru)**
Hæreð	**Hildeburh**		**Halga**
Hygd			**Hroðulf**
Hereric (?)			**Heremod (?)**

For the name *Hocings* see Widsið 28; the author of the Beowulf evidently accounts them Scyldings; presumably their royal house was Danish through a female line (1069a). For the apparent exception *Freawaru* see above.

There is one other exception to the rule: the names *Beowulf* and *Ecgþeow* do not alliterate. This has long puzzled students of the monuments and several theories have been advanced to account for it. We have so little to go on here, though, that theory becomes little else than speculation. I do not purpose to discuss the matter at this point. It will suffice to say that in spite of the want of alliteration in this particular case the existence of the practice of using alliterative names within a given family may be considered established, and the presence or absence of alliteration can be scientifically used in testing the authenticity of names otherwise doubtful (see Olrik, DH. I 22 ff.).

Returning now to our problem, we find ourselves confronted by a most curious situation. For on the face of it the woman in the case is a Scylding, and certainly the husband is a Scylfing. Yet, whatever the actual names involved, no Scylding could possibly have a name which would alliterate with that of any Scylfing, while on the other hand unless the names of husband and wife alliterate the line goes without alliteration entirely. Two impossibilities thus stare each other in the face. There is evidently something rotten in the State of Denmark. What is the solution of this difficulty? We find the clue in Saxo, who knows nothing of any daughter of Halfdanr but furnishes us with a perfectly good daughter-in-law in the person of Yrsa, the widow of Halfdanr's son Helgi (OE. Halga); this prince had died young, as we know from the Beowulf and from the Scandian monuments. As to Yrsa, she was probably a historical person (Olrik, DH. I 151 ff.), and her name obviously meets the alliterative requirements of the line. We must of course further assume that the poet mistook the daughter-in-law for a true daughter. — The Yrsa emendation was first suggested by Miss Clarke (see cap. XI below), but she, unlike me, regards Yrsa as a true daughter of Healfdene.

On the basis of our emendation, how would the line read in its restored form? As my colleague Professor Klaeber has pointed out to me (orally), the simplest restoration, and the one involving least violence to the text, would be a restoration achieved by inserting "Yrse wæs" into the line at the point where the gap obviously occurs. If we do this, the line reads as follows:

hyrde ic þæt Yrse wæs Onelan cwen.

For other possibilities compare Trautmann, Anglia, Beiblatt X 261 (but see Klaeber, Mod. Phil. III 243).

Before leaving the passage it is necessary to devote some attention to the reading proposed by Kluge (ESt. XXII 144 f.), based on the fact that the Hrólfssaga kraka gives Halfdanr a daughter Signý who is married to a certain jarl Sevill. Kluge accordingly reads the line thus:

hyrde ic þæt Sigeneow wæs Sæwelan cwen.

The objections to this reading are conclusive. *Sigeneow* is no proper name for a daughter of Healfdene, whose other children's names, like those of all the Scylding family, begin with H. Sevill is not a Scylfing, and so does not meet the requirements of l. 63. Furthermore, as we shall see below, both Signý and Sevill are late additions to the Fróðaþáttr (the Hrólfssaga episode in question), Signý being derived from the Völsungasaga and Sevill getting his name from the German Sabene (OE. Seafola). Finally, Kluge's emendation flies in the face of the 10th century Hyndluljóð, which clearly connects Áli (Onela) with Halfdanr, as we have seen already. All this being so, Kluge's reading can hardly longer be taken seriously.

Does the Beowulf offer any further indication of the existence of a daughter-in-law of Healfdene identifiable with Yrsa? At any rate a most curious name appears, for which no plausible explanation has heretofore been found. I refer to Wealhþeow, the wife of Hroðgar. The name itself means 'Gaulish slave' (compare Icel. *Val-land* 'France,' *Valir* 'inhabitants of France'), and thus fits in admirably with Yrsa's origin, for according to Olrik (DH. I 153f.) Yrsa was probably a native of France, and the Northern monuments inform us that she was captured by Helgi in a Viking expedition. Among the English the word of course might be interpreted as having reference to Wales, but its ending *-þeow* shows that it was of Scandian formation and so referred originally to Gaul. The attempt to connect Wealhþeow with the Ögn of the Hrólfssaga kraka and the English noblewoman of the Skjöldunga has been proved abortive (O. L. Olson, op. cit p. 97), and the theory of her British origin has not a leg to stand on.

Turning now to the references to Hroðgar's wife in the English poem itself we find an extraordinary contradiction between her name and the statements made about her. The more important of these statements may be tabulated as follows:

615a freolic wif 'chief wife; freeborn wife'
620b ides Helminga 'lady of the Helming family'
641a freolicu folc-cwen 'free-born folk-queen'
2017a friðu-sibb folca 'peace-bringer between peoples'
2174a þeodnes dohtor 'king's daughter'.

These references do not comport well with the name *Wealhþeow* 'Gaulish slave,' although some of them may be explained away as stock phrases. The epithet *ides Helminga* deserves special attention. Widsið 29b tells us that *Helm (weold) Wulfingum.* The Wulfings (or Wylfings) are also referred to in the Beowulf, as we have seen, and the tribe is to be located in South Scandinavia (see above, and cf. Björkman 120 ff.). If Hroðgar's wife was a Wylfing princess we have an explanation of the Danish king's success as peacemaker between Ecgþeow and the avengers of Heaðolaf (470 ff.). The connexion with the Wylfings here assumed may also serve to explain the epithet *Ylfingr* applied to Helgi in the Elder Edda, and to Hrólfr and Hjörvarðr in the Ynglinga (cap. 37), where it seems to be used as a synonym of Skjöldungr. But under these circumstances the name *Wealhþeow* becomes quite impossible. No descendant of Helm could have borne such a name.

In my opinion the name *Wealhþeow* is an appellative or nickname properly belonging to Yrsa, and used in the Beowulf, by mistake, with reference to the wife of Hroðgar. The poet, who was weak on women's names anyhow, remembered that Halfdanr had a daughter-in-law called a 'Gaulish slave,' but gave her the wrong husband. His error here goes well with his other error (on the present hypothesis) in assuming that the wife of Onela was a true daughter of Healfdene.

Before proceeding further with the discussion it will be well to point out how admirably the hypothesis that Yrsa was the wife of Onela accounts for the hitherto obscure features of the political situation as it then existed. We understand thoroughly why the Geats allied themselves with the enemies of Hroðulf (Hrólfr) among the Danes. The intimate relations between Hroðgar and the Geats rendered any other course impossible. But what was the reason for the enmity between the Geats and Onela? If Onela had been married to a true daughter of Healfdene, we should still be at a loss to account for the political grouping, as this marriage would not bind him to either of the Danish factions — in itself, at least. If however he was married to Healfdene's daughter-in-law Yrsa, the mother of Hroðulf, we have at once a perfect explanation for the whole situation. Hroðulf's step-father would necessarily be Hroðulf's ally, and as such would be an enemy of the Geats. It now becomes clear why Eanmund and Eadgils when defeated at home turned to the Geats for help, and why they got it. Beowulf's motives for breaking faith with Onela now become clearer; his loyalty to Hroðgar played an important part here, and the campaign against Onela was only the necessary preliminary to the later campaign against Onela's step-son Hroðulf. We shall see in the following discussion how these plans were upset by the action of Yrsa herself.

Let us now turn to the Scandinavian sources. What do they say about Yrsa's activities as a widow? They all agree that she married a second time, but make Aðils (Eadgils) her second husband. What are we to conclude from this? The answer is simple. From the Beowulf we know that Aðils defeated and killed Áli (Onela). From the Scandinavian monuments we learn that he married Yrsa. But Yrsa was Áli's wife, if our emendation of the Beowulf line holds. Ergo, Aðils married Áli's widow. Here we have a striking correspondence to the Ermuthrud of Saxo. At this point it may be well to stop for a moment to point out a peculiarity of the Hamlet Tale which so far as I know is unique. I refer to the repetition of the faithless widow motif. Hamlet's mother marries her husband's murderer. Hamlet's wife does the same thing. Therefore if when we have gathered up all our historical material we find that it contains elements which would call for such a repetition, we may feel with some confidence that we are on the right track. More of this anon.

At present our case for Yrsa as the wife of Áli rests on an emendation of the Beowulf — an exceedingly plausible emendation, it is true, but still an emendation. It would strengthen our position enormously if we could find corroborative evidence from other sources. Now by all odds the most important source bearing on the matter is the famous story of Hrólfr kraki's expedition to Uppsala. Olrik (DH. I 38) believed that Hrólfr made this expedition in order to avenge the death of Áli. Let us examine the tale, and see what we can make of it.

As told in Saxo the story runs as follows. Hrólfr gave his mother Yrsa in marriage to king Aðils, but Yrsa found her husband stingy and began planning to escape back to Denmark. She pretended to hate her son and persuaded Aðils to invite him to the Swedish court, ostensibly to receive gifts but in reality to be put to death. As a matter of fact, though, she intended to invoke her son's assistance when he came and thus escape, taking along with her as much treasure as she could lay hands on. Hrólfr was invited and came. His mother treated him with the greatest coldness, at which he protested. He thrust himself upon his mother, sitting beside her at table in spite of Aðils's objections. After the meal conversation became general in the hall. Hrólfr was asked what virtue he considered to be the greatest, to which he answered, endurance. Aðils, asked the same question, replied, generosity. It was now insisted upon that each be put to the proof. Hrólfr was tested by being placed close to the fire, which was made roaring hot for the purpose. He stood the test well. Aðils showed his generosity by giving his stepson much treasure and a great ring. After three days Hrólfr and Yrsa fled by night, carrying with them Aðils's hoard, which Yrsa had stolen. They were pursued, but saved themselves by having their followers strew gold along the way, on the principle of the golden apples in Atalanta's race. This strewing was done at Yrsa's bidding. — Snorri's version of the tale (Skáldskaparmál 43) omits Yrsa's plotting, substituting, as motive for the expedition, Aðils's failure to reward Hrólfr's champions for their assistance to him in his struggle with Áli. Yrsa also loses much of her initiative, and does not accompany her son on his flight. The Hrólfssaga version motivates the expedition as an attempt to collect from Aðils Hrólfr's paternal inheritance; the tale is expanded by the introduction of much supernatural material. In both the Icelandic versions Hrólfr's champions, unknown to Saxo, appear, and play an increasingly important part. In my judgment the Saxonian version is the more primitive not only as a whole but in practically every detail (but see Olrik, DH. I 181).

This expedition of Hrólfr's is certainly a most extraordinary affair, especially as told in Saxo, and so far the commentators have n't been able to make heads or tails of it. It contains all sorts of contradictions.

Thus, Yrsa complains of Aðils's parsimony, but his actual conduct anything but bears this out. Again, Yrsa's arrangement with her husband is inconsistent with her behavior towards her son, for if she were supposed to be leading him into a trap she would certainly be expected to behave cordially towards him, if only to avert suspicion. Besides, there is absolutely nothing to indicate how she could make her husband believe of her so unnatural a sentiment. Looked at from the other side, too, her scheming strikes one as unnatural in the extreme; why was it necessary to pretend to plot against her son? Her methods would certainly involve him in a very dangerous situation, and all uselessly enough, as a simple visit to the court on his part, without any plotting, would serve her purpose just as well — the narrator gives us no hint that apart from Yrsa's plotting the relations between stepfather and stepson were other than amicable. On the whole what happens in the tale is hard to reconcile with the motivation set forth by the narrator. Hrólfr's talk about endurance and Aðils's counter-praise of generosity evidently have more than the surface meaning given them by the poet. All explanation is wanting of how the gifts held out as bait to Hrólfr were motivated to their recipient. Finally, it is noteworthy that Saxo does not say that Yrsa accompanied her son back to Denmark, though she was with him in his flight, while the other sources agree that she did not accompany him.

What is the key to this mystery? Chapter 28 of the Ynglingasaga throws some light on it. Here it is related that king Aðils, one summer while in viking, came to Germany and captured a maiden wonderfully fair, named

Yrsa. He took her home with him and made her his wife. This tale is usually told of Helgi, and properly belongs to him. That it is here told of Aðils, however, indicates that some memory lingered of the fact (if it was a fact) that Aðils had taken his wife by force on a military expedition. Let us assume, then, that Aðils after defeating and killing Áli takes possession of Áli's wife Yrsa, the mother of Hrólfr, and let us see what we can make of the expedition to Uppsala on this basis.

What is Hrólfr to do? Avenge his stepfather Áli, of course, and rescue his mother Yrsa from Aðils's clutches. He sets out to do this, but his fleet has hardly reached the Fýri (the river on which Uppsala is located) before he learns to his disgust that his mother has married her husband's murderer. This marriage changes the situation altogether. Hrólfr does not relish the idea of waging war on his own mother (the two are birds of a feather anyway, as we shall see, and must have been especially sympathetic to each other). At the same time he remains loyal to Áli, and is determined somehow or other to avenge his death. He finally decides to come to terms with Aðils; this will enable him to get in touch with his mother, and he may succeed in persuading her to abandon her unnatural alliance and flee with him. An opportunity may also be found for taking direct vengeance on Aðils, who by the conclusion of a peace will be lulled into a false security. It will be observed that Hrólfr's methods are not over honorable. The two kings now confer. The conversation in the hall about the greatest virtue represents the negotiations. Hrólfr in praising endurance means to say two things: that his wrongs are great and that he is not a man easily turned from his purposes. Aðils answers him by praising generosity, i. e., he urges Hrólfr not to judge his mother too harshly and promises him wergeld enough to reconcile to the situation even a man of his 'endurance.' This exchange may well be historical; nothing is more characteristic of primitive peoples than a fondness for the indirect or even riddling approach, especially on state occasions. Hrólfr accepts the wergeld offered, an apparent reconciliation is thus effected, and Hrólfr becomes the guest of Aðils. His mother greets him coldly because she knows how he feels about her marriage and resents his attitude. He tries to get a private word with her, but Aðils, still none too sure of his man, is on the watch and Hrólfr is unable to do more than sit beside her. At every point Aðils guards himself as well as he can — he evidently knew his Hrólfr! — and Hrólfr finds himself at first unable to effect anything against him. He does finally win his mother over, however, and they manage to flee, carrying with them Aðils's hoard, which they have stolen. Hrólfr doubtless intended to fight it out with Aðils after rejoining his army, but his flight was observed, he was pursued, and only by abandoning his plunder and finally his mother as well was he able to reach his ships and safety. The expedition was thus a total failure — a fiasco, indeed.

The story, thus analyzed, fits in admirably with the other exploit of Hrólfr's preserved to us in the Bjarkamál — his overthrow of his cousin Hrœrekr. In both exploits he shows himself very bold — and very unscrupulous. In both he is lavish with treasure, though for different reasons. In both his opponent acquires a reputation for niggardliness. The character of the man shines plainly through in both stories, and it is the same Hrólfr that we see in each case. We have here, then, another explanation of why his slaying of Ingjaldr was so quickly forgotten. There was nothing specially characteristic of him in this deed, nothing Hrólfian (if I may coin a word). And as to his own death, there was a compelling poetic fitness in the manner of it, that he fell victim to the same treachery that he was accustomed to mete out to his opponents.

The question now naturally arises, how did the facts get so obscured? This question is not so hard to answer as might at first appear. In the first place, it is obvious that the story of a defeat could not well be sung in court as it stood. It would have to be carefully altered to avoid making the hero something less than a hero. Nor could the hero's mother be pictured as a bad woman, as that would taint the hero himself. Yet a story that involved gold-strewing would be irresistible to the skalds, who always advocated lavishness, and that for very good business reasons! What would happen to the tale, then? Yrsa's method of acquiring a new husband would clearly have to be omitted, which meant that in course of time the very existence of her other husband would be forgotten. The theory that she pretended to hate her son but really wanted to escape would serve to motivate her actual coldness toward Hrólfr and her actual flight, and would make excuses for her presence in Uppsala, which would thus become a species of durance. The elimination of Ali would leave Hrólfr no motive for his expedition, and the wergeld he received would become meaningless; this difficulty was solved by making him the intended victim of a plot, in which the wergeld functioned as bait to entice him to Uppsala. Even so, however, the want of any real reason for his receiving gifts, and the retention of Uppsala as the scene of action, reveal clearly enough that originally he was the aggressor. As Hrólfr's opponent, Aðils was subject to depreciation, and the usual Skaldic imputation of niggardliness was therefore attached to him and combined with Yrsa's imputed desire to escape. In general, with Hrólfr in the role of victim, his activities would tend to be transferred to others, but as Aðils himself could hardly be changed from victim to aggressor without smashing the story to bits, Yrsa was the only person available for the part. She was therefore made the sole cause of all the trouble between the two kings, who apart from her plotting are not represented as hostile. Especially striking is the way in which she is put in charge of the flight.

Why did n't Áli resist elimination more strenuously? In Selund, which is far from Sweden, neither he nor the other Swedish kings had ever got much attention (Olrik, DH. I 203), and as his relations with Hrólfr were not of a dramatic sort there was no reason why his memory should have been preserved. In Norway, on the other hand, a great interest in the Swedish royal house existed, and this resulted in the preservation of the material found, for example, in the Ynglingasaga and -tal. Áli was therefore not forgotten in Norway, and his relations with Aðils and even with Beowulf were not lost. However, when the latter, by virtue of his intimate connexions with the Danish royal house, became, under the name Bjarki, a retainer of Hrólfr, he continued to function as supporter of Aðils in his final struggle with Áli, but brought this support into connexion with Hrólfr, who, as Bjarki's overlord, had to take sides against Áli. Under these conditions vengeance for Áli's death became unavailable as motive for the Expedition to Uppsala in Norway, in spite of the fact that the Norwegians had preserved some memory of Áli. At the same time another motive arose to take its place. From our study of the English poem we have already come to the conclusion that Beowulf broke with Eadgils after the overthrow of Onela, because he granted protection to Weohstan, his own kinsman but Eadgils's most hated opponent. When Beowulf became Bjarki his break with Aðils was not lost, although the causes of it became obscured; it will be remembered that it was not Hrólfr who quarreled with Aðils in Snorri's version of the tale, but Bjarki and the other champions. When therefore the Danish version of the Expedition to Uppsala came to Norway, the Norwegians adopted it but changed its motivation so as to make this conform to their own traditions in the matter. That this is what occurred is pretty obvious from the fact that the motivation in the Icelandic versions is that appropriate to a military expedition, but the story of the Expedition itself is anything but the story of a campaign and must be derived from a source in which the motivation as well as the tale is non-military. Accordingly, when Olrik assumes (DH. I 181) that Yrsa's plotting is a comparatively late addition to the tale, the internal evidence does not bear him out; in fact, he has himself admitted that the dialog between Yrsa and her son has a "vist gammelt præg." Indeed, on a priori grounds one would be likely to assume that the plotting motivation was a first clumsy attempt to account for the historical facts, still so well remembered that the inconvenient ones could not easily be discarded, though the underlying historical situation was no longer understood or had to be ignored to avoid offending the audience. — The absorption of Beowulf into the Hrólfr cycle thus accounts for the peculiarities of the Snorra version. The fact that Yrsa's marriage to Aðils actually took place prior to the Expedition resulted in a complete reversal of the order of the historical relations between Hrólfr and Aðils. Historically Hrólfr was first hostile, later friendly to Aðils. In the saga he is first friendly, later hostile.

Yrsa is the central figure in the Saxonian version of the Expedition to Uppsala. This is a shift of emphasis only in that she has become the chief actor; in the historical situation, as I have reconstructed it, she is no less the center about which the action revolves, although her own activities are indirect. She loses much of her importance, it is true, in the later versions of the tale, which magnify the champions of Hrólfr at the expense both of Yrsa and of the king himself, but this is a development common to all the tales of the cycle. Anyhow, this later period does not greatly concern us here. For us the important thing is the initiative which the Saxonian Yrsa had undoubtedly acquired. In addition to the considerations previously brought forward there must have been something inherent in the woman herself which favored this development. However excellent her opportunities, no ordinary woman, placed in the same story with men like Aðils and Hrólfr, could have come to dominate it as Yrsa came to dominate it. Yrsa was assuredly no ordinary woman. Let us look at her for a moment in this the height of her power. Destitute of the finer virtues, incapable of love or selfsacrifice, plotting against her husband, using her son like a pawn, without a thought for his safety in the dangerous game she was playing, unscrupulous, even a thief, she yet possessed in abundant measure virtues of another sort: courage, initiative, determination, ability to lead and control — in a word, strength. Clearly this woman has her points of kinship with Þryð herself, and her historical prototype under favorable conditions might have drawn to her a veritable Þryð story.

What are the facts? We have already seen that the Jutes adopted as their own originally Anglian and Geatish kings. Among the former was Offa, of whom in England two stories were told, viz., the story of his fight at Fifeldor and the story of his wife Þryð. Now in Saxo the first of these tales is still told of Uffe (Offa), but the story of Þryð is not. What became of it? As the wife of Amleth is called Ermu-thrud (d = ð), and as her story is largely nothing more than a version of the Þryð tale, there is every reason to assume that the story originally told, in Jutland, of Uffe's wife was later transferred, in Jutland, to Amleth's wife. How did this happen? Clearly the character of the Hamletian lady was the magnet that drew it over. Nothing could be easier than a psychological association between the faithless widow and the woman who is the death of her suitors. What we have learned about the character of Yrsa from our study of the Expedition to Uppsala tends to confirm this theory of transfer, and certainly it seems unnecessary to go all the way to England in search of the source of a Jutish tale the original home of which was in the

Jutland peninsula! But see Müllenhoff, Beovulf 81 f., Olrik, KS. II 177 f. The latter assumes that Ermuthrud was a late addition to the saga. Some of the motifs attached to her are undoubtedly late. The Þryð story, however, is very early, as Olrik himself points out, and in view of the fact that Amleth's wife belonged to the historical complex there is every reason to suppose that the tale from which her saga name was derived became early attached to her. If so, it is best explained simply as an Anglian inheritance. As to the name itself, the German form in which it appears is simply an example of the 'fortyskning' process to which Danish names (and the Danish language) have been subjected from pre-Saxonian times almost to the present day.

Chapter VI.

Ørvendill.

So much for Onela's wife. What of his father? In the Beowulf he is called Ongenþeow; in the Widsið, Ongendþeow (31 b). This name would correspond to a Scandian **Anganþér*. No such name occurs in the monuments, however. The nearest approach to it is the name *Angantýr* of the Hervararsaga etc. That the two names actually correspond is rendered practically certain by l. 116 b of the Widsið: *Hliþe ond Incgenþeow*. This is generally recognized as a reference to the half-brothers Hlöðr and Angantýr III of the Hervararsaga. See especially Björkman 93 f. and the references there given. Nevertheless, the Swedish king whose position in the genealogy corresponds to that of the Beowulfian Ongenþeow is called Egill in the Scandian monuments (Ari's Íslendingabók and Historia Norwegiae; Snorri's Ynglingasaga; Þjóðólfr's Ynglingatal). There can be no doubt that the Ongenþeow of the Beowulf and the Widsið is the same person as the Egill of the Scandian monuments. Furthermore, if our Hamlet theory holds, the same king appears in Jutland under a third name, Ørvendill. What was his original name, and how can we account for its replacement by other names so different in form?

We had best begin with the etymology of the word *Agantýr*. The second element of the name is clearly the name of the god Týr. The first element is connected with OHG. *Angan-*, OE. *Angen-*; further, with OHG. *Engin-*, OHG. and Burg. *Anga-*. Förstemann relates this *Anga-* to OHG. *ango*, OE. *ongā*, Icel. *angi* 'prickle, sting, goad.' See Björkman 92 f. In West Germanic the word might also mean 'a kind of spear' and such a name as *Ongenþeow* on this interpretation would mean 'servant of the spear' or 'warrior.' The English poet perhaps interpreted in this sense the name of the Swedish king. In reality, though, as I see it, the king's name had a very different meaning. In the North *angi* never came to mean 'spear' but was used exclusively in the sense 'stimulus, prick, sting, goad.' The name-element *Angan-* was used, so far as we know, only in the name *Angantýr*; a variant of this name, **Anganþér* may likewise have existed, of course, but our only evidence for its existence is the occurrence in OE. and in German of etymologically equivalent forms. Now since the god Týr was the husband of Nerthus and had a function in a vegetation cult we are justified in assuming the possibility of a connexion between this fact and the appearance of his name in composition with Angan-, especially since at this early period the names of gods were very rarely compounded. I therefore interpret *Angan-* as 'phallus' and the names *Anganþér* 'servant of the phallus' and *Angantýr* 'phallus-Týr' as designations appropriate to the representative of Týr in the yearly Nerthus celebration. We know very little of the primitive Swedish form of the Nerthus cult, but it is not unreasonable to suppose that the representative of the god in the celebration was the king himself. Certainly Tacitus states explicitly that the king of the Sviones was an absolute monarch; we may infer that all the functions of the state (including the high-priesthood) were concentrated in his hands. Again, at least one of the legendary kings, Domaldi, was put to death as a ritual act to ensure a good harvest (Ynglingasaga cap. 15). From the description of the Nerthus cult in Tacitus it is clear that ordinarily slaves were used for sacrificial purposes, but the Swedish story shows that if this method did not prove efficacious the king himself might be sacrificed. This feature of vegetation rites is of course familiar enough, and I need not dwell on it here. It will suffice to say that if the king actually functioned as representative of Týr, either in person or through a deputy, he might well be given a by-name to correspond. On this interpretation Egill was the king's true name, *Anganþér or Angantýr his by-name. Of the two forms of the by-name the Christianized English would naturally make use of the form which did not contain the name of the god. — It is possible enough that the forms *Ongenþeow*, *Angandeo* are not primitive at all, but are pure euphemisms introduced after the Christianization of the English and the Germans. If so, no such form as **Anganþér* is to be postulated for the North, of course. — A word *angan* 'delight, joy, pleasure' occurs in the Völuspá (e. g., 53, 4: þar mon Friggjar falla angan), and this word may possibly have had some influence on the development of *Angan-* to its meaning 'phallus.'

Several questions now arise. In the first place, why did this by-name get attached to Egill and to no other king? The reasons for its want of popularity and its special association with Egill are closely connected. We have already seen that with the development of Nerthus to a bi-sexual deity Týr was forced out of the cult and

Ing brought in as son of Nerthus. In the OE. Runic Poem this development is clearly associated with Denmark (ll. 67 ff.), although a Vandilian origin may be hinted at (l. 70). Moreover the Beowulf, which calls the Danes *Ingwine,* gives no indication that the Swedes likewise were worshippers of Ing. Procopius too reports the inhabitants of Thule (Sweden and Norway) as worshippers of Ares (i. e., Týr). Eventually however, as we know from the Scandian records, the cult in its new form found its way to Sweden also. Its penetration was hardly a peaceful one, though. On the contrary, a cult war seems to have taken place. The story of Álfr and Yngvi (Ynglinga cap. 21) is, I think, a reminiscence of this cult war.

The equation Yngvi = Freyr offers no difficulties, of course (see Ynglinga cap. 10). The equation Álfr = Týr is harder to establish, and before we can establish it we shall have to examine the history of the word *alfr.* The two chief etymologies proposed connect *alfr* with IE. roots meaning 'white, shining' and 'cunning, skilful' respectively. And both these etymologies, curiously enough, find support in the characteristics attributed to elves in our sources. On the one hand the elves appear as beautiful, radiant, beneficent beings, associated with the day, the sun etc. Thus, *Alfröðull* 'elf-ray' is a sun heiti (Vafþrúðnismál 47, 1); the *Alfr* of Hyndluljóð 18, 4 is of the race of Dagr; in OE. we find such words as *ælf-sciene* 'elf-radiant.' Everywhere *alf-*, as name or name-element, is appropriate to a king or hero; cf. our own Alfred. On the other hand the elves may be represented as cunning dwarfs, often with a pejorative development into maleficent creatures of darkness, bringers of disease etc. For a specific contrast of the two kinds of elves see Gylfaginning 17. The contradiction is best explained by assuming the correctness of both etymologies of the word. That is to say, there were probably, to start with, two distinct types of beings, and two names to correspond. In the course of time, through the operation of phonetic laws, the two names were leveled, and this leveling brought in its train a confusion of the two types, which now bore the same name.

It is well known that Yngvi-Freyr had many characteristics appropriate to the old sky-god. See among others Mogk 318 ff. A current theory accordingly makes Freyr a hypostasis of Týr. The theory is hardly tenable, however, since Freyr is clearly a development of Ing, and Ing cannot be looked upon as a hypostasis of Týr but must originally have been the eponymous ancestor of the Ingvaeones. Freyr is to be interpreted, then, not as Týr's double, but as his successor, and he got his Týr-like qualities by virtue of his succession. One of his functions or rather possessions is of particular interest to us here. According to Grimnismál 5, the gods gave Alfheimr to Freyr, in days of yore, as a tooth-gift. Freyr originally belonged in Vanaheimr, of course. Who, then, was the original possessor of Alfheimr? We can hardly go far wrong in assuming that Týr was this original possessor, and that *Alfr* 'the radiant one' was an epithet eminently appropriate to the old sky-god. Cf. Mogk 322.

Let us now turn to the story in the Ynglinga. Here Álfr and Yngvi are the sons of the Swedish king Alrekr. They are apparently half-brothers. Nothing is said about the mother of Yngvi. The mother of Álfr is Dag-heiðr 'day-heath' and her father is Dagr. Álfr's maternal ancestry undeniably points to a connexion with the sky-god, of whom Dagr is generally considered a hypostasis. Again, Álfr is married to Bera 'she who bears.' From her name one would judge Bera to be simply the fertility goddess in euhemerized form. Her relations with Álfr, then, are parallel to the relations of Nerthus with Týr. The story proper runs as follows. Yngvi is a viking; he comes home from abroad and wins Bera's love; in consequence, he is attacked and slain by Álfr, who however likewise falls. I interpret this story thus. Ing, already at home among the Swedes as an eponymous ancestor, is imported from abroad in the new capacity of chief deity of the Nerthus cult; this cult in its foreign form wins adherents among the Swedes but is forcibly suppressed by the Swedish king, who however loses his own life in the course of the struggle. The king, as the representative of Týr, bears Týr's by-name Álfr (a name which because of its vocalic alliteration was particularly suitable for a Swedish king). His wife Bera is Nerthus under another name.

Who was the historical prototype of the Álfr of the story? According to the present theory Egill was this prototype. We know from the Beowulf that Egill was overthrown and his kingdom overrun by the Gauts under Hugleikr. Now Snorri represents this very Hugleikr as Álfr's successor on the Swedish throne. In my opinion the appearance of Hugleikr at this point in the Yngling genealogy is a reminiscence of the historical course of events. There are other curious parallels. Historically Egill was succeeded by his son Ohthere, upon whose death Onela usurped the throne, driving into exile the true heirs, the brothers Eanmund and Eadgils. Later, in a battle with the brothers, Onela is victorious, Eanmund being killed and Eadgils being forced to flee. Still later Onela himself falls and Eadgils succeeds to the throne. Now according to Snorri Álfr was succeeded by his son Hugleikr, upon whose death Haki usurped the throne, driving into exile the true heirs, the brothers Eiríkr and Jörundr. Later, in a battle with the brothers, Haki is victorious, Eiríkr being killed and Jörundr being forced to flee. Haki himself, however, was mortally wounded in the battle, and after his death Jörundr succeeded to the throne. Here Onela's two battles, the first with Eanmund and Eadgils, the second with Beowulf and Eadgils, have apparently been fused into one, and there are other discrepancies too, of course, but nevertheless the parallel is too close to be accidental. It can best be accounted for on the theory that the career of the Bardish hero Haki was early remodeled on the pattern of the career of the more famous hero Áli. The form of the Álasaga used for the purpose must obviously have been a very primitive one.

The fact that the Hakasaga appears where it does in the Ynglinga, then, casts light upon the identity of king Álfr. What further information about the cult war can we glean from the Ynglingasaga? In the first place, it is worth noting that Aðils's doublet Jörundr is called 'son of Yngvi' while Aðils himself is referred to as 'kinsman of Freyr.' It would appear, then, that Aðils was particularly connected with the Freyr cult, and that this cult triumphed with his accession to power. If so, his allies the Geats must likewise have been Freyr (i. e., Ing) worshippers. On this point, unhappily, the Beowulf is silent, but see below. On the other hand, Egill's doublet Álfr is called 'descendant of Dagr' while Egill himself goes by the kenning 'kinsman of Týr;' both of these epithets appear in the Ynglingatal itself, and cannot be constructions of Snorri's. If to the epithets we add the by-name *Angantýr* we can hardly avoid the conclusion that Egill was an adherent of the Týr cult, and that his capital was a center for that cult. Now Ari calls Egill by the nickname *Vendilkráka* 'Vendel crow,' and this nickname Stjerna (50 ff.) has shown to be derived from the stronghold Vendel in the Uppland district of Sweden, the *fæsten* mentioned in the Beowulf (2950) where the king was slain. Egill's son Óttarr was apparently buried at Vendel; at any rate a burial-mound there still bears his name. His other son Onela likewise seems to have been connected with Vendel, if one may judge by his nickname 'inn upplenzki.' It therefore seems plausible to suppose that Vendel was a center for Týr worship, and, if not the actual capital, at any rate the original seat of Egill's dynasty. However it may be with Vendel, there can be no doubt that the chief seat of the Freyr cult was Uppsala, and here it is of some significance to note that the first historical Swedish king unquestionably identified with Uppsala was Aðils, with whose accession to power, as we have seen, the Freyr cult probably first became supreme in Sweden. — Eanmund = Aun was also associated with Uppsala (see Ynglingatal 19), but this was probably because he was Aðils's brother.

From both accounts in the Ynglinga (caps. 21—23 and 26—29) one would conclude that Egill's two sons were Týr worshippers (though perhaps not persecutors of the Freyr cult, like their father), and that the Freyr cult won the final victory with Aðils. As to Onela, we have only his enmity to Eadgils to go on (and perhaps the epithet 'inn upplenzki'). As to Óttarr, we have the curious fact that both the story of his father's death and the nickname Vendilkráka are attached to him in the Ynglingasaga. How did this come about? If he was a Týr worshipper the by-name Angantýr would naturally be applied to him in his priestly capacity, and this may have caused him to be confused with his father in later times. See further below.

We may conjecture that the worshippers of Týr tried to suppress the newfangled cult of Freyr which was making its way into Sweden, but that they in the end proved unable to do so. The triumph of the new cult would of course bring with it the elimination of Týr from the vegetation rites and the name Angantýr would be eliminated along with the god to whom it had reference. This explains the rarity of the name and its legendary atmosphere. A name which had long since gone out of use and which accordingly to later generations sounded strange would naturally acquire unhistorical associations. As the name Angantýr was connected with hostility to the (new) gods, its development in legend would be governed accordingly. And in fact we find it used much as the analysis above would lead us to expect. Thus, Freyja 'the lady of the Vanir' appears in the Hyndluljóð as hostile to Angantýr the rival of Óttarr; further, Angantýr I of the Hervararsaga is represented as sprung from giant stock (like Týr himself in the Hymiskviða), and the giants of course were the traditional enemies of the gods.

Why did the name cling especially to Egill? This

can be accounted for only on the supposition that he was looked upon as the great representative of Týr, the great champion of the old cult in its fight for existence. What is the evidence? We have already seen that Egill can with some plausibility be identified with Álfr. The passage from the Ynglingatal quoted in cap. 26 of the Ynglingasaga provides us with further information. I follow the translation of Schück (SY. 109), which reads substantially as follows: "and famous out of the land fled the kinsman of Týr because of the might of the toothed one, but the giant's yoke-beast reddened the boar's snout's sword on Egill, who long before in the east with fire had destroyed the temple. But sheathless the male beast's sword struck the heir of the Scylfings to the heart." The boar here referred to is to be identified with Freyr's chariot-boar Slíðrugtanni (Gylfaginning 49), who was precisely a yoke-beast — a part which boars ordinarily do not play! Historically Egill was killed by the Geatish champion Eofor, whose name means 'boar,' and if Egill during his lifetime actually was an enemy of Freyr it is easy to see how in the course of time his death might come to be referred to a true boar and interpreted as an act of vengeance on the part of the offended god, who used as his instrument the animal sacred to him.

The account of the king's struggle with the beast clearly falls into two stages. In the first he flees before the boar; in the second he is slain by the boar. This is parallel to the account in the Beowulf, where Egill flees before the Geats but is finally overtaken and slain. There is however a difference between the two versions here: Egill flees out of the land according to the Ynglingatal, whereas according to the Beowulf he flees to his stronghold. We must of course accept the Beowulfian version as the correct one. Where did Þjóðólfr get his information, then? If we are to find out we must examine the Beowulfian account more minutely. The English poet tells the story of the entire campaign in which Egill met his death. The exact course of events is obscure, but the following stages are clearly distinguished:

1) Onela and Ohthere make pirate raids into Geatish territory.
2) The first Geatish army, under Hæðcyn, makes a surprize attack on Sweden. Hæðcyn captures the Swedish queen with her valuables. The surprize was evidently complete, and we have a right to infer that the king's hall was taken. The king himself, however, seems to have made his escape.
3) Ongenþeow attacks, defeats and kills Hæðcyn and rescues his wife. He encloses in a wood the remnants of Hæðcyn's army.
4) The next morning Hygelac comes up with the second Geatish army, rescues his brother's army and puts the Swedes to flight. Wulf and Eofor attack and kill king Ongenþeow.

The verses in the Ynglinga confine themselves to stage 4) above. The statement that Egill fled out of the land, however, seems to be based on the events of stage 2). That Ongenþeow actually fled out of the land is not likely, as stages 2) and 3) are connected in the Beowulf by the word *sona* (2928 a). He certainly had to abandon his capital, however. Moreover, as we shall see later on, Egill actually had been driven into exile in the course of a previous war with the Geats. It was thus natural enough that the king's loss of his hall should be interpreted as involving the loss of his kingdom, a loss already familiar from the story of the earlier war. The complexity of the historical account would inevitably be simplified as history became tradition; here the process reduced to one the two Geatish wars and left the boar as the king's sole opponent.

The motivation for the boar's attack evidently lies in the statement that, long before, Egill had destroyed the temple in the east. Now, since the boar goes back to the Geatish champion Eofor, the temple the destruction of which he is avenging was probably a Geatish temple, especially in view of the fact that, as I shall show below, the Geats in Scandian tradition came to be located in the east. Furthermore, the temple destroyed was presumably one of a cult to which the king was hostile, and if my identification of the boar with Slíðrugtanni holds, it becomes likely that Geatland, Eofor's land and hence the boar's land, was devoted to the worship of Ing (Freyr) and that the temple destroyed was a Geatish temple of Ing. If so, Egill must have been an opponent of the Freyr cult. That the Geats were worshippers of Ing is borne out by other indications, in themselves indecisive, as the intimate relations of Geats and Danes and the southern location of the Geatish kingdom; cf. also Beowulf 2577 and Saxo VII 224.

The boar is called 'the giant's yoke-beast.' From this it appears that Ing was made over into a giant — the giant cannot be original, since giants and temples do n't go together. Why was Freyr edited out of the tale? The reason becomes clear when we remember that Egill was the grandfather of the Freyr worshipper Aðils and a member of the Yngling family. It would hardly do to sing in court a lay which represented the king's ancestor as an enemy of the king's god; furthermore, the later poets would look upon such an enmity as inherently improbable and so would substitute an enemy more innocuous and at the same time from their point of view more appropriate. For the same reason court tradition would avoid the by-name Angantýr with its bad associations and would substitute something less objectionable. Schück (SY. 119 f.) has suggested a line of least resistance whereby such a substitution might have come about. The name may have occurred in the genitive in some early version of the tale. The genitive form, *Angantýs*, would lend itself readily to analysis as *angan Týs* 'loved of Týr' and from this kenning the change to the kenning *Týs ǫttungr* (which we actually have in the passage) would be easy. Certainly Þjóðólfr uses this kenning nowhere else, and its appearance in connexion with Egill can hardly be accidental.

According to Saxo king Fróði III of Denmark was gored to death by a female troll disguised as a 'sea-cow.' Her enmity was due to the fact that he had ordered her house torn down. Here, as Schück points out, Saxo's troll woman must stand for a goddess, and her house for the goddess's temple. Likewise the sea-cow goes back to an animal sacred to the goddess. The connexion with the sea is probably primitive as well. All these signs point to Nerthus as the deity concerned. Her sanctuary was on an island, and her connexion with the sea is borne out by Gylfaginning 23, which says of Njörðr: "Hann ræðr fyrir göngu vinds, ok stillir sjá ok eld; á hann skal heita til sæfara ok til veiða." From

Tacitus we learn that Nerthus made her yearly progress in a wain drawn by cows. But why should she be hostile to Fróði? We have seen that Ing early supplanted Nerthus as the chief deity of the cult. There is every reason to suppose, however, that the old conception of Nerthus as a female deity lingered for a time in parts at least of Denmark. In such regions there would be a cult rivalry, of course, which seems to have resulted in the triumph of Ing and the degradation of Nerthus to a witch or female troll. The relations between Ing and the troll would be anything but friendly, it is clear. Now later on Ing became identified, in Danish tradition, with the vegetation spirit Fróði (for the name see Björkman s. v. Froda and the references there given). Fróði in Danish tradition plays in many ways the same part as does Yngvi = Freyr in Swedish. Having absorbed Ing, Fróði fell heir to Ing's enemy the witch that once was Nerthus. Still later a euhemeristic process made Fróði into an early Danish king. Now even as a vegetation spirit Fróði was mortal; indeed, he was annually slain, as a ritual act. This situation gives his enemy her chance. We have no means of knowing the primitive rationalized form of the story of Fróði's death, but it seems altogether likely that this story represented him as meeting his fate at the hands of the witch, who was embittered against him because he had superseded her in the vegetation cult. The tearing down of the witch's house goes back to the forcible suppression of her cult in the districts where it had maintained itself.

The Saxonian story just analyzed is obviously similar to the story of Egill's death, but the resemblance is just as obviously fortuitous. Any consideration of the incident in this connexion would therefore be superfluous were it not for the fact that Schück (SY. 110 ff.) assumes it to be a Danish version of the Egill story. Supporting himself on Tacitus's statements about the Aestii and on the word *austr* of our passage, he further assumes a Swedish expedition to Esthonia in the course of which the temple of the Aestian goddess is destroyed. The sacred boar of the goddess expels the Swedes, however, and later comes to Sweden and kills Egill. There are several objections to this theory. In the first place, one would naturally interpret the phrase *ór landi* as referring to Sweden, the king's land, and as we have seen this interpretation finds support in the Beowulf narrative; Ari and Snorri take it in this sense as well (and their interpretation is indicative of the content of the lost portions of the passage). Schück, however, makes it refer to Esthonia. Secondly, on Schück's hypothesis we must suppose that the boar first expelled Egill from Esthonia, and then, long afterwards, came to Sweden and finished the job. This is a most peculiar method, and I am unable to find any parallels to it. Why did n't the boar complete his task in the first place, and, granting that he let Egill off with expulsion from Esthonia, why did he change his mind many years later, cross over to Sweden and kill the unfortunate king? The boar's activities become much more intelligible if we suppose all the action to have taken place in Sweden: the boar puts Egill to flight and upon the king's return to the attack kills him. The long interval indicated by the text clearly occurs between the burning of the temple and the attack of the boar, not between the two stages of this attack. Thirdly, the story undoubtedly originated in Sweden. Accordingly (if for the moment we accept Schück's two-version theory), we should expect the account derived from the Swedish version to be the more primitive account, especially since it is much older than the Saxonian story. Þjóðólfr knows nothing of a goddess, however; his giant would more naturally go back to a male divinity. And though we do find a degraded goddess in Saxo, her sacred beast is the cow! Furthermore, as we have seen, the whole story of Fróði's death can be derived without difficulty from native Danish tradition, and has no true connexion of any sort with the Egill story. Apart from the word *austr,* then (for which see below), there is in reality not one scrap of evidence in favor of the Esthonian origin of the boar that killed Egill, but much that is contradictory to that theory.

We have now established Egill with some plausibility as an opponent of the Freyr cult. After his death things seem to have cooled down. We have no evidence that his sons took an aggressive stand in the matter, and it is clear that his grandson Aðils was identified with the new cult (see above). The character of Egill, the 'terrible Ongenþeow' of the Beowulf (2929 a), thus marks the end of an era, and must have made a deep impression on the entire North. It is therefore not surprizing that the story of his death should meet us at every turn. We have in fact no less than eight versions of the tale. I have already analyzed three of them: the Beowulfian version, which is substantially historical, and the Álfr and Egill versions, so called because in them he goes by the names in question. I now proceed to the Angantýr I version, as contained in the Hervararsaga and the Örvaroddssaga.

In spite of the identity in name, Angantýr I is not usually recognized as the same person as Ongenþeow alias Egill. And certainly the differences between the historical and the mythical hero are considerable. Schück, however, in his *Studier i Hervararsagan,* has greatly lessened these differences by proving that Angantýr I did not originally belong in the saga at all. In the following I will assume that the reader is familiar with Schück's essay, and will confine myself to points which in my opinion still need clearing up. Angantýr is represented in the story as one of the twelve sons of Arngrímr and Eyfura. There are certain indications, however, that he did not originally belong in the family at all. Thus, although said to be the foremost among the brothers his name does not head the list — a violation of Schütte's law which should make us suspicious. Secondly, his brothers were berserkers of long standing. He himself, however, was no true berserker. On one occasion, it is true, a berserksgangr came on him along with the rest (for which see below), but the author of the Örvaroddssaga specifically contrasts him here with his brothers, stating that it had never happened to him before (M. 26). Thirdly, he clearly was not originally a rival of Hjálmarr for the hand of Ingibjörg, for when his suit proved unsuccessful he proceeded to marry another woman — a poetical impossibility if he from the first had been the rival. The primitive leader among the brothers was probably Hjörvarðr, who in the Cod. reg. version is retained as Hjálmarr's rival. Again, as Heinzel has pointed out, the graves of the sons of Arngrímr are called Hjörvarðshaugar. It is true, Hjörvarðr does not head the list of brothers, though he comes second in some of the lists. However, the brother who does come first, Hervarðr, has a name suspiciously like that of Hjörvarðr. It is unlikely that when the story arose there were 12 brothers available. The list was therefore swelled to the orthodox poetical number by doubling up (compare the two Haddingjar). Hervarðr is thus probably only a variation on Hjörvarðr. One may reconstruct the primitive story, then, as follows. The berserker Hjörvarðr, one of 12 brothers, made suit for the hand of the princess Ingibjörg. The king was intimidated by the brothers, but the hero Hjálmarr came to the rescue, himself became a suitor, and was accepted as the lady's champion against the berserkers. He fought and killed all 12 but was himself slain. Ingibjörg died of a broken heart.

Let us now examine the details of the so-called duel between Angantýr and Hjálmarr. We see at once that it was no duel, but a battle. It began with an overwhelming victory for Angantýr and his brothers (i. e., followers). This was followed by the berserksgangr mentioned above. The peculiar feature of this is that it came on, not before or during the battle, but after it. All this corresponds precisely to Ongenþeow's overwhelming victory over Hæðcyn and the berserksgangr which came on him, after the battle, at Hrefnesholt. Hjálmarr and his comrade Oddr now came up and converted Angantýr's overwhelming victory into an equally overwhelming defeat. This is parallel to the arrival of the second Geatish army, under Hygelac but seemingly led by Wulf and Eofor, who even in the Beowulfian account overshadow Hygelac and are evidently well on their way to taking his place in the story altogether. At the end Angantýr stood alone, facing his two opponents Hjálmarr and Oddr. He and Hjálmarr then fought while Oddr stood idly by. This too is strictly parallel to the first stage of the fight between Ongenþeow and the sons of Wonred. Here, however, the parallelism ends, for Hjálmarr kills Angantýr but himself receives his death wound. It will be observed, however, that he has a comrade, though to the comrade was assigned the duty of fighting Angantýr's brothers rather than Angantýr himself.

It is clear that here two stories have been combined: the story of Ongenþeow's two-day struggle with the Geats and the story of Hjálmarr's fight with the 12 berserkers. What brought them together? Ongenþeow's ferocity would make him fit well into the Arngrímr family, of course, once he got there, but of itself would hardly have put him there. The chief link, I think, was the name *Eofor,* which corresponds to a Scandian *Jöfurr.* This word originally meant 'boar' but later became a heiti for 'prince.' The development was due to the fact that chieftains wore helmets adorned with the figures of boars. The word thus came to mean 'boar helmet, army helmet' whence finally 'man wearing such a helmet, chieftain.' But the name Hjálmarr means precisely 'army helmet.' It might therefore have been substituted for Eofor on some occasion, and this would draw Ongenþeow and Hjálmarr together. Again, both Eofor and Hjálmarr obtained in marriage a king's daughter, although themselves simple warriors, and this obviously constitutes another link.

We now see how Ongenþeow developed in popular (as distinguished from courtly) tradition in South Sweden (i. e., among the old Geatish population). The ferocious king of the Beowulf became a half-giant, a berserker, a figure inspiring plenty of terror but little of anything else. The temple burner of the Ynglingatal lost his royal estate; his enmity to the gods was inconsistent with the priestly functions of a king. His memory was preserved well enough, but only as the villain of the story of the Wonredings. In this role his name Angantýr, so carefully deleted by the court poets, would of course be particularly in place, and *Egill,* reserved for the man in his royal capacity, would fall into disuse.

We now come to Óttarr, son of Egill. We know little about this king. The Ynglinga tells us that he succeeded his father on the Swedish throne, from which we may conclude that he was the elder brother. Furthermore, since a grave-mound at Vendel still bears his name that stronghold was probably his capital. Our primary interest, however, is in the various accounts of his death. The Beowulf gives us no information here. The account in the Ynglingatal reads as follows (after Schück): "Óttarr fell under the eagles' claws, the brave one before the weapons of the Danes, when the war-vulture (Óttarr) at Vendel spurned with bloody foot the one from afar. I learned that these deeds of Vǫttr and Fasti became a tale for the Swedish people, that the jarls of Fróði's island (Selund) had killed the champion." Ari's account reads thus: Cui (Egill) successit in regnum filius suus Ottarus, qui a suo aequivoco Ottaro Danorum comite et fratre eius Fasta in una provinciarum Daniae, scilicet Wendli, interemptus est. Snorri tells us further that Óttarr had the nickname Vendilkráka 'Vendel crow.' Schück equates this with the kenning *hergammr* 'war-vulture' which Þjóðólfr uses to denote king Óttarr and concludes, I think correctly, that the nickname was a title of honor, although Snorri interprets it as a contemptuous epithet applied to him by his enemies the Danes. See Schück, SY. 126 ff.

Turning now to the Beowulf, we find that the story of the death of Ongenþeow there told corresponds point for point to the story of the death of Óttarr given in the Scandian monuments. One would expect to find this story somewhere in the North; it was too good a tale to be thrown away. And after the sacred boar cut it loose from Egill who could be a more appropriate person for it to get attached to than Egill's son? On the point see also above. But before rushing to a conclusion let us compare the English and Scandian versions in detail. In the first place, we have Geats in the Beowulf, but these are replaced by Danes in the Scandian accounts. This substitution occurs so frequently in the monuments that it may be called regular; the earliest clear case is that of Gregory of Tours (died 594), who calls king Hygelac a Dane. The reasons for the confusion have been debated at great length, principally in connexion with discussions as to the home of the Geats, for which see above. As to the facts, however, there can be no dispute. In the present case at least the identification of Geats and Danes is easy to account for. When all memory of the existence of an independent Geatish nation had died out the Geatish opponents of the Swedish kings were left without a country. They were therefore identified with those later enemies of the Swedes, the Danes. If there actually was a Geatish migration to Jutland, as we have many reasons for supposing, the associations thereby established would of course also play an important part here.

This brings us to the location of the battlefield. Both Snorri and Ari make the fight occur in the Jutish district Vendel. In the Ynglingatal, on the other hand, the Dane whom Óttarr spurned with bloody foot at Vendel is said to have come from afar. This points to the Swedish Vendel, the ancient royal seat in Uppland, for if the battle took place in Denmark it would be Óttarr, not his opponent, who came from afar. Still more important as evidence here is the burial-mound at Vendel in Sweden bearing Óttarr's name. If he had fallen at Vendel in Jutland he would hardly have been buried at Vendel in Sweden. The battlefield is to be located in Sweden, then, and the location given by Ari and Snorri is to be explained as due to their ignorance of the existence of a Swedish Vendel and their familiarity with the Danish Vendel. Now in the Beowulf the last fight of Ongenþeow takes place at his fæsten in Sweden, and so as to the location of the battlefield the two stories are in agreement.

Let us now examine the details of the king's death. He was killed by the Danish jarls Vǫttr and Fasti, according to Þjóðólfr, or Ottarus and Fasti according to Ari. Ari further makes these jarls brothers. In addition, Schück has shown (SY. 133) that Fasti was a heiti for 'boar' and so can be equated with the name Eofor of the English poem. Finally, it is important to note that the king's slayers are below him in rank;

they are subjects, not rulers. Compare the brothers Wulf and Eofor of the English poem, who are likewise subjects, not rulers. For the name Vǫttr see Schück loc. cit. The Ottarus of the Historia Norwegiae is probably a mistake for Vottarus or some such form; the work is by no means an exact reproduction of Ari! The two brothers are the eagles under whose claws Óttarr fell. In the course of the struggle, however, the king spurns one of them with bloody foot. In plain prose, the king is slain by the brothers, but manages to wound one of them severely before he is struck down. The correspondence of the English and Scandian versions is evidently complete, for this is just what happens in the Beowulf, where Ongenþeow succeeds in severely wounding Wulf before he himself falls.

It remains to consider the nickname Vendilkráka. Snorri applies it to Óttarr, and as we have seen this has some support in the kenning *hergammr* 'war-vulture' of the Ynglingatal. However, as the whole story originally belonged to Egill, the nickname presumably belonged to him too. This becomes certain when we turn to Ari, for Ari both in the Íslendingabók and in the Historia Norwegiae applies the epithet to Egill, not to Óttarr. Why was Egill called by such a name? Here as in so many other cases the Beowulf gives us our answer. One of the most striking passages in that poem is the passage which tells of Ongenþeow's counter-attack on Hæðcyn and his Geats. I will quote the passage in full (ll. 2928—2941 a):

Sona him se froda fæder Ohtheres
eald ond egesfull ondslyht ageaf,
abreot brim-wisan, bryd aheorde,
gomela io-meowlan golde berofene,
Onelan moder ond Ohtheres;

ond þa folgode feorh-geniðlan,
oð-þæt hi oðeodon earfoðlice
in Hrefnes-holt hlaford-lease.
Besæt þa sinherge sweorda lafe,
wundum werge; wean oft gehet
earmre teohhe ondlonge niht;
cwæð, he on mergenne meces ecgum
getan wolde, sume on galg-treowum
fuglum to gamene.

Both followers and foes of such a man must have felt intensely the need of an epithet which would sum up the sheer ferocity of his character, and *Vendilkráka* is just such an epithet. It was not applied to him in contempt; by no means; rather in fear and trembling! For king Ongenþeow was a war-vulture indeed!

What would be the development of the nickname on Jutish soil? In the first place, *Vendilkráka* would inevitably be associated with the Jutish district Vendel. Furthermore, when the crow ceased to be considered a noble bird and the *kráka* thus became disrespectful it would be dropped. I attach no great weight to this last point, however; from the beginning the nickname would be subject to analysis and to reduction to a simple *Vendill*, giving some such phrase as *Egill the Vendel* (i. e., a man hailing from that district). The use of the epithet *Vendill* in connexion with the hero would naturally be especially popular in Jutland, since it would serve to give the Jutes a claim to him, and they would not fail to put in this claim, as his fame would do them credit. Indeed, a tendency might well become operative to make of him an eponymous ancestor, in which case the epithet would become the true name and the original true name would eventually be lost. There were other factors involved, however, and these served to complicate matters. Thus, Egill as the representative of Týr was known as Angantýr, but among the Vendel-folk this nickname might easily have been supplanted by the name *Ørvendill* (Icel *Aurvandill*), which, as we have seen (cap. I), was the name of a hypostasis of the god, and which, by virtue of its form, not only would be especially popular in the Vendel district but also would be especially suitable for application to a man who, like Egill, already bore the by-name *Vendill.* Again, Egill must have had a certain amount of competition for the position of eponymous ancestor (or first king). The Beowulf mentions (l. 348) a certain Wulfgar, prince of the Wendlas (i. e., the inhabitants of the Jutish district Vendel). Wulfgar describes himself as Hroðgar's "ar ond ombiht," and was obviously a vassal of the Danish king. Upon the death of Hroðgar, Wulfgar presumably entered the service of Hroðgar's son and successor Hreðric. The short form of Wulfgar's name might have been either Wulf or Gar (Danish Ger). If it was the latter, the Beowulfian *Gar Wendla* may with some plausibility be identified with the Saxonian *Gervendill*, who, to judge from his name, derives from the district Vendel, and who, according to Saxo, was a vassal of king Røric (OE. Hreðric). Now it is obvious that while Egill, by virtue of his nickname, would tend, as his tradition developed, to become a Jutish king, he would have, in the person of Wulfgar, a formidable rival for the position of eponymous ancestor or first king of the Vendel-folk; above all, Wulfgar would have the advantage of being on the ground from the beginning, and this would more than counterbalance Egill's greater fame. And in fact the competition (if it took place) seems to have been settled in Wulfgar's favor. Egill was not thrown aside, however; his nickname brought him into the dynasty as Ørvendill the son of Gervendill.

Let us now turn from name to saga. What was the development of the Egill story in Jutland? The Beowulf tells us that Egill was defeated by the Geatish king Hygelac. Some memory of this king is preserved to us in Saxo, as we have seen. He would naturally be remembered among the Geats for his great victory over the Swedes, and this victory is duly recorded in Saxo. We find no reference to Ongenþeow in Saxo's account, however. Hygelac is represented as having defeated in a sea-fight two Swedish "tyrants" named Omod and Ogrim. These names look like insulting appellatives, meaning 'no fight in him' or thereabouts, and their originals may well have been Onela and Ohthere, the two sons of Ongenþeow, whose harryings brought on the war and who were possibly Hygelac's opponents in the first day's fighting. For the sea-fight cf. Beowulf 2472 ff. If our thesis as to the development of the Geatish tradition is correct, it is easy to see how these two figures, who played an important though subordinate part in the conflict, took the place originally occupied by Ongenþeow. The latter, when he became a Geatish king by virtue of the fact that he was the father of Onela, could no longer serve as antagonist of the Geatish hero Hygelac. His sons, however, whose true relationship to Ongenþeow would be obscured and finally lost through the use of their nicknames in this connexion, could continue to serve as Hygelac's antagonists and even take over their father's role. However this may be, the fact remains that in Saxo no trace of Ongenþeow as antagonist of Hygelac is to be found, and for us this evidence of his actual elimination from the Hygelac saga is of the utmost importance.

We have seen that the Beowulfian account of the death of Ongenþeow appears in the Ynglinga attached to his son Óttarr. Turning now to Saxo, we find the same account, but Ongenþeow's grandson Aðils has become the victim, while Wulf and Eofor appear as Ket and Vig, the sons of the originally Anglian king Frøvin (OE. Freawine), who in Saxo is known as duke of Slesvig. Ket and Vig are represented as avenging on Aðils the death of their father, whom Aðils had slain in battle. Weyhe (ESt. XXXIX 21 ff.) has already called attention to the fact that although this story forms a part of the originally Anglian saga of king Uffe, and accordingly belongs to the Jutish tradition, it nevertheless is clearly Geatish in origin. He therefore inclines to the opinion that Jutland was the home of the Geats. Schütte's theory of a Geatish migration to Jutland accounts equally well for the development here, of course. The exact nature of this development cannot however be made clear without a preliminary survey of the Jutish saga-complex as a whole, and such a survey will now be attempted.

The Jutish saga-complex, as we find it in Saxo, is made up of two distinct sagas, viz., a Geatish Amleth saga and an Anglian Uffe saga. These two sagas must have come into contact before the development of either had proceeded far from the historical complex itself. What happened? Neither hero got the upper hand, that is clear. Each remained the center of a saga of his own, and the two sagas are entirely separate. The course of development may briefly be described as follows.

Uffe had from the earliest times been essentially and primarily a national hero, the defender of the realm against outside attack. His fight at Fifeldor of which the Widsið tells was a fight of this sort. Consequently he tended to attract to himself saga-stuff which had to do with national attack and defense. The historical Onela, on the other hand, waged no national wars as such. His life centers about his struggle for the crown against his nephews Eanmund and Eadgils. This was a civil war, not a war against outside enemies. And accordingly the Amleth saga centers about a struggle within the realm and between near kinsmen. In such a struggle the Geatish material concerned with foreign wars would have no place, and so would readily be transferred to the national hero Uffe. What was this material? Apart from Hygelac himself, whom Uffe never succeeded in absorbing, we have the slaying of Hæðcyn by Ongenþeow, the slaying of Ongenþeow by Wulf and Eofor the sons of Wonred, and the disastrous defeat of the Geats by the Swedes which led to the destruction of the Geatish kingdom and (on Schütte's theory) to the migration to Jutland of a certain proportion of the Geatish population. This defeat may have been administered by Aðils, or by some later Swedish monarch; as to this we have no historical information. The Saxonian account, however, gives us some right to infer that tradition credited or came to credit Aðils with the exploit, and in the following we will assume, for convenience in presentation, that Aðils was the Swedish king who finally overthrew the Geatish kingdom. Now historically the slaying of Ongenþeow came first, the victory of Aðils last. Poetically, however, the order would obviously have to be reversed, as otherwise the slaying would be unmotivated and the defeat unavenged. Such a reversal could be effected neatly enough by associating with Aðils not only his own victory over the Geats but also that of his grandfather. That this association was actually made is indicated by the fact that Wulf and Eofor were in fact taking vengeance for the latter victory when they slew Ongenþeow. When Ongenþeow ceased to be known as a Swedish king, then, his grandson Aðils, the great enemy of the Wægmunding house, took over his part as antagonist of the Geats, and the two Swedish victories became one.

How did the development then proceed? Before the story was attracted over into the Uffe saga-group one important change certainly had already taken place — Wonred had become the victim of the Swedish king. For as we have the tale in the Beowulf it is good history but poor poetry! The brothers Wulf and Eofor kill Ongenþeow. Why? In the old days any man with a spark of poetic feeling would know the answer at once. They must have been avenging their father. And so they are in Saxo. The development here was obvious and easy. Ongenþeow actually killed Hæðcyn, but as the tale developed he would come to be represented rather as the slayer of Wonred. Hæðcyn and Wonred might conceivably have become identified, of course, but the actual versions of the tale as we have them show conclusively that this was not the way in which the poets worked the problem out. For in none of the versions are Wonred and his sons represented as royal. In the Beowulf they are nobody in particular. The Ynglinga promotes the brothers to the rank of jarls.

Saxo makes them the sons of the duke of Slesvig. But everywhere they are subjects, not monarchs, and when the family gets identified with the Anglian king Frøvin and his sons the result is a reduction of the king to the rank of duke. Clearly Hæðcyn furnished nothing except his death. Indeed, it may be that he did not furnish even this; the story of the slaying of Wonred may well have arisen from the mere fact that his sons kill Ongenþeow. — The factors which prevented the Wonred story from appropriating Hæðcyn are obvious enough. As we shall see later on, Hæðcyn was remembered not so much for his death as for certain events in his life, and these events tied him to the Amleth saga with bonds that could not be loosened.

What was the link that effected the transfer of Wonred and his sons from Amleth to Uffe? A link of some sort there must have been. Uffe undoubtedly had strong powers of attraction, but these could not become operative until contact had been established. We have already seen that the Widsið (96) mentions a king Eadgils of the Myrgings, and (42) makes the Myrgings the enemies of the Angles in the fight at Fifeldor. Later the Myrgings seem to have migrated and the Swæfe to have taken the lands they vacated, as also their role as traditional enemies of the Angles. This last development took place on the Continent after the migration to England of the bulk of the tribe. It is therefore not reflected in English tradition. Among the Angles left in the peninsula, then, king Eadgils came to be remembered as king of the Swæfe, and the Myrgings were forgotten altogether. Now a confusion of name between Swæfe 'Svebi' and Sweon 'Swedes' is easy, and in fact occurs in medieval monuments. It is hardly necessary, however, to postulate with Weyhe an actual war between Freawine and Eadgils. Such a war may well have occurred, of course, but the facts which we actually possess are sufficient to account for the identification of Wonred and his sons with Anglian princes. In the first place, the bearers of the Anglian tradition, when they heard for the first time the Geatish story of king Eadgils, his crimes and final end, would naturally associate it with the king Eadgils that they were familiar with, viz., the king of the Swæfe. The antagonists of Eadgils in the tale, on the other hand, would be entirely strange, and the low rank of Wonred and his sons would seem to them intrinsically improbable and unworthy of the poetic art. A new version of the story would therefore arise in the south, in which Eadgils was given proper antagonists, drawn from the ranks of his hereditary enemies the Angles. Who were available here? Uffe was already pre-empted. Vermund was unavailable because both a father and sons were needed. King Freawine and his son Wig were therefore utilized, along with an additional son, Ket, either given him by the poets to fit the tale, or else a true son whose name is not otherwise preserved to us. In this manner the introduction of the Anglians may well have come about. They lost their royal rank, however. The tenacity with which the Wonredings were remembered as subjects reduced Freawine from king to duke, and this reduction in rank, which gave him Vermund, father of Uffe, for an overlord, brought the tale within range of the Uffe saga-group. For the further development of the tale see Olrik, KS. II 185. In any case, however, the important thing for us is the fact that the actual slayers of Ongenþeow in the course of time became totally disconnected from him in Jutish tradition and attached to another victim.

We have seen that in the Jutish tradition as preserved in Saxo neither the Hygelac story nor the story of the Wonredings preserved the slightest trace of the historical antagonist, viz., Ongenþeow. Yet die he must. The proper function of a hero's father is to be killed, in order that the hero may have a chance to avenge him. The father's own deeds are likely to be forgotten, or transferred to the son; thus, Sigmundr originally killed the dragon, as we know from the Beowulf, but in the later accounts his son Sigurðr gets the credit for the deed. The father's death, though, cannot be taken away from him, but rather becomes the all-important event of his life — in many cases the only event about which we get much information. Who could his slayer have been? We have eliminated Hygelac and the brothers Wulf and Eofor. There remains only one historical antagonist. Tradition must have made Hæðcyn the slayer of Ongenþeow.

This conclusion seems at first sufficiently startling. For in the historical account Ongenþeow kills Hæðcyn! When we have considered the matter, however, we shall see how natural it was that the tradition should have developed as I assume it to have done. In the first place, just as Ongenþeow, after he had become a Geatish king, could no longer serve as antagonist of Hygelac, so Onela could no longer serve as antagonist of Hygelac's son Heardred. What happened? Heardred was lost altogether; no trace of him is to be found outside the

Beowulf. But the memory of Onela's deed was not so easily disposed of. Heroes do not readily get shorn of their heroic accomplishments. The knowledge that Onela had slain a Geatish king must have persisted, and must have brought Onela into competition with his father for the honor of having slain Hæðcyn, the only other king available. In such a competition the hero, not his father, would gain the victory, and Ongenþeow would be stripped of his laurels — a fate not uncommon to heroes' fathers anyhow, as we have seen. But if Onela slew Hæðcyn there must have been a reason for it, and the orthodox reason was vengeance on his father's slayer. Thus Hæðcyn became the villain of the tale. And if ever a man lived who was specially made for the part, Hæðcyn was that man. The Beowulf tells us how by accident he killed his elder brother Herebeald, the heir to the throne, and how the old king died of grief and Hæðcyn, profiting by his deed, ascended the throne. With this elder brother Ongenþeow became identified (see below), an appropriate place being thus found for the hero's father in the historical royal house. We learn further (2930) how Hæðcyn in the course of his expedition to Sweden captured Ongenþeow's wife. Historically she was later rescued by her husband, but when Hæðcyn became her husband's slayer her rescue obviously no longer fit into the situation and so was necessarily eliminated from the story. If in addition we recall that the faithless widow motif was already present in the historical complex and would infallibly influence the development of the relations between Hæðcyn and his captive, we cannot escape the conclusion that we have before us the nucleus of the Hamlet Tale.

Chapter VII.

The Hervararsaga.

Is there any external evidence confirmatory of the development I have outlined above? Yes. Such evidence is to be found in the Hervararsaga. I have already shown that Angantýr I of that saga is to be identified with Ongenþeow. I will now prove that the other two Angantýrs in the story are derivable from the same source. First, however, we shall have to go rather far afield — apparently, at least. In the OE. and Scandian monuments is preserved a name for the Goths which does not occur elsewhere. This is the much discussed *Hreiðgotar* etc. For the variant forms see Chambers 225f. It is certain that the original diphthong in the first element was *ai*, which would give Icelandic *ei*. The corresponding sound in OE. would be *æ* (with i-umlaut). And a form with *æ* actually occurs in the Widsið (120 a). The ordinary OE. form however is *Hreð-*. The substitution of the close for the open vowel was due to a popular etymology. The meaning of the element *Hræð-* being unknown, a meaning was forced upon it; it was popularly connected with *hreð* 'glory' and the name *Hreðgotan* thus came to be interpreted as 'glorious Goths.' Such an interpretation would fit in admirably with the reputation of the Goths, of course, and the violence done to the vowel would hardly be great enough to disturb the folk-etymologists! Popular etymologies of this sort, and sound-changes resulting from them, are among the most familiar of linguistic phenomena, and I need not dwell on the matter further, except to mention a parallel case, *acorn* for *akern*, where the vowel suffered much more severely than in the case under discussion.

Turning now to the Beowulf, we find in l. 445 a the name *Hreðmen* applied to the Geats. The half-line, which reads *mægenhreðmanna*, is best divided as *mægen Hreðmanna*, parallel to the *Geata leode* of 443 b. The usual argument against this division, based on the *m*-alliteration, seems to me unsound. There is no need to assume that the *m* of *Hreðmanna* alliterates at all, or that *Hreðmen* was felt as a compound any more than *Englishmen* is felt as a compound today. The close *e* of *Hreðmen* is to be explained on the same basis as that of *Hreðgotan* etc. The Beowulfian name, then, is of some significance to us, for, taken in connexion with the *Gautigoths* of Jordanes, it shows that the name *Hreðgotan* might well originally have been used to designate the Geats. Was it actually so used? No such form as *Hreðgotan* occurs in the Beowulf, and where it does occur in OE. it is used with reference to the Goths, not the Geats. This usage is no doubt secondary, and due to the fact that the name *Gotan* early ceased to be applied (in England, at least) to the Gothic tribes of Scandinavia. Nevertheless, our theory remains theory unless we can find further support for it. The evidence here must be sought in the Scandian monuments, where one would expect the original usage (if it was original) to maintain itself longest. The earliest Scandian reference to the Hreiðgotar occurs in the Rök inscription, which Bugge has dated at c. 835. The passage in which the name occurs reads as follows: þat sakum onart huaR fur niu altum on *on* urþi fiaru miR hraiþkutum auk tu miR on ub sakaR 'let us say that in the second place, where nine generations ago Øn lost his life, (viz.) among the Hreiðgotar, and (he) died among them furthermore on account of a feud.' The Øn here referred to is to be identified with the Swedish king Aun of the Ynglingasaga, who according to the story in cap. 25 of that saga took refuge among the Geats and lived among them as an exile for a long time. As we have seen (cap. III), this Aun became confused with his great-grandson the Eanmund of the Beowulf. Now the Beowulf tells us how Eanmund took refuge among the Geats and was there slain by the Geatish warrior Weohstan. The exact circumstances of his death are not related, but apparently it took place in the course of a battle between the Geats and the Swedes, Weohstan being then in the service of Onela, the Swedish king. The hostilities were induced by the fact that the Geats had given asylum to Eanmund, who was a claimant to the Swedish throne. The feud was really one between Onela and Eanmund, but the fact that Eanmund met his death at the hands of Weohstan seems to have caused the tradition to develop to what we get in the inscription. The author of the inscription, however, although he transmitted the tradition faithfully enough, evidently did not know the true meaning of the name *Hreiðgotar,* for he tacks onto the passage quoted a strophe about Theodoric, the famous Ostrogothic king; in other words, he identifies *Hreiðgotar* with *Ostrogoths.*

From the passage itself, nevertheless, the original meaning oft he word is manifest. For other interpretations of the passage see especially Studier i Nordisk Filologi III. 8. 14 ff. and Schück, SY. 103 ff. The latter, like me, refers the tradition to Aun, although for reasons very different from those I have given. For further evidence pointing to the equation *Hreiðgotar* = *Geats* see Bugge, Antikvarisk Tidskrift för Sverige V 35 ff.

Let us now return to the Hervararsaga. There king Angantýr III is represented as ruler of the Hreiðgotar. Who was this king? He began his reign by suppressing a servile insurrection, and Schück (SY. 115 ff.) has shown that this corresponds to the servile insurrection which Egill suppressed at the beginning of *his* reign. We are therefore justified in tentatively equating him with the father of Onela. How did he become king of the Hreiðgotar? If these were originally Geats the process is clear enough; as the father of Onela he would naturally become a king of the Geats when Onela became one, and this change of nationality is a fundamental part of the present Hamlet theory. The change of meaning which *Hreiðgotar* underwent does not offer any serious difficulties. The Geats, whom Jordanes calls *Gautigoths*, were more usually known by the first element of that name only, and eventually their rather distant kinship with the Goths proper was forgotten. Even so early a monument as the Beowulf makes no use of the compounded name, though perhaps we have no right to assume too much from its silence on the point, which may well be accidental or due to the English environment. As to *Hreiðgotar,* then, I conceive the term to have been employed originally with reference to the

Geats, but later used to refer to the Goths proper on account of the second element of the word. In this way Angantýr in his capacity as king of the Hreiðgotar was transplanted far to the east and became identified with the Ostrogothic royal house, the Amalungs. The part which Angantýr III plays in the Hervararsaga, then, is a notable confirmation of the present Hamlet theory, and indeed can be explained only on the assumption of the validity of that theory. — For a collection of references to the Hreiðgotar in Scandian monuments see Heinzel 469 ff.

Before we go on to Angantýr II a few points remain to be gathered up. In the first place there is the curious statement in the Hyndluljóð (24, 1) that Angantýr I was born *í Bolm austr*. The word *austr* may of course refer simply to Sweden, as distinguished from Norway, but taken in connexion with the passage in the Sturlaugssaga starfsama (FAS. III 633) which locates Ingibjörg *í Görðum austr,* i. e., in Russia, it looks very much as if the poet had the Goths in mind. If so, here too we can explain the eastward shift only by using the Geats as a link. Again, we have already noted that the temple that Egill destroyed was located in the east. Yet for various reasons, already brought forward (see cap. VI above), we have concluded that the temple which he destroyed was a Geatish temple. The location of the temple in the east is thus most extraordinary. It can be explained readily enough, however, if we assume that *Hreiðgotar* originally had reference to the Geats. Finally, the contradiction between Snorri's two references to Reiðgotaland (Gylfaginning 4 and Skáldskaparmál 65) can easily be explained on the present hypothesis. In the Gylfaginning Snorri identifies Reiðgotaland with Jutland; in the Skáldskaparmál he locates it in Sweden. But the Geats originally lived in what was later South Sweden; when their kingdom was overthrown by the Swedes a considerable Geatish migration to Jutland seems to have taken place. There was thus every reason for uncertainty in tradition as to the home of the Geats, and as we have seen a confusion actually took place. To this confusion Snorri's location of Reiðgotaland in both Jutland and Sweden is beautifully parallel. As we proceed with the discussion other cases will appear the obscurities of which can be cleared up by a utilization of our theory of the traditional transfer of Geatish kings to the east.

We are now ready to examine the career of Angantýr II. Here we discover at once that he has no career, except to die at the hands of his brother Heiðrekr, and this makes us suspect that he was inserted in the tale simply because some narrator had heard a version of the death of Angantýr different from the one he was familiar with and so had supposed the new version to refer to a different man, presumably a relative or descendant of his own Angantýr. At any rate, Angantýr II appears as grandson of Angantýr I. Neither he nor his brother and slayer Heiðrekr belong in the saga at all, which would be greatly improved by their absence and which in its primitive form, according to Schück, knew nothing of them. The source of Angantýr II has never been discovered. Heiðrekr, on the other hand, clearly goes back to a saga dealing with Guðmundr á Glasisvöllum and his family (see Heinzel 447 f.). According to the Saga af Þorsteini Bæjarmagni (FMS. III 197) he was a son of this Guðmundr, who in all the monuments appears as Guðmundr the wise. Heinzel has pointed out that Guðmundr's son Heiðrekr must also originally have been wise, and in fact he appears as such in his riddle match with Óðinn. For the most part, however, he shows himself wild and reckless to a degree, and this change of character must have been brought about by outside influence of some sort. Angantýr's character too is anything but what one would expect of a man with such a name. He is pictured as mild-mannered and gentle! It is a far cry to the 'terrible Ongenþeow' of the Beowulf and the berserker Angantýr I.

To my mind it is clear that the story of Angantýr II and Heiðrekr in the Hervararsaga is identical with the story of Herebeald and Hæðcyn in the Beowulf. The two stories both run thus: an elder brother, beloved by his father and heir to the throne, is killed, accidentally, by the younger brother, who is not dear to his father (Beowulf 2467). There is also a correspondence in names. For *Herebeald* we have ***Angantýr***, for *Hæðcyn Heiðrekr,* it is true, and in neither pair can the names be equated phonetically. But the substitution of *Angantýr* for *Herebeald* is precisely what one would expect to find, on the present Hamlet theory, which assumes that the father of Onela was identified with Hæðcyn's victim. The substitution of *Heiðrekr* for *Hæðcyn* can also be explained with some plausibility. In the Beowulf the Geats are once (l. 1983) referred to as *Hæne* 'wilderness-dwellers.' The name doubtless had reference to the original home of the Geats in pre-historic times, before their conquest of the valley of the Götaelf. Some such title as 'lord of the heath' would thus be particularly appropriate for a Geatish prince. Now the name *Heiðrekr* means precisely this, and in addition seems to have been an appellative, or at any rate no true personal name. It may thus be explained as an epithet or title which belonged to Hæðcyn by hereditary right and which served as a link to identify him with the mythological Heiðrekr of the Guðmundr line when the sagas of the two came into contact. To be compared is the *Gautrekr* of the Ynglinga (cap. 34) and of the Hrólfssaga Gautrekssonar; the name *Gautrekr* seems to have been, in origin, an epithet or title meaning 'lord of the Geats.' More direct evidence of a confusion of the names *Hæðcyn* and *Heiðrekr* is to be found in the *Heaþoric* of Widsið 116 a, a name which is usually referred to the Heiðrekr of the Hervararsaga but which in form represents a Scandian *Höðrekr*, i. e., a contamination of *Höðkon* (the Scandian form of *Hæðcyn*) and *Heiðrekr*. For the etymology of *Hæðcyn* here followed see Björkman s. v. — The name *Hæne* may be interpreted as meaning 'barbarians' and as having been applied to the Geats by their enemies and later subjects the more civilized tribes of the plain (mentioned in Jordanes; see above, cap. I). This interpretation need not disturb our argument, however, of course.

Returning now to our episode, we find that no less striking than its correspondence to the Beowulf account in plot and names is its correspondence in the characters themselves. That anybody named Angantýr could be mildmannered and gentle in disposition is astonishing enough, and nothing in the Hervararsaga serves to explain this most curious development. Such a development however is just what we should expect in the

Hamlet tale, where the son is the hero and the father's only function is to be killed. The poetic tendency here would be to make the victim a sympathetic person, and Ongenþeow's ferocity would thus have to go. Indeed, eventually the by-name Ongenþeow itself, because of its ferocious associations, was replaced by the colorless Ørvendill, and it is altogether probable that for similar reasons Ongenþeow, when he was identified with Herebeald, was given the personal characteristics of that prince. The form of the story as we have it in the Hervararsaga is thus very primitive, and this is reflected in its close correspondence to the Beowulf — a correspondence far closer than that of the Hamlet saga of Saxo, where Feng is a villain pure and simple.

This brings us to Hlöðr and the problems connected with his name and career. Here we shall have to begin with Angantýr I—III. The historical Ongenþeow was known among the Geats as Angantýr rather than as Egill on account of his religious or anti-religious activities, of which they had to bear the brunt. Even among the Geats though there were two sides to his shield. On the one hand was the temple-burning ferocious enemy, the antagonist of the Geatish hero Eofor. On the other hand was the father of Onela. As we have seen, Onela through his connexion with the Wægmunding house became, in Geatish tradition, a Geatish king, and his father naturally was adopted with him. There was thus every stimulus to the differentiation of Ongenþeow into two persons. This differentiation became a certainty when Eofor was identified with Hjálmarr. For this identification brought the opponent of Eofor into the Arngrímr house, and changed him from a king to a half-giant and berserker. The historical Ongenþeow thus became differentiated into a berserker, Angantýr I, and a king, Angantýr III. As king of the Hreiðgotar (Geats, later Ostrogoths), Angantýr III was soon transferred to the east, losing his connexion with Onela and becoming associated with the Gothic kings of the house of Amala. In this connexion it is interesting to note that Jordanes mentions a branch of the Ostrogoths living in the immediate vicinity of the Gautigoths. It may be that the Geatish kingdom included this tribe and that it was in this way that the Geatish kings acquired their title of king of the Hreiðgotar. This would of course also facilitate the transfer of Angantýr III to the east. As traditional king of the Goths, Angantýr now became the hero of the great victory over the Huns actually won by king Valamir. He likewise attracted to himself the story of the sword Tyrfing. This story may be outlined as follows (for a full discussion see Schück). A king forces a dwarf to forge for him a magic sword. The dwarf obeys, but lays upon it the curse that through the sword one of the two sons of the king's daughter will become the bane of the other. To prevent this from happening the king, just before he dies, orders the sword to be buried with him. This is done. The king's daughter has two sons. One of them at an early age goes abroad (the Hlöðr of our story, who is brought up among the Huns). The other stays at home (the Angantýr III of our story). Upon reaching manhood the latter demands of his mother her father's sword, and she, ignorant of the curse laid upon it, removes it from the king's grave and gives it to her son. He in the course of his adventures as a warrior meets his brother, whom he does not recognize, and kills him in a duel. The mother thus unwittingly causes one of her sons to kill the other. In our story the plot outlined above appears in a much corrupted form. The fight between the brothers is brought into connexion with the battle between Goths and Huns, with Angantýr III as king of the Goths and his brother Hlöðr as one of the leaders of the Huns.

It has already been pointed out that when Ongenþeow became a Geatish king he was made brother of Hæðcyn. Now historically he killed Hæðcyn, and if we go back far enough we must come to a time when this was remembered. The story of Tyrfing then probably got attached to Angantýr III because he killed Hæðcyn and Hæðcyn was thought of as his brother. That this was a very early development is clear from the fact that the story is referred to in the Widsið. In Jutland, however, with the development of Onela at the expense of his father, the latter was later identified with Herebeald and this resulted in a reversal of the historical facts: Hæðcyn is represented as killing Ongenþeow. This later version appears in the Hervararsaga as well (see above).

If Hlöðr, the brother and victim of Angantýr III, actually goes back to Hæðcyn, there ought to be further evidence pointing in that direction. Such evidence is to be found in Saxo, who knows a Danish king named Hlöðr (Lotherus).* That Hlöðr appears as a Danish king is in itself indicative, in view of the well-known confusion of Danes and Geats. Furthermore, the story of this king seems to be little more than a Saxonian version of the life of Heiðrekr, the king with whom Hæðcyn had become identified in Götarike. Saxo begins by telling how Hlöðr gained the throne by plotting against his elder brother Humli (Humblus), defeating him in battle and dethroning him. This trait apparently represents a fusion of three distinct episodes in the life of Heiðrekr, who accidentally killed his elder brother, gained a throne by plotting against his father-in-law Haraldr and defeating and killing him in battle, and, later on, waged war successfully against his second father-in-law Humli. In the tradition known to Saxo the two father-in-laws are reduced to one, who answers to Haraldr in that he is plotted against, defeated and deprived of his throne, but answers to Humli in name, and in the fact that he is only defeated, not slain. This fusion-product is further made into an elder brother. The development may have been due to a confusion of Angantýr II with Heiðrekr's colorless brother-in-law and rival heir the son of Haraldr; Heiðrekr killed this brother-in-law along with Haraldr, and father and son may have become fused in some tradition. At any rate, Humli appears with much the same characteristics as those given to Angantýr II in the Hervararsaga, while Hlöðr in character is almost a double of Heiðrekr. The way in which Humli and Hlöðr are set over against each other and contrasted in the Saxonian account reminds one irresistibly of the passage in the Hervararsaga where Angantýr II and Heiðrekr are compared. Saxo now goes on to tell how Hlöðr, become king, alienated the affections of his more important subjects by robbing them of their property and even, in some cases, of their lives; they accordingly rebelled against him and overthrew him. His son nevertheless succeeded to the throne, apparently without difficulty. Humli is forgotten; he might as well be dead! The situation becomes more intelligible when we compare it with the corresponding account in the Hervararsaga. Here the elder brother of Heiðrekr is actually dead, while the rebels are war-captives, who before their enslavement were men of great consequence and who bore ill the loss of their freedom. As slaves they would naturally have no share in the choice of a new king, and in fact they are represented as fleeing the country as soon as they had slain Heiðrekr, whose son succeeded to the throne without popular opposition. Saxo's conversion of the slaves of noble birth into native lords deprived of their goods makes an inconsequence of the peaceful succession of the murdered king's son; this peaceful succession, however, he retains nevertheless, and its presence casts suspicion upon the fidelity to tradition of his (or his source's) account of Hlöðr's fall. The Saxonian form of the story here is usually explained as due to influence from the story of Heremod (Sievers Berichte, Sächs. Akad. 1895 p. 175ff.). However this may be, Siever's equation Lotherus = Heremod manifestly becomes doubtful, in view of the parallels developed above.

But whence comes the name *Hlöðr*? It is best derived, by metathesis, from **Hróþilaʀ*, the primitive form of the Beowulfian *Hreðel*. In the resulting form, **Hlóþiraʀ*, one would expect the first element to develop to **Hlœð-*, it is true; the shortening was doubtless due to association with *Höðr*, or with *Hlöðvér*, the latter a name actually confused with *Hlöðr* in the mss., the former a person actually confounded with *Hlöðr* in the sources (as Messenius). The original length seems to be preserved in the OE. form *Hlíþe* = **Hlýþe* (Heinzel 491), where *y* is to be interpreted as an attempt to represent the foreign *œ*. As to the second element, we may suppose an early loss of the ultima vowel between the *r*-sound, followed by simplification of *-irʀ* to *-iʀ* and consequent attraction into the *ja*-stem group. This development would be supported by the analogy of the numerous *ja*-stem proper names in *-iʀ*, whereas there would be no analogical support for a name in *-irʀ* (or *-irr*). Finally, with the shortening of the first syllable of the name, the internal *-i-* would be lost by syncope. — As to the early syncope of the ultima vowel here assumed for the position between *r*-sounds, cf. the name-elements *-marr* and *-ārr*, where the *i*-syncope must have taken place earlier then *i*-syncope in general; indeed, in *-arr* two syncopes must have occurred, yet both these took place so early that no umlaut appears. We therefore have some basis for our supposition that in the position between *r*-sounds the *ă*-syncope took place at an earlier date than *ă*-syncope in general. To be compared is the regular loss of an unstrest *-a-* between *r*-sounds in the spoken Icelandic of today. The phonetic explanation of this syncope is obvious, of course.

If my etymology of *Hlöðr* is sound, we must suppose that Hreðel and his son Hæðcyn were confounded in popular tradition. What was the reason for this development? It is probable that Hæðcyn usually went by the short form of his name, i. e., by its first element, which in Scandian form would be *Höðr*. The phonetic similarity between *Hlöðr* and *Höðr* might well result in a certain amount of confusion. Again, father and son seem to have had the same opponent, viz., the Swedish king Egill. The opposition Hæðcyn : Egill is of course well known. As however the Beowulf tells us practically nothing about Hreðel's career the very possibility of his having had a war with Egill has hitherto escaped attention. Nevertheless the story of Egill's death as told in the Ynglingatal ought to have made us suspicious. If Egill, long before he died, burned a Geatish temple, he must have had hostile relations with the Geatish king of the period, who could hardly have been other than Hreðel. It behoves us, then, to search for further evidence. This we find in the Swedish chronicler Messenius (see Sarrazin, Anglia XIX 392 ff.). I quote from Sarrazin, the original not being accessible to me: Lotherus igitur, Danorum rex, ab Othino vehementer infestatus, et ope suorum propter nimiam destitutus tyrannidem, superatusque in Jutiam profugit. Caeteri porro Danorum, et praesertim Siaelandi, victoribus se accommodantes, Balderum Othini filium, pro rege acceptarunt. Is protinus in loco Bredebliche, sub Lethra prope Roschildiam sito, novum Diis sacrificandi morem instituit. Here Baldr is out of place, his introduction being due to contamination from the Höðr story (for which see below); indeed, even as the account stands Óðinn is obviously Hlöðr's true opponent, and if we had an uncontaminated version we should undoubtedly find him Hlöðr's only opponent. But why should Óðinn be hostile to Hlöðr? Snorri tells us a good deal about a war between the Æsir and the Vanir, i. e., a struggle for supremacy between the cult of Óðinn (imported from the south) and that of Ing or Freyr. This cult war was doubtless historical; all the evidence we have goes to confirm Snorri as to the main point. It had however been preceded by another cult war, a war between the followers of Týr and those of Freyr. The memory of this earlier war was preserved in the story of Álfr and Yngvi, as we have seen, and the degradation of Týr which was its result finds expression in the Týr kenning *átniðr jötna* (Hymiskviða 9, 1) and in Loki's taunt (Lokasenna 40). Nevertheless, Scandian tradition, on the whole, did not keep the two cult wars separate. The two opponents of Freyr were put in the same camp, and the one subordinated to the other. Týr was naturally the god subordinated; he was made one of the Æsir, and became Óðinn's son and follower, in the tradition which the Snorra Edda has preserved to us. I conceive the same process to have taken place in the tradition represented in Messenius: Óðinn came to wage Týr's wars as well as his own.

For Óðinn, then, let us substitute Týr in the Messenian account. The account at once becomes much more readily explicable, for obviously the part played by the god must historically have been played by Egill, the great champion of the Týr cult and the bearer of the by-name Angantýr. If in addition we assume the usual confusion of Danes and Geats we are able to reconstruct the historical basis of the Messenian story. This story in all probability goes back to a cult war between the Swedish king Egill and the Geatish king Hreðel. The latter was a worshipper of Ing; many of his subjects, however, continued to adhere to the old cult of Týr. Hreðel's persecution of these Týr-worshippers won him the name of tyrant and caused his victims to call to their aid the Swedes, whose king Egill had remained faithful to the old cult. In the conflict which followed Egill was victorious, and Hreðel was forced to flee to Jutland. It was at this time that Egill did the temple-burning told of in the Ynglingatal.

Messenius continues: Sed Lotherus, interim auxiliaribus ex Suecia, Norvegia et Jutia copiis in hostem impetratis, cum eo animose congreditur, et Balderum regno atque vita simul exuit. Itaque Othinus mortem vindicaturus filii, et Daniam recuperaturus, Vectam Saxonum et Boum Russiae principes, filios suos in subsidium advocat, bellum instaurat; Lotherum, non Hotherum, trucidat, et victor Daniam, Sueciam et Norvegiam occupat ante Christum anno XXIV. This is for the most part the story of Höðr, in spite of Messenius's denial of that fact. From it nevertheless we can glean the conclusion of the Hlöðr story: Hreðel returned from exile and recovered his kingdom. A more complete account can be made by piecing together the scraps of evidence found in other sources. According to the Ynglinga Egill was defeated and driven into exile as a result of a servile insurrection. This insurrection is no doubt historical, but the proportions which it assumes in Ari and Snorri seem much too considerable, especially when compared with the more modest account of the matter in the Hervararsaga. Furthermore, in the latter account Egill's exile does not occur at all, while Þjóðólfr connects the exile with the Geatish war (for the correspondences in Saxo see below). Supporting ourselves on these discrepancies, and on the Swedish auxiliaries of Lotherus mentioned in Messenius, we may conjecture that Egill had to contend with two insurrections, the first a servile revolt or rather plot at the beginning of his reign, the second a rebellion fomented by the Ing-worshippers, whom he doubtless persecuted much as Hreðel persecuted the Týr-worshippers. Hreðel seems to have taken advantage of the second rebellion to attack and defeat Egill, thus recovering his throne and driving Egill into exile. Egill fled to the Danes. These seem to have been in alliance with their co-religionists the Geats (cf. Beowulf 1865 and Saxo III 75, where Höðr = Hlöðr), but, alarmed perhaps at the power of Hreðel, they now changed sides (Beowulf 1855 ff.; Saxo loc. cit.; Ynglinga, cap. 26). Egill accordingly through their aid was able to win back his kingdom (Ynglinga loc. cit.). — Hreðel upon his conquest of Sweden seems to have introduced there the worship of Ing (cf. Saxo III 74 bottom). His formal recognition of the cult must of course have been preceded by a period during which Ing worship was practiced unofficially or surreptitiously. — Hreðel's overthrow of the terrible Ongenþeow must have made a deep impression on the Scandian skalds, for we find *hlöðr* used in verse as an epithet meaning 'prostrator.'

The war between Hreðel and Egill thus ended with each in possession of his own kingdom. Certainly the two kings must have managed somehow or other to patch up their differences, for according to the Beowulf Hreðel did not die in battle, but in his bed, and apparently in a time of peace. As we have already seen, he died of grief over the slaying of his eldest son Herebeald. A reminiscence of this grief seems to be the passage in Saxo (III 75 bottom) where Höðr (= Hlöðr), overcome with despair, abandons his kingdom and flees alone to the wilderness (cf. Beowulf 2444 ff.).

The reconstruction given above enables us to explain the tyranny attributed to Hlöðr both in Saxo and in

Messenius. The tradition that he was a tyrant grew out of his persecution of the Týr-worshippers. Messenius puts the tyrannical conduct in its right place, viz., at the beginning of the story. Saxo, on the other hand, whose Hlöðr had been remodeled on the pattern of Heiðrekr, was able to retain the tyranny only by substituting it for the servile conspiracy which terminated Heiðrekr's career. In neither case do we need to assume any influence from the saga of Heremod; all the facts can be accounted for from the reconstructed historical basis itself. The Heremod theory has always rested on an insecure foundation, inasmuch as Heremod, unlike Hlöðr, is not credited with a brother, and, far from being supported by the Jutes, is betrayed among them. And this in addition to the total lack of correspondence in name! In view of the new parallels now brought forward, the theory that Heremod and Hlöðr have any connexion with each other must be regarded as dubious indeed. Of course, however, I would not claim for my own theory in the matter anything more than plausibility; my reconstruction is after all a reconstruction, and the evidence on which it is based gives but an insecure foundation for the erection of any kind of superstructure!

We were compelled to reconstruct most of the historical career of Hreðel. The outlines of his son Hæðcyn's life, on the other hand, are given us in the Beowulf. Hæðcyn accidentally kills his elder brother Herebeald and thus becomes heir to the Geatish throne, to which he succeeds upon the death of his father. Hardly has he become king when he is plunged into a war with king Egill of Sweden, then an old man. After some sea-fighting he invades Sweden and has a considerable initial success, capturing Egill's wife and hall. Egill however at once makes a counter-attack, defeats and kills Hæðcyn and rescues his wife. If we put the names into the shortened Scandian forms phonetically corresponding, we get a series of events something like this: Höðr accidentally kills his brother Baldr, but is himself slain by Egill. We have already seen that in Jutish tradition Onela probably took the place of his father as the slayer of Hæðcyn. With this alteration the series would read: Höðr accidentally kills his brother Baldr but is himself slain by Áli. And in fact this form of the story appears in Snorri (note especially Gylfaginning 30, where the avenger of Baldr is called "Áli eða Váli"). In connexion with the Eddic account it is important to remember that Höðr had no intention of killing his brother; the slaying was entirely accidental, so far as he was concerned. This feature of the tale is peculiar, since the original myth must have been to the effect that the god of light was slain by the demon of darkness, and such a slaying could hardly have been looked upon as accidental even though the demon were represented as blind. The sympathetic treatment of Höðr, too, and the use of Loki as the true villain, are secondary developments that comport ill with such Váli kennings as *hefniáss Baldrs, dólgr Haðar, bani Haðar,* and with the Baldr kenning *dólgr Haðar.* These kennings must be survivals of a form of the tale in which Höðr, not Loki, was the true villain. The primitive myth may thus be reconstructed somewhat as follows. Baldr, god of light, is slain by the blind demon of darkness. The demon in turn is slain by Baldr's mourners, later made into one person, Váli 'the wailer' (for a different etymology see Detter, PBB. XIX 503). The myth probably received dramatic representation, as a ritual, connected with the vegetation rituals or at any rate closely parallel to them. This is not the place, however, for a discussion of the Baldr myth, which would take us too far afield. For such a discussion see Kauffmann, Mogk or the handbooks. We are here interested primarily in the contamination which took place when the myth came into contact with the historical tale of the death of the Geatish prince Baldr. The name of the god and the name of the prince were identical in the nominative singular; this fact, together with the similarity of the two stories, resulted in the development of a new story in which the myth and the historical tale were combined. To the latter, then, we owe the extant name of the demon, his kinship to his victim, the representation of the death as accidental, the sympathetic treatment of the villain, and Snorri's Áli as an alternative name for the avenger. The appearance of Áli here is of course a notable confirmation of my theory of the development of the Hamlet tale, according to which Onela in Jutish tradition took the place of his father as slayer of Hæðcyn. — The original name of the demon of darkness may have been Nari or Narfi, the name of that son of Loki who was disemboweled by his brother Váli (Gylfaginning 50) or Áli (Skáldskaparmál 16). The disemboweling is interpreted as part of the vengeance taken on Loki for his treachery. This has a secondary look, however; the person actually disemboweled was probably the original villain. The equation Áli = Váli, too, corresponds neatly enough to Gylfaginning 30. Narfi the son of Loki is further to be identified with Narfi the father of Nótt (Gylfaginning 10; Vafþrúðnismál 25, 2).

(Hotherus), as contained in Saxo (books II and III). Here we had best begin by outlining the tale, with omission of the manifestly mythical traits. 1) Höðr is born in the East; 2) his father is king Hothbrod of Sweden; 3) his youth is spent with his foster-father Gevar, a Norwegian king; 4) Höðr and Nanna, the daughter of Gevar, love each other; 5) Baldr, son of Óðinn, falls in love with Nanna, and becomes Höðr's rival for her hand; 6) Höðr asks for Nanna's hand, but Gevar denies him, for fear of Baldr; 7) Gevar tells Höðr how to obtain Miming's sword, with which the otherwise invulnerable Baldr may be killed, and Höðr, following Gevar's instructions, gains the sword; 8) Baldr wooes Nanna, but she refuses him; 9) Höðr attacks and defeats Baldr, though the latter is aided by the gods in person; 10) Höðr takes Nanna, leads her home to Sweden in triumph, and becomes king of Sweden; 11) Höðr is defeated by Baldr and compelled to flee to Gevar; 12) Höðr becomes king of Denmark and unites that kingdom with Sweden upon the death of his brother Aðils; 13) Baldr wins Denmark from Höðr; 14) Höðr attacks Baldr, but is defeated and flees to Jutland; 15) Höðr returns to Sweden in despair, abandons his throne, and retires alone to the wilderness; 16) Höðr attacks the Danes under Baldr, and mortally wounds Baldr, who dies after three days; 17) Óðinn begets Bói on Rindr, daughter of the king of Russia, and Bói avenges his brother Baldr by killing Höðr, but is himself killed in so doing.

An important discrepancy between this tale and

that told in Iceland is in the person of the avenger. Instead of Áli or Vâli we have Bói. The difference makes no rea[illegible] represents the 'mourners' or participants in the ritual funeral of the dead god, so Bói represents these same participants, the inhabitants or neighbors in the particular district where any particular rite was celebrated. The avenger, instead of being called the 'wailer,' is called the 'inhabitant, neighbor.' One may easily imagine the ritual in progress: the god and his murderer played by slaves, perhaps; the god slain, and mourned by the assembled neighbors, who then tear to pieces the slayer. In later times effigies probably took the place of the slaves, or mock slayings were introduced. In any case the name Bói is appropriate enough for the avenger.

For a discussion of the general characteristics, inconsistencies, etc. of Saxo's version, see especially Olrik, KS. II 13 ff. Here it must suffice to say that the story is essentially a fornaldarsaga, with Höðr as its hero. In Saxo, as in Messenius, Hreðel (Hlöðr) and Hæðcyn (Höðr) have been fused into one, but whereas in the Messenian version the composite hero goes by the name Hlöðr, in the Saxonian version he is called Höðr (the Lotherus of Saxo is another story, going back to a different line of tradition). Let us try to separate Saxo's tale into two parts, grouping together on the one hand the episodes properly belonging to Hreðel, on the other hand those properly belonging to Hæðcyn. This can be done if we assume the following: 1) that Hreðel and Hæðcyn had the same historical antagonist, viz., the Swedish king Ongenþeow = Egill; 2) that this antagonist became identified with Herebeald, as in the Hamlet tale of Saxo and the Angantýr II episode of the Hervararsaga; 3) that through contamination with the Baldr myth Herebeald appears as the god Baldr and is supported by the gods in his struggle with Höðr. Evidence for these assumptions has already been presented, and further evidence will appear in the course of the argument. In the following the numbered references are to the traits or episodes enumerated in the outline of the story given above.

According to trait 1) Höðr was born in the East. As an Eastern origin could be attributed to any Geatish prince, this trait applies equally well to Hreðel and to Hæðcyn. Trait 2) however properly belongs to Hæðcyn, for the parentage given doubtless goes back to the identity of the first elements of the names (cf. Hroðgar and his son Hroðmund in the Beowulf). The love story, and the first two battles with Baldr, undoubtedly belong to Hæðcyn (traits 3—11). Particularly striking is the correspondence of traits 9) and 10) to the Beowulf account, where Hæðcyn defeats Ongenþeow and takes his wife from him. This is followed, just as in the Beowulf, by another battle in which Baldr (Egill) is victorious. Historically Egill kills Hæðcyn in this battle (trait 11). We have already seen, however, that his deed was transferred to Onela as the tradition developed.

At this point the story of Hreðel begins; the break here is manifest, and is made emphatic, indeed, by the disagreement of traits 10) and 12) as to the person of the ruler of Sweden (cf. Olrik, KS. II 36). Traits 12) to 15) inclusive go back to the historical career of Hreðel as already reconstructed. His great victory over Egill is omitted, it is true. The situation in 12) however can be explained only by presupposing the omitted victory. Furthermore, its aftermath is reflected in 13), where Baldr goes (i. e., flees) to Denmark and persuades the Danes to change sides and support him in his conflict with Höðr. Trait 12) is further to be interpreted as a reminiscence of the earlier alliance between Geats and Danes. Trait 14) is chronologically misplaced; here Messenius has the right order of events. For 15) see above. — With trait 16) Hæðcyn returns; here it is significant that he does not slay Baldr in battle, but in a chance encounter. Cf. the accidental death of Baldr and Herebeald in the Icelandic and English accounts. The battle scene is thus probably secondary. For Bói as avenger see above.

We have now finished our examination of the literary history of Hlöðr. Let us, then, return to the Hervararsaga and to Heiðrekr. From the Saga af Þorsteini Bæjarmagni loc. cit. and the Flateyjarbók I 279 the Guðmundr line in what seems to be its primitive form can be reconstructed. I give it below, together with the pre-Angantýr Arngrímr line:

Guðmundr	**Arngrímr**
Heiðrekr	**Hjörvarðr (and 11 brothers)**
Hjörvarðr	
Hervör	

The two Hjörvarðrs seem to have crossed paths more or less, since when Angantýr I took the place of Hjörvarðr Arngrímsson as the leader among the brothers he also replaced Hjörvarðr Heiðreksson, who indeed completely vanishes. With the differentiation between the Angantýrs Angantýr I held his place in the Arngrímr house and brought Hervör over as well, while Angantýr III became son of Heiðrekr. The exact chronology here is beyond my powers to determine. In the course of time, however, Angantýr I attracted to himself the sword Tyrfing, which in the extant versions of the Hervararsaga was buried with him. This development was doubtless due to the desire to establish some sort of blood-relationship between the two Angantýrs, whose original connexion must have been dimly remembered. On this theory Hervör became the wife of Heiðrekr. Certainly she removed the sword from her father's grave, and so ought to have been Heiðrekr's wife. This (hypothetical) stage may be represented as follows:

Guðmundr		Angantýr I
Heiðrekr	=	Hervör
	Angantýr III	

Later on a story developed about an Angantýr who was killed by his brother Höðkon (to use the Scandian forms of the names). As there were already two Angantýrs in the Hervararsaga, and as that saga dealt with the slaying of one brother by another, the poets felt the necessity of incorporating the story of the new Angantýr also, but as his story was entirely different from those of his namesakes he could not be identified with either of them but had to be given a place of his own. He therefore took the place of Angantýr III as son of Hervör, his brother Höðkon was identified with Heiðrekr, who thus became likewise a son of Hervör, and, in order to keep Hervör as the wife of a son of Guðmundr, a double of Heiðrekr was manufactured and given the name Höfundr. Höfundr was thus the son of Guðmundr, the husband of Hervör and the father of Angantýr II and Heiðrekr. Angantýr III kept his place as son of Heiðrekr and so was shifted forward a generation. This stage, the one extant in the Hervararsaga, appears as follows:

Guðmundr		Angantýr I
Höfundr	=	Hervör
Angantýr II		Heiðrekr
		Angantýr III.

Höfundr, the double of Heiðrekr, retained the latter's original character and was known as *the wise.* Heiðrekr retained the character of Hæðcyn, the man with whom he had been identified. Like Hæðcyn, he was a reckless, dare-devil sort, not given to heeding the rights of others and not finding favor in the eyes of his father, yet not vicious or a genuine villain. He had the makings of a villain in him, however, of course. That he did not develop in that direction was due partly to the dash of the original Heiðrekr which he retained and partly to the fact that he was the father of Angantýr III, the true hero of the story. For Hervör II see Heinzel 448; I see no reason to suppose two women of that name, however. Both Hervörs in the Hervararsaga can be derived from the Hervör of the Guðmundr line.

It remains to account for Onela's absence from all these stories. In the first place it is clear that Onela could never have had any connexion with Angantýr I, the hero of the Eofor tale. This Angantýr owes his existence in saga simply and solely to the fact that he was Eofor's opponent, and with his death and his conqueror's reward the story ends. As to Angantýr III, he became a Geatish king through his son, it is true, but when later on he was metamorphosed into a king of the Goths this cut his connexion with Onela and Geatland in general. Finally, the story of Angantýr II arose in Jutland, not in Gautland. In Jutland it is intelligible enough, for it forms the basis of the Hamlet saga by furnishing both victim and villain. In the Hervararsaga, however, as we have seen, it is out of place. Its introduction spoils the story, in fact, by taking away the point of the fight between Angantýr III and Hlöðr. Very clearly it was with violence inserted into the tale from the outside, by some narrator or other who had heard the Jutish version of the death of Angantýr and, looking upon the Hervararsaga as primarily a collection of stories about all heroes named Angantýr, thrust the additional version in as best he could. He found the job sufficiently hard as it was; if he had tried to put in Onela as well he would have smashed to bits the tale he was operating on. Furthermore, from the primitive form in which he knew the story it is clear that the development of Hæðcyn into a villain had hardly more than begun, and in any case this development would have been inconsistent with the new environment of the story, which knew Heiðrekr as a hero, not as a villain. Hence the introduction of a son of Angantýr II as avenger of his father was out of the question. — It is conceivable that another factor may have had some influence in keeping Onela out of the Gothic story. The primitive form of his name was *Anala*, and this would be easy to confuse with *Amala*, the legendary founder of the Gothic royal house. If such a confusion took place, it would help to explain both Angantýr's transformations into an Amalung and Onela's absence from the saga — as an exceedingly remote legendary monarch Amala could of course have no part to play in the events around which the story grew up. It is tempting, indeed, to account for the *m* of Hamlet's name as being a result of this confusion, and the Danish *amlingestikker* 'pranks of an Amalung' (?) seems to point in that direction. But although phonetically all that could be desired, the explanation otherwise is far-fetched and on the whole not so plausible as the one advanced earlier in the discussion (cap. II).

Chapter VIII.

Feng: Geruth.

We can now say with some assurance that Ongenþeow in the course of time became identified with the Geatish prince Herebeald under the name Ørvendill. In this manner Hæðcyn became his brother and slayer. Hæðcyn, however, appears in the Amleth saga under the name Feng. How did he acquire the new name? It occurs in Reginsmál 18 as an Óðinsheiti. Let us see what we can make of the passage:

Hnikar hétu mik, þas hugin gladdi,
Völsungr ungi, ok vegit hafði:
nú mátt kalla karl af bergi
Feng eða Fjölni — far vilk þiggja.

'They called me Hnikarr, when one made glad the raven and fought, O Sigurðr. Now thou mayest call the old man on the mountain Fengr or Fjölnir — I will take passage.' The speaker is Óðinn, the 'old man on the mountain' who wishes to take passage on Sigurðr's ship. A severe storm is raging at the time; when Sigurðr takes Óðinn aboard, however, the weather becomes good again. Here the contrast is clear between *Hnikarr,* on the one hand, and *Fengr* and *Fjölnir,* on the other. *Hnikarr* is a name for Óðinn in his capacity as the god who brings death in battle. *Fengr* and *Fjölnir* on the contrary denote him in his capacity as one who stills the tempest. Furthermore, it is clear that *Fengr* and *Fjölnir* are equivalent epithets, with the same essential connotation. In the only other passage where *Fengr* occurs (SnE. II 266) it is also associated with *Fjölnir*. Similarly, Amleth, who kills Feng, also kills a certain Fjaller, i. e., Fjölnir (Bugge's etymology). The deed stands entirely isolated, and in my opinion is simply another version of the death of Feng, a version left without motivation because of its fragmentary character. If so, we may set up the equation Fengr = Fjölnir.

Turning now to the Ynglinga, we find Fjölnir to be a son of Freyr and pretty clearly his father's double. How then did the heiti *Fjölnir*, which ought to belong to Freyr, get attached to Óðinn? The two gods must have had conflicting jurisdiction in some respect, else such a change could not have taken place. As it happens, our passage shows us just where the overlapping occurred. A vegetation deity (not to mention an heir of the sky-god) would have to have control of the weather, of course. But Óðinn was originally a storm demon; on this point Helm says (I 264): Als ein vergöttlichter Sturmdämon und Totenführer ist Wodan also ursprünglich aufzufassen. Consequently the storms which originally were stilled by Freyr could no longer be conceived of as under his control when the storm god became chief of the gods, although vestiges of the old beliefs might remain, of course. The control of storms, then (or at any rate of such storms as involved danger of death), was taken over by Óðinn himself, who thus became not only a stirrer up of storms but also a storm stiller, and in his new capacity as stiller of storms he was called by the same heiti that in an earlier period had been used to designate Freyr.

It follows that *Fengr* too was earlier a Freyr heiti,

used in a similar way. And the meaning of the word fits the interpretation. For *fengr* means 'gain, advantage (in general), take or catch (of fish), provision.' It is thus associated with prosperity and good fortune, with increase in one's possessions. Cf. Ynglinga caps. 10 and 11. *Fengr's* special reference to fish is noteworthy here. Obviously, fishing requires good weather and a god who stilled storms would very appropriately indeed be called *Fengr* 'the one who insures a catch.' In this connexion it may be pointed out that Njörðr, the original vegetation deity, to the last retained some connexion with storm-stilling and the chase (Gylfaginning 23), although his son Freyr controlled the weather ordinarily (Gylfaginning 24).

On this interpretation, then, Ørvendill was at one time thought of as having been killed by Freyr. This of course fits in admirably with my identification of Ørvendill and Angantýr-Egill, who, as we have seen, according to the Ynglingatal was killed by Freyr through the instrumentality of his sacred boar (originally Freyr himself in theriomorphic form). In the Jutish tale, however, Eofor played no part, as his opponent had become disconnected from the royal house. There is no reason to suppose that the Swedish tale had any influence on the Jutish, either; both grew independently out of the same historical situation, viz., Egill's hostility to the Freyr cult. In Jutland Egill's death was confounded with that of Herebeald; as this was an accidental death it was natural enough to blame a god for it, and the god chosen would naturally be the king's historical enemy Freyr. In this way Hæðcyn, the instrument of the god's vengeance, came to be called by a Freyr heiti.

We come now to Amleth's mother. As I have already indicated, her change from captive of her husband's murderer to the murderer's wife was doubtless partly due to influence from the story of Ermuthrud, though the customs of primitive peoples are such that much influence was hardly needed. Her name also is to be derived from the same source. We do not know her original name; it is not given in the Beowulf, probably because it had already been forgotten. The hero's mother had to have a name, however, and as a faithless widow her career was sufficiently like that of Ermuthrud to suggest a name like hers, *Geirþrúðr*, which later by a process of phonetic change became *Gerruth* or *Geruth* (Saxo uses *d* and *th* indiscriminately for *ð*). The loss oft he *þ* between *r*'s is a native development, and goes to confirm our contention that Ermuthrud herself is an inheritance from the Angles rather than an importation from Germany or England.

Saxo makes Geruth a Danish princess. How did she gain that distinction? It probably came to her from Ermuthrud, like her name. As we know, the historical Yrsa, as the widow of the Danish prince Helgi, was a Danish princess, but in origin she was no Dane, but rather a Frank (see Olrik, DH. I 153). Now it was hardly to be expected that this complexity of provenience would maintain itself in the saga, and since in Jutland she attracted to herself the Þryð story already current there her foreign origin (in itself favorable to her identification with Þryð) received all the emphasis. Her role as Danish princess was inconsistent with her role as Þryð, and its transfer to Geruth was all the easier since this development would put Danish blood into Amleth's veins — a consummation devoutly to be wished by poets with Danish audiences. As to Geruth herself, she was always a tame creature, so far as we can judge — a pale reflection of Ermuthrud, so remodeled by the poets on account of a superficial resemblance between the careers of the two women historically. We may be sure then that no Þryð story was ever attached to Geruth, in spite of the name which she acquired by the line of least resistance.

Chapter IX.

Amleth.

We now come to the most interesting question of all. How did Onela become mad Ole? First let us look at the evidence for his physical prowess. As we have already seen, the Hyndluljóð calls him the 'strongest of men.' In the Ambalessaga (Gollancz 74) it is said that 'á vexti og abli var hann umfram alla sem í borginni vóru.' The Saxonian version lays the emphasis on his cleverness rather than on his physical strength, it is true, but this emphasis is hardly original; the reasons for the shift will become obvious in the course of the discussion. How would Anle's great strength express itself? The story answers the question. He became a strong fool, or 'dummling,' as the Germans call it. Over-strong men are usually more or less stupid anyhow, witness Hercules himself. But the thing that made Onela develop so vigorously in the direction of stupidity was the emphasis which the saga plot inevitably put on his youth. For the fratricide and faithless widow combination makes the widow young. Hence the son who is to avenge his father's death must be pictured as growing up. Such a situation has, besides, an irresistible poetic appeal, so that in the hands of the skalds it would naturally be dwelt upon and elaborated. Now in the world of saga the youthful exploits of heroes have the same essential characteristics that we find to this day in stories about boys. Our boys' tales are tales of pranks, mischief-making (rebellion against constituted authority), combined with sayings amusing by virtue of their naiveté and freshness of outlook — a freshness often illuminating enough, too, and by no means to be despised, however much laughed at. The follies of youth, then, in word and deed, are different in kind from ordinary follies, being due simply to inexperience and immaturity, and having in them in many cases a certain originality interesting both in itself and as a presage of future achievement. Indeed, we are prone to seek signs of greatness in the boyhood records of great men, and when, after the event, these signs are sought with sufficient diligence, they are usually found, whatever the actual state of the records! Our fore-fathers were not so different from us in these matters. If the youthful exploits told of their heroes differ from our tales of bad boys etc., it is because primitive peoples are more interested in physical prowess than are we, and so make more of feats than of wiles. In any case, however, youthful prominence is necessarily a prominence in folly of one sort or another; real achievements are not to be expected of striplings. Hence, as a hero must be prominent in all periods of his life, his youth among our ancestors was notable for great folly, either inert stupidity, like Beowulf and Offa, or stupidity of a more active sort, exhibiting itself in breaches of decorum and general wild unorthodox behavior, as with Grettir and Amleth. But the circumstances under which Amleth grew up were peculiar, and so it was natural or indeed inevitable that the stories about his youthful pranks should take a peculiar turn. With a stepfather who hated and feared him and a mother completely under her husband's thumb he would naturally become a species of male Cinderella. Unlike Cinderella, however, he would not accept his lot meekly and do what he was told. In the development of the story his strength would not desert him, and his uncowed spirit would express itself in all sorts of wild outbreaks which finally would earn for him the name 'mad Anle.' This name, once given, became the decisive factor in the further development of the tale. When first applied to the boy it was not at all with the idea that he was really mad but simply a consequence of his wild behavior, just as we might nowadays use the word 'crazy' loosely enough. However, the whole saga situation was such that, once given a starting-point the idea of simulated madness would quickly take root and permeate the story. For vengeance was after all from the beginning the keynote. It could not be otherwise, given the point of view of the Northmen, for whom to avenge one's father was a sacred duty that must be performed at any cost. Every hearer of the tale would know instinctively that the boy thought of little else, that he bent all his efforts to the accomplishment of this righteous and pious deed. Hence if he did wild things and made a fool of himself, it must be for a purpose. If he seemed mad, there was a reason for it. And the reason lay near at hand. He was living in the house of his father's murderer. How could he, a helpless dependent, escape his father's fate and be ready to take his chance for vengeance when it came? Evidently only by using his wits, by brain rather than brawn. What scheme did he actually hit upon? His wild behavior furnished the answer. He simulated madness.

In this manner I conceive the saga to have acquired its most characteristic feature.

We have now passed definitely from history to legend. The chief characters in the story, Amleth, Ørvendill, Geruth, Feng, Ermuthrud, all go back to historical prototypes, and the relations existing among them, if not historically accurate, at least have some historical basis. With the introduction of the feigned madness motif, however, we come to something new, something not contained in the historical complex at all but a development from it due to poetic compulsion (or inspiration, if you will), a saga-creating instinct at work. This instinct had already altered the complex in many ways. It now gave to the complex a new element, unifying and dominating. It is probably impossible to determine just how a saga comes into being, just how much of it is a group product and how much is contributed by individuals as such. Any changes in the tale would naturally be made by narrators. One may easily picture a story-teller drawing inspiration from the group spirit which he shares with his audience and so improving his tale as he tells it, while on another occasion his contribution may be more premeditated and personal. At any rate sagas do spring up, and change, and many of the motifs which they contain cannot be explained otherwise than as having become attached to the historical nucleus by psychological association or suggestion. Sometimes the new element fits into the old material so well that one is justified in comparing the change to the growth of a plant, where the finished product already lay in embryo in the seed. A change of this sort was the development of the feigned madness motif, as I have tried to show above. Even here, howewer, our simile exaggerates the deterministic features of the process, and for most of the motifs which we shall have to consider such a comparison would be entirely inappropriate. For these it would be better to look upon the nucleus of the tale as a kind of magnet, which of the various motifs that happened to come its way drew to itself those for which it had a peculiar affinity. This kind of growth, though real enough, leaves the motifs a certain individuality of their own and even a capacity for independent existence, while not preventing the development of a wellknit coherent tale.

Our theory assumes that Amleth's follies were in origin boyish pranks. Are they in fact so represented in any of the monuments? Hardly in Saxo, where Amleth, though young, is nevertheless by no means a child. We have no right, then, to assume that Saxo's account is in this respect unprimitive, unless we can adduce other versions of the story in which our hero does appear as a child or a callow youth. These other versions will be considered in the following chapter.

Chapter X.

Helgi.

So far our discussion has been based on the Amleth saga of Saxo (books III and IV). The story of this saga, reduced to its simplest terms, reads as follows. A certain king was killed by his brother, who thereupon married his victim's widow and ascended the throne to the exclusion of his nephew, the son of the former king. The son, in order to save his life and make ready to avenge his father, feigned madness. His ruse was successful and he eventually succeeded in killing his uncle and winning the crown. Later he married a foreign princess. He was finally killed in battle and his widow married her husband's murderer. This version will hereafter be called version A. We have already accounted for all its general features as outlined. Let us now turn our attention to another saga, the Helgasaga, making our basis that version of it (hereafter known as H) contained in the Hrólfssaga kraka. The story of H may be outlined as follows. A certain king was killed by his brother, who thereupon married his victim's widow and ascended the throne, to the exclusion of his nephews, the two sons of the former king. The sons were rescued and kept in hiding by faithful retainers until they were grown; then they took vengeance on their uncle and won back the crown. Later the elder brother was killed by a cousin; the younger brother avenged his death. The younger brother married a foreign princess. He was finally killed by treachery and his widow married her husband's murderer. The points which the two tales have in common are obvious. It will be our task to account for the differences. In so doing it will be convenient to divide the saga into two parts. The present chapter will be devoted to a consideration of the vengeance stories which comprise the larger part of the tale. In cap. XI the love story will be taken up. As regards the vengeance stories, H differs from A in the following fundamental respects: 1) the elder brother; 2) the faithful retainer; 3) the use of concealment instead of madness. These differences will be taken up and accounted for in turn.

Version H is not the only version of the Helgasaga. The most important of the other versions are the portions of the Skjöldungasaga dealing with Helgi (SS = Snorri's, AS = Arngrímr's version), the Bjarkarímur (BR), the story of Harald and Haldan in the 7th book of Saxo (HH), the story of Brjám (B) and the folk-tale which was the chief source of the Ambalessaga (X; the Ambalessaga itself will be referred to as AB). In addition to these there are several other brief accounts or references which have a more or less important bearing on the history of the saga. The resemblances and differences of the various versions will appear in the course of this discussion.

The Helgasaga, like the Amleth saga, is based on historical events. The historical complexes of the two sagas are different, however. In other words, the sagas themselves were originally distinct. They remained so in Denmark. In Norway and Iceland, however, they coalesced, giving us the various versions of the Helgasaga named above. The Helgasaga, then, is the Amleth saga of the West Scandinavians.

The historical complex on which the Helgasaga is based includes a war between Danes and Bards and a feud within the Danish royal house. The war between Danes and Bards may be divided into two stages, separated by an uneasy peace of uncertain length. In the first stage king Fróði of the Bards was killed, apparently by the Danish king Hróarr. Our rather uncertain information here is derived from the Beowulf (2020 ff.). Later Hróarr tries to patch up a peace between the two peoples by giving his daughter in marriage to king Ingjaldr of the Bards, the son of Fróði. The marriage does not have the results expected, however; on the contrary, it accentuates the friction and finally Ingjaldr attacks the Danes in an effort to avenge his father's death. In this effort he proves unsuccessful, and is himself defeated and slain by Hróarr and Hrólfr. The Bards now disappear from history. They seem to have been absorbed by their conquerors; at any rate their kings in the later tradition appear as Danish monarchs, which would indicate a fusion of the two peoples.

The adoption of the Bardish kings did not do away with their hostility to the historical Danish kings. This hostility, however, received a different interpretation; the struggle between Bards and Danes became a fratricidal strife within the Danish royal house (the Scylding house). The development in this direction was aided by the second feature of the historical complex, mentioned above, viz., the feud within the Scylding family. After the war with the Bards had been brought to successful completion, the two victors, king Hróarr and his nephew Hrólfr, fell out. We are not informed in the OE. monuments what the issue of the quarrel was.

All that we can be sure of from them is that there was a break between the kinsmen and that it had tragic consequences. For the material here, and bibliographical references, see especially Chambers 81 ff. The Scandian monuments, on the other hand, although they are of much later date than the Beowulf and Widsið and so preserve less of the historical setting, do give us unmistakable testimony as to the results of the feud. Perhaps the oldest of them is that version of the Bjarkamál given by Saxo (II 59 ff.) in Latin translation. This poem is primarily a poem in praise of Hrólfr, who had become the Danish national hero. It might therefore be expected to omit all reference to so dastardly a deed as the slaying of Hróarr (if Hrólfr did slay him). And in fact no reference to Hróarr is to be found in the whole poem. We do get an account, however, of Hrólfr's slaying of Hróarr's son Hrœrekr. Interesting here is the justification given for the deed. The kinship of the two men is omitted, of course. Hrœrekr is represented as an avaricious and unwarlike king who deserves overthrow, while Hrólfr is the soul of generosity and for that reason the rightful occupant of the throne. No attempt, however, is made to motivate Hrólfr's deed as an act of vengeance. Clearly the murder of Hróarr had not yet become ascribed to Hrœrekr, as it was in the Icelandic accounts. Both the poet's silence as to Hróarr and his manner of justifying the slaying of Hrœrekr are thus indicative.

From the Bjarkamál it is clear that if Hrólfr slew both Hróarr and Hrœrekr the two deeds did not take place at the same time. For Hrœrekr is represented as the ruling monarch. Hrólfr is the leader of a fleet; he attacks the capital from the sea. That the struggle between Hrœrekr and Hrólfr was naval appears also from the accounts in Saxo (II 53 and VII 220), where Helgi-Haldan (i. e., Hrólfr) defeats and kills Hothbrod-Erik (i. e., Hrœrekr) in a sea-fight. The death of Hróarr, on the other hand, had no connexion with the sea. In Saxo VII 220 Harald (i. e., Hróarr) is defeated in three battles and killed in the fourth; similarly, in Saxo II 52 Roe (i. e., Hróarr) is three times forced to give battle and is slain (presumably in a fourth battle). In the Hrólfssaga, Hróarr is defeated and slain as a result of a surprize attack made on his hall. In none of the accounts is the sea referred to. Further information as to Hróarr's relations with Hrólfr may be obtained by an examination of the Hrani incident in the Hrólfssaga version of the Expedition to Uppsala. The sagaman identifies this Hrani with Óðinn, it is true, but inasmuch as *Hrani* appears also (earlier in the tale) as a nickname of Hróarr's we are justified in examining the incident for traces of a primitive identification to correspond. Hrani is represented as Hrólfr's friend and benefactor; Hrólfr however repays him with ingratitude, and this changes their friendship into enmity. Parallel to the three battles of Saxo are the three nights which Hrólfr and his followers spend in the house of Hrani, where they undergo and sustain as many severe supernatural tests, as a result of which their numbers are finally reduced to Hrólfr himself and his immediate followers. To Saxo's fourth battle corresponds Hrólfr's fourth and last encounter with Hrani, when the break between the two men definitely occurs. Bjarki tries to act as peacemaker here, but in vain, for Hrani and his hall disappear at the crucial moment. This disappearance is part of the supernatural machinery, of course, but it may be based on a historical event parallel to the death of Hróarr as recounted in the Hrólfssaga. Similarly, Bjarki's role as peacemaker may be historical, though the Beowulf gives us no information on the point. More significant is Bjarki's advice to Hrólfr not to take part in any more battles. Evidently the disappearance (i. e., death?) of Hrani was looked upon as a turning point in Hrólfr's career, and the king's treatment of his benefactor was to prove his own bane. That Bjarki gives the warning is to be brought into connexion with the political situation as given in the English poem, which shows Beowulf in close alliance with Hroðgar.

We may now venture upon a tentative reconstruction of the historical course of events. Hrólfr rebels against his foster-father and benefactor Hróarr and after three indecisive battles finally defeats and kills him, perhaps in a surprize attack. Hróarr's son Hrœrekr succeeds in making his escape; perhaps he was in service at the Geatish court at the time (cf. Beowulf 1836 ff.) and so did not participate in the struggle. Aided by the Geats, and perhaps by a revulsion of feeling in Denmark itself, Hrœrekr now attacks Hrólfr, forces him to flee, and takes possession of the throne. Hrólfr becomes a 'sea-king' or viking. As time goes on, Hrœrekr's objectionable qualities make him unpopular; Hrólfr takes advantage of the situation, brings his fleet to Denmark and taking Hrœrekr unawares overthrows and kills him. — The career here assigned to Hrœrekr serves neatly enough to explain the curious fact that in both Danish and Icelandic tradition a Hrœrekr appears as Hrólfr's successor. Saxo knows two kings named

Røric (i. e., Hrœrekr): the Røric of II 62 is Hrólfr's predecessor; the Røric of III 82 ff., the successor of Hother, appears in Sweyn as the successor of Hrólfr. This second Røric, nicknamed Slyngebond, is generally identified with the Hrœrekr Slöngvanbaugi of BR and the Raerecus of AS, as also with the two Hœrekrs of the Langfeðgatal. He is also to be identified with Saxo's first Røric (cf. Olrik, DH. I 33). The development of two Hrœrekrs is best explained on the assumption that in fact Hrœrekr both succeeded Hrólfr (drove him from the throne) and, later, was succeeded by him (was overthrown and killed by him). — The part played by Hrólfr likewise fits in well with the freebooting career of his father Helgi, the traditional slayer of Hrœrekr in the Icelandic monuments. Along with his son's deeds Helgi took over his son's viking activities as well.

The Bjarkamál was probably composed early in the 10th century; Olrik dates it at c. 900. Another 10th century monument which refers to the history of Hrólfr is the Grottasöngr, and inasmuch as the author of this poem has no case to plead we are justified in expecting from him a less one-sided and biassed account than that of the Bjarkamál. The Grottasöngr is the story of a magic quern owned by king Fróði, the euhemerized vegetation deity. This king was the mythical father of Halfdanr, and must not be confused with the Bardish king of the same name, who belonged to a different and hostile line. The relations envisaged in the poem will be better understood if first we list the kings of the line to which Halfdanr belonged; I add, for purposes of comparison, the corresponding genealogy in the English monuments:

Skjöldr	Scyld
Fróði	Beow(ulf)
Halfdanr	Healfdene
Hróarr Helgi	Hroðgar Halga
Hrœrekr Hrólfr	Hreðric Hroðulf

It will be observed that the euhemerized deity has taken the place of the Beow of the OE. records. Who this Beow was is a question into which I will not go here; see Olrik, DH. II 254 ff.

To return to our story. King Fróði owned a magic mill and two giant slavegirls to keep it going. They ground out gold for him on the quern and made him enormously rich and otherwise prosperous. He would give them no rest, however, so finally they began grinding him curses instead of gold. These curses, as Olrik has pointed out, for a crescendo. They culminate in two curses upon Fróði's descendant Hrólfr kraki, contained in the following stanza:

Mölum enn framarr! mun Yrsu sonr
við Halfdana hefna Fróða;
sá mun hennar heitinn verða
burr ok bróðir: vitum báðar þat.

'We grind on! The son of Yrsa shall avenge Fróði on the Half-Danes; he shall be called her son and brother: we both know that.' The first curse is a terrible one. Hrólfr is doomed to act as avenger of Fróði, the king of the Bards and enemy of the Danes. Normally the avenger would be Fróði's nearest of kin, of course. To make the avenger Hrólfr, who was an enemy of Fróði and all his race, was a terrible curse indeed. The full horror of it, however, becomes manifest only when we realize who had killed Fróði. The identity of the slayer is not absolutely certain, but the Beowulf passage from which we get our information can hardly be interpreted otherwise than that the slayer was Hróarr. But the Grottasöngr speaks of Half-Danes, implying that there was more than one victim. And true enough, from the Bjarkamál we learn that Hrólfr killed Hrœrekr. The terrible nature of the curse now becomes clear. Hrólfr was doomed to kill Hróarr, his own uncle and foster-father, and Hrœrekr, his cousin and Hróarr's son. Halfdanr, then, is a synonym for Scyldings, just as in the Beowulf (1069), and in the Grottasöngr passage it refers to Hróarr and Hrœrekr, the particular Scyldings that Hrólfr (himself a Scylding) was doomed to kill. One might think that the giant maidens would rest content with this, but no, they lay on the unfortunate Hrólfr a second curse, worse still. His mother will also be his sister. In other words, he will be born of an incestuous marriage. Here Olrik adds (DH I 150), Vi kan fortsætte denne tanke: "Yrsas sön" maa blive den sidste mand i sin æt; slægten kan efter dette ikke fortsættes. The ultimate aim of the curses thus becomes clear: the race of Fróði must come to a catastrophic end, an end of shame and horror. And in the next stanza, appropriately enough, the quern bursts asunder. — For a different (and untenable) interpretation of the stanza see Olrik loc. cit. and compare Heusler, HZ. XLVIII 69. Previous interpreters have sought to get a meaning out of the stanza by emending the text. My translation however is based on the text as it stands.

Halfdanir (Healfdene) as a synonym for Scyldings occurs only in the Beowulf and (on my interpretation) in the Grottasöngr. When it went out of use its proper reference in the old songs naturally ceased to be understood. It was taken to refer to king Halfdanr and so was doubtless regularly changed from plural to singular. Thus, in Saxo we find it stated that Halfdanr killed Hróarr. This astonishing statement becomes correct enough if we put it back into its original form: the Halfdanir (in this case Hrólfr and his fellow Scyldings, i. e., Danes) killed Hróarr. Similarly, the opposition Halfdanir: Fróði became Halfdanr: Fróði and king Fróði accordingly was shifted from his proper historical position as opponent of Hróarr and became the opponent of Hróarr's father Halfdanr. In a similar way the opposition Halfdanir: Ingjaldr became Halfdanr: Ingjaldr. Here Halfdanir originally meant Hróarr and Hrólfr (Widsið 45). This explains the uncertainty as to the proper opponent of Halfdanr that we find in the texts. When Saxo makes Halfdanr kill Hróarr and Scatus, this reflects the fall of Hróarr and (apparently) Hrœrekr at the hands of their fellow-countrymen. The enmity in the Skjöldunga between Halfdanr and Ingjaldr goes back to the fight at Heorot, and the enmity between Fróði and Hróarr in the same source gives us a genuine survival of the historical situation, although in order to be able to retain Fróði in his proper position here it was necessary to make him the son instead of the father of Ingjaldr!

So far we have taken up two early interpretations of Hrólfr, both sympathetic. In the Bjarkamál we have an enthusiastic apology and eulogy, with the judicious selection of incident which that involves. As Hrólfr's chief virtue was generosity, his generosity becomes the central theme of the poem. His treachery is explained away where possible; in the other cases the deeds are left out altogether. Very different is the treatment in the Grottasöngr. Here the facts are faced boldly enough, but they are accounted for in a way both highly poetic and favorable to Hrólfr, who is represented as a tool in the hands of fate, foredoomed to his deeds by the giant maidens whom his ancestor Fróði had oppressed. The ancient theme, the sins of the fathers shall be visited upon the sons, even unto the third and fourth generations, here appears in all its austerity. Hrólfr, the tool of fate, born in incest, murderer of his kin, avenger of his enemies, becomes a tragic and sympathetic figure. And this all the more since his downfall is more than a personal one: it is the downfall of the Scylding race, the tragedy of the greatest of the royal houses of the North.

We now come to monuments composed at so late a date that little of the historical setting remains. What do they tell us about the death of Hrólfr? In all the accounts without exception he dies a violent death at the hands of a kinsman. The evidence may be tabulated as follows:

monument	murderer(s)	relationship
Saxo II, 51	Haldan	brother
Saxo II, 52 f.	Hothbrod	cousin
HH	Eric	cousin
H	Hrókr	cousin
AS	Hrœrekr and Fróði	half-brothers

Here Hothbrod is to be interpreted as a personification of the Bards, the Heaðobeards of the Beowulf (see Bugge, HEP. 160). Hothbrod, then, as well as Fróði, is correctly enough represented as an antagonist of Hróarr; as however the latter was completely victorious over the Bards and survived his Bardish enemies (Widsið 45 ff.), he could not have been their victim. As for Haldan, and Hrœrekr or Hrókr, the one was his father, the other his son! Erik, like Hrókr, is to be identified with Hrœrekr (see Olrik, KS II 82 and DH I 169 ff.). The later sources are thus clearly wrong as to the identity of Hróarr's murderer. Their unanimous testimony that he was murdered by a kinsman is nevertheless significant, especially since it is not contradicted by any of the earlier monuments and (on my interpretation) is confirmed by the Grottasöngr. Besides, the OE. sources point to Hrólfr as the murderer and the silence of the Bjarkamál probably means that Hrólfr's relations with Hróarr were not easily defensible. We are therefore justified in concluding that in all probability Hrólfr was the actual murderer of Hróarr. It remains to account for the ascription of the crime to those named above.

Before undertaking this task, however, let us go back for a time to the Grottasöngr. This poem tells us that Hrólfr avenged Fróði on the Halfdanir or Scyldings. This obviously presupposes an earlier struggle (referred to in the Beowulf, as we have seen), in which the Halfdanir kill Fróði. With the substitution of Halfdanr for Halfdanir, the tradition may be stated thus: 1) Halfdanr kills Fróði; 2) Hrólfr kills Halfdanr. The first stage is represented in Sweyn Aagesön's account, where Halfdanr kills his brother Fróði. The second stage, however, does not appear in any genuinely Danish account. As we have seen, it was originally a highly poetic conception, an interpretation of the historical facts probably first made by the author of the Grottasöngr itself. This author was a Norwegian skald, and his interpretation gained currency in Norway and Iceland but not in Denmark. Nevertheless it must have seemed nonsense to the more prosaically minded among his fellow-skalds, who would be very likely to miss the poetic point. One can fancy them saying with a superior smile, "the man evidently got this backwards: Hrólfr could not have avenged Fróði on the Halfdanir; he must have avenged the Halfdanir on Fróði." And in their dull prosaic way they were right enough. Hrólfr certainly did not have in mind Fróði, the enemy of the Danes, when he killed Hróarr and Hrœrekr. His conscious avenging would be on an alien, not a kinsman. But in a very real and poetic sense he avenged Fróði nevertheless, as I have tried to show above.

Under the influence of this misinterpretation and consequent 'correction' then our stages took the form: 1) Fróði kills Halfdanr; 2) Hrólfr kills Fróði. Later Helgi took the place of his son Hrólfr as the avenger. With him the Amleth of Jutish tradition became identified. As a result the typical Hamletian motifs of the helpless position and simulated madness of the avenger were attached to Helgi. Still later, as in Sweyn, Fróði and Halfdanr were made brothers. The reasons for the substitution of Helgi for Hrólfr are clear enough. The natural person to avenge Halfdanr was his son, not his grandson, while the poetic interest in the father of Hrólfr (as Olrik has pointed out) would attract to him any saga-stuff with which he could plausibly be connected. The introduction of Helgi in turn led to the introduction of his elder brother Hróarr. Hróarr came in originally as a second victim, however, as I shall show, and in version X this remained his only part. In H too he is strictly subordinated to his younger brother, and in other respects the part he plays is best explained as due to the fact that in a more primitive form of the story he was only a second victim of Fróði. His greater prominence in HH, H and AS was due to the incorporation into the saga of another account of his death which had arisen as an independent story. The use of this story made it impossible to represent him as having been killed (along with Halfdanr) by Fróði. In consequence he was made Helgi's associate in avenging Halfdanr's death.

What was this other story and how did it arise? It is obvious that when Hrólfr became a national hero a strong tendency would set in to clear his character. The murder of his uncle and foster-father Hróarr was a particularly atrocious deed, and his apologists would have every incentive to transfer it to others. While the historical facts were still well remembered the only recourse would be to use euphemistic expressions like 'the Halfdanir' for the names to be avoided. In this way the Saxonian tradition came into being according to which Halfdanr (i. e., Hrólfr and his followers) slew Hróarr and Scatus. Similarly the Grottasöngr, instead of telling the facts outright, says, euphemistically enough, that Hrólfr was destined to avenge Fróði on the Halfdanir (i. e., on Hróarr and Hrœrekr). Later other devices could be employed. A natural one would be to make Hróarr's historical enemies the Bards do duty here. Hence Saxo's Hothbrod and the Fróði of AS. The neatest solution, however, and the one which gained the widest popularity, was that which made Hrœrekr the murderer. This solution cleared the character of Hrólfr both by relieving him of the murder of Hróarr and by justifying his murder of Hrœrekr, which thus became an act of vengeance. Naturally, however, no such story could arise untill the exact degree of kinship between Hróarr and Hrœrekr had been forgotten, as a story in which a son murdered his own father would hardly have been invented by any skald of the period, and certainly no such story could have been the ancestor of the story of Hróarr's death as we actually have it in the monuments. Since Hrœrekr occurs as villain only in HH and the Icelandic sources, it would seem that he was made the villain in Norway or Iceland. An earlier villain, in all probability, was Hothbrod, who appears both in Saxo and the Elder Edda. Bugge has conjectured that Hothbrod was the invention of some Danish viking poet in England, the story being carried thence to Denmark on the one hand and, eventually, to Norway and Iceland on the other (HEP. 160; cf. 157 ff.). This is a very speculative matter, however.

In all the extant forms Helgi, not Hrólfr, is the avenger of Hróarr. As, however, we know from the Bjarkamál that Hrólfr killed Hrœrekr, it is certain that in the Hrœrekr versions at least Helgi was substituted for an earlier Hrólfr. Perhaps this substitution was partly due to contamination with an originally independent Hothbrod story in which Helgi was from the beginning the avenger of Hróarr. Our information here, however, is not sufficient to enable us to reconstruct with assurance the course of the development; the history of the Eddic versions is particularly obscure, so much so that I have not included them at all here but refer the curious to Bugge, HEP., and to Detter, Die Hamletsage, HZ XXXVI 13 ff. It needs to be emphasized that in none of its versions does the story of Hróarr's death have any organic connexion with the story of Halfdanr's death. In the latter Hróarr probably at one time appeared, it is true, but only as the fellow-victim of Fróði, and without playing any active part. This the primitive form of the saga is still preserved to us in AB. In H, HH and AS, however, the story of Hróarr's death at the hands of Hrœrekr was added on to the original saga, and this addition changed the Hróarr of the saga from the fellow-victim of Fróði to the fellow-avenger of Halfdanr. This change brought in its wake other changes of considerable importance which will be taken up in due course.

The discussion so far has been devoted primarily to an attempt to account for the fact that the Helga-saga, though a version of the Hamlet tale, has two brothers as avengers. We have seen that originally there was only one avenger, viz., Hrólfr; that later Hrólfr was displaced by his father Helgi, who corresponds to Saxo's Amleth; that inasmuch as Helgi had an elder brother Hróarr this brother was inevitably brought into the tale, but was at first used simply as a second victim of Fróði; that in some of the versions an independent story of the death of Hróarr was incorporated into the saga, making impossible the further use of Hróarr as an additional victim and necessitating his use as fellow-avenger. The identification of Amleth and Helgi, then, if it took place at all, must have taken place while Hróarr was still a victim. Otherwise no identification could well have taken place, as the story of two brothers who avenge their father's death is essentially different from the Hamlet tale. More direct evidence on the point is to be found in AB, where the elder brother is a victim along with his father, while the younger brother is called

Amlóði. It may, however, be asked what the evidence is for connecting AB with the Helgasaga at all, as none of the names of the characters correspond and there are important differences in the plot as well. In order to establish the relationship it will be necessary to dispose of these objections, of course, and this will now be attempted.

The Ambalessaga (AB) is a modern literary production, based on a lost folk-tale (X), supplemented by Saxo's Amleth saga and heavily padded with conventional romantic material drawn from various sources (or from the author's own imagination). This analysis of the saga has been pretty generally accepted since the publication of Olrik's *Amledsagnet paa Island* (AfnF. XV 360ff.). We are primarily interested in the folk-tale X, of course. It is unfortunately not extant, except as incorporated in AB, but we are able to reconstruct it, in part at least, by a comparison of AB and B. The latter is a folk-tale formerly current in North Iceland and recorded in 1705. As Gollancz says (p. lxix), "The interest attaching to Brjám is mainly due to the fact that it substantially agrees with the Ambales saga where the saga diverges from Saxo." This apart from the romantic padding, of course. However, B could not have been a source of AB, which was written in South Iceland. The folk-tale actually used by the author of AB is generally identified with that mentioned by the South Icelander Torfæus (born in 1636) in his *Series Regum Daniae*. Torfæus says (I quote from Gollancz lxiii, the original not being accessible to me): Ad Saxonis Amlethum quod attinet, ego in patria puer a vetulis anibusque et ejusdem furfuris homuncionibus Amlodii historiam narratam audivi, inque tenerrima illa aetate pro fabula tantum aestimavi. etc. Obviously we have here a folk-tale handed down in oral tradition only and apparently current chiefly among the lower classes. We may expect then a story of a primitive type, reduced to its simplest elements and with the characters anonymous. By comparison with the story of Brjám we find that all this holds good, with the exception of the hero of the tale, who is given a name. Even this though is not a true exception, for *Amlóði* was used as a common noun meaning 'fool,' and the name was doubtless preserved only because it was felt as a characterization. The same probably held good of the name Brjám used in B, a name which Olrik accounts for on the basis of its resemblance to *bjáni* 'idiot.' Except for the name of the hero, then, the names of the characters in AB were not derived from X but were supplied by the author of the saga. This point is obviously of great importance in determining the ultimate origin of X.

The plot of X may be reconstructed as follows. A certain king was slain by a king hostile to him, who then established himself in his victim's place. The former king had two sons. The elder of these was put to death along with his father, but the younger escaped by pretending to be witless. He finally avenged his father and succeeded to the throne. This story is to be referred to the Helgasaga rather than to the Amleth saga. Particularly noteworthy are the elder brother and the lack of kinship between villain and victim. The latter is in accord with both the Grottasöngr and the first vísa in H (cf. Heusler, HZ. XLVIII 75):

Öll er orðin ætt skjöldunga
lofðungs lundar at limum einum . . .

Nor does Amlóði's mother marry her husband's murderer in X (although in AB a chaste marriage takes place). This is in accord with HH and the Grottasöngr. Version X can readily be accounted for on the assumption that it goes back to the Helgasaga in a form more primitive than any we meet in the literary versions. In this more primitive form Helgi had been identified with Amleth but the identification of the other characters had not yet been carried through: Halfdanr and Fróði were not yet brothers, the wife of Halfdanr played no part in the story, and the elaboration had hardly begun. The preservation of so primitive a version of the story was due to the fact that it became a folk-tale. Here the anonymity of the characters aided powerfully in preserving it from contamination with the literary versions.

What caused the identification of Helgi and Amleth? Each avenged his father's death, it is true, but otherwise the two stories, in their primitive forms, had no compelling resemblances. In my opinion the decisive link was the woman in the case. Yrsa's two husbands were rolled into one. Here version X does not help us out, it is true; it knows nothing of Yrsa. Her elimination however was undoubtedly secondary, and due to the fact that the orthodox folk-tale must make the hero marry the princess and live happy ever after. Instead of the Yrsa story, then, we have an orthodox happy ending tacked on to the revenge story (in which Yrsa at no time played any part). The history of Yrsa will be taken up in detail below, after the analysis of the father-revenge story.

We now come to the second fundamental difference

between A and H, viz., the faithful retainer. The most primitive form of this motif appears in an incident told in HH, where Haldan is defeated in battle by Eric and, severely wounded, seeks refuge with a wizard named Viðolfr, who through his magic arts saves him from capture and keeps him in hiding until his wounds are healed. Viðolfr is represented as an old man, a retired retainer of Haldan's father. That Haldan should be defeated by Eric is most extraordinary, and if we compare the whole incident with the corresponding incident in H (where Viðolfr has become Vifill) we can hardly escape the conclusion that the original victor in the battle was not Eric but Fróði. If so, the two Haralds (Halfdanr and Hróarr in H) must have been killed by Fróði in the battle, as Haldan (Helgi in H) is represented as the sole survivor. In H, it is true, both Helgi and Hróarr survive, but as both the Grottasöngr and X know only one avenger and X makes the younger brother (the Helgi of H, the Haldan of HH) the sole survivor, we are justified in concluding that the form of the incident given in H is a later development, especially since H as it stands is actually some 200 years younger than HH. It may further be objected that the vengeance story as we have it in the various versions of the Helgasaga is essentially a youthful exploit, whereas the battle with Eric presupposes mature participants. Undoubtedly the story of Helgi's vengeance on Fróði eventually became the story of a youthful exploit, but this was not its original character. The historical events underlying the tale, viz., Hrólfr's slaying of Hróarr and Hrœrekr, were not youthful exploits, and the avenger is not made a youth in the Grottasöngr. We have already (cap. IX) found reasons for believing that the whole conception of the youth of the hero properly belonged in the pre-Saxonian Amleth saga. The actual appearance of this motif in the Helgasaga, then, makes us conclude that it, along with the feigned madness, was simply introduced from the Amleth saga after Helgi and Amleth had been identified. On the point see further below. — For Viðolfr see especially Olrik, KS. II 82 and DH. I 177 note.

The original form of the faithful retainer story in the Helgasaga, then, can be reconstructed as follows. King Halfdanr and his elder son Hróarr fall in battle against king Fróði. Halfdanr's younger son, Helgi, is severely wounded in the same battle, but he is saved and healed by the faithful retainer and wizard Viðolfr. With this story is to be compared the incident in AB where Amlóði is severely wounded (Gollancz 88). The AB account in other ways reminds one of the course of events in HH; thus, the Thor of HH has a certain resemblance to the Drafnar of AB, and both Haldan and Amlóði are taken for gods and sacrificed to. Nevertheless the parallelism is not complete, and it would not be safe to press the point. More important here is the development of the story just outlined. With the introduction from the Amleth saga of the youthful exploit idea the sons were made into children and so the battle scene as it stood could no longer be used. In H therefore the battle setting was entirely abandoned, so far as the children were concerned, although retained in the death of the father. In HH just the opposite choice was made: the father's death was accomplished by assassination, and the battle was attached to Haldan (the

Helgi of H); this necessitated its postponement to the period after the vengeance on Fróði (as Haldan could hardly fight a regular battle till he was grown), and in consequence Eric became the antagonist. In AB the battle seems to have been used twice, although the one in which Amlóði figures is changed into a victory for him, and otherwise modified, so that we cannot be sure that it really goes back to the primitive account.

The name Viðolfr is preserved in HH, the oldest and in some respects the most primitive version. In H, however, the wizard appears under the name Vifill. This name is derivable from the Amleth saga, although it does not appear, on the face of it at least, in version A. From the Kalfsvísa we know that one of Áli's retainers was named Vifill; a Vifill also appears in the 8th book of Saxo, and here too he is an associate of Ole, i. e., Áli. We are justified, then, in examining version A more narrowly, to see if, in spite of that anonymity which the Jutes seem to have been so fond of, some trace of the name of Áli's retainer has not nevertheless survived. Now the only person in A who could well be identified with Vifill is Amleth's foster-brother. This foster-brother is represented as a retainer who, though in the service of Feng, is at heart loyal to his rightful master Amleth. On one occasion he saves Amleth's life by warning him of a trap into which he otherwise would have fallen. The warning in question was a most peculiar one, and has never received a satisfactory interpretation. The story goes as follows (Elton's translation): For this man (the foster-brother), . . . found a straw on the ground and fastened it underneath the tail of a gadfly that was flying past; which he then drove toward the particular quarter where he knew Amleth to be; an act which served the unwary prince exceedingly well. The token was interpreted as shrewdly as it had been sent. For Amleth saw the gadfly, espied with curiosity the straw which it wore embedded in its tail, and perceived that it was a secret warning to beware of treachery (Saxo III 90). Later on, after Amleth, through his foster-brother's warning, had succeeded in outwitting his enemies, we find another reference to this extraordinary method of conveying a message. I quote again from Elton's translation: Then he who had marked the gadfly in order to give a hint, wishing to show Amleth that to his trick he owed his salvation, observed that latterly he had been singly devoted to Amleth. The young man's reply was apt. Not to seem forgetful of his informant's service, he said that he had seen a certain thing bearing a straw flit by suddenly, wearing a stalk of chaff fixed on its hinder parts. The cleverness of this speech, which made the rest split with laughter, rejoiced the heart of Amleth's friend (Saxo loc. cit.).

What is the joke here? I conceive the reply to be a punning reference to the foster-brother's name, which I assume to be Vifill. The name means 'a kind of beetle' (cf. Eddica Minora XXXIV note) and certainly on this interpretation Amleth's reply is intelligible enough, and a palpable hit in its coarse way. No wonder the rest split with laughter! As to the warning itself, which, taken as it stands, is something quite impossible and quite inexplicable, we need only assume that the joke arose first and we have an explanation of the warning which leaves nothing to be desired. After the foster-brother's name had been lost to the story the pun lost its point, of course. It thus came to be taken literally, and gave rise to the warning as we have it.

We have now established Vifill as one of the characters in version A, and this of course greatly strengthens our identification of Amleth with Áli, since we know from the Kalfsvísa that Vifill was a retainer of Áli. We can now also explain the origin of the Vifill of H. His usurpation of Viðolfr's role was perhaps due to some supernatural connotation of the name Vifill (cf. *dwarf*, which seems originally to have meant 'insect'). But Viðolfr-Vifill is not the only faithful retainer in the Helgasaga. In H we find a certain Reginn, to whom correspond the Regno of HH and perhaps the Gamaliel of AB. All these, like the nameless retainer of A, were in the service of the new king although at heart faithful to the dispossessed heir(s). Reginn and Regno are represented as the brothers' foster-father. Reginn rescues them when their father is killed and entrusts them to Vifill, who keeps them in hiding for a time. Later they find refuge with their elder sister Signý and her husband Sevill. In their vengeance they are greatly aided by Reginn, who in truth does practically all the work. In HH unnamed protectors save the boys and keep them concealed at first; later Regno appears as their protector. He plays no part in the vengeance, however, even warning Fróði of what is afoot, though in the story this is explained away and not considered a betrayal. Traces of a similar betrayal are to be found in H. In this connexion it is noteworthy that jarl Sevill and his wife do not appear in HH, their part being played by Regno.

It is probable that Reginn-Regno was originally a faithless retainer (perhaps a malevolent dwarf), who after the death of his lord entered the service of the new king. This faithless retainer served as contrast to Viðolfr, who did not enter the service of the new king but lived in retirement and saved the life of the son of his old master. The Amleth saga, however, offered a new interpretation of the faithless retainer. In that saga his faithlessness was only ostensible; in reality he was as loyal as ever. When Amleth and Helgi were identified, then, Reginn's conduct was seen in a new light and his career was remodeled accordingly. In HH the process has not proceeded so far but that we can see the original form of the story pretty plainly. In H on the other hand only slight traces of the former faithlessness remain, the Hamletian interpretation having won an almost complete victory.

The interpretation given in the preceding paragraph is based on the assumption that Reginn, like Viðolfr, was already present in the pre-Hamletian form of the Helgasaga. This would be the most plausible assumption, I think, even if we had only the Regno of HH to account for. It becomes the only plausible assumption when we consider the situation in H, where, since Vifill answers partly to the Viðolfr, partly to the Regno of HH, it seems clear that in the primitive Helgasaga there were two characters with whom the Hamletian retainer might be identified.

Bugge has pointed out (HEP. 176f.) that jarl Sevill was originally a faithless retainer. He did not note the fact, however, that as such he was simply a doublet of Reginn. We are of course not justified in assuming two faithless retainers in the primitive story, except as a bare possibility. It is a much sounder method to see if we can discover any reason for doubling up. A stock example of the faithless retainer was Sabene (OE Seafola), and Bugge has shown how this name might have come into the Helgasaga in the form Sevill (as we have it in AS and the first vísa of H). Now it is conceivable enough that a tendency might arise to call Reginn, the faithless retainer, by this other and more familiar name. This would not normally result in the development of two persons having the same function, however. Ordinarily one or the other of the two names would gain the victory, nothing more. In this case, however, an unusual factor affected the development. It will be remembered that the original avenger in the saga was Hrólfr. Now Yrsa, the mother of Hrólfr, was also his sister, as the Grottasöngr specifically states. When Helgi displaced his son as avenger, Yrsa likewise vanished from the vengeance story, of course. Her place was taken by Signý. But which place? Her predecessor occupied two! In HH she became the mother, in H the sister. In consequence we find no sister in HH. However, although the hero could do without a sister, he could not do without a mother, so in H the element *Sig-* was used to make up a name, Sigríðr, which would fill the gap. The same two women appear in AS, which tells us further that Ingjaldr (the Fróði of H and HH) gave Signý in marriage to Sevill, evidently in reward for his villainy. This throws some light on the development of the story. When Sevill came in as an alternate name of Reginn, a differentiation began, Sevill becoming the actually faithless, Reginn the ostensibly faithless retainer. Hence the almost total loss of faithlessness in the Reginn of H. Sevill's marriage to Signý, however, eventually caused a reversion, and in H we find him a supporter of his brothers-in-law, although certain indications remain of the villainy so clear in AS. — The character used to replace Yrsa probably goes back to the Signý of the Völsungasaga, whose career presents certain parallels to that of Yrsa.

Before completing our discussion of the faithful and faithless retainers, it will be convenient to consider the third fundamental difference between A and H, viz., the use of disguise instead of madness. In H the brothers, far from being brought up in Fróði's court, are concealed, first with Vifill, then with jarl Sevill. Even when they go to Fróði's hall to execute their vengeance they retain a disguise, which they throw off only at the last moment. Nevertheless, one trace remains of a different form of the story. On the way to the hall Helgi, the younger brother, is mounted on an untamed colt, sits facing towards the animal's tail and in general plays the fool as he rides along in this curious fashion. This procedure of Helgi is specifically contrasted with the conduct of Hróarr, who rides in the orthodox manner. The contrast is of some importance in determining the history of the motif, as we shall see. It is obvious that Helgi's mad behavior does not fit in with the disguise motif, as it serves to attract attention to him. Turning now to HH, we find the brothers kept hidden, first with unnamed protectors, later with Regno. The latter eventually betrays them and they fall into the hands of Fróði but save themselves by pretending to be mad. The next night they carry out their vengeance.

If we are to understand the history of the Helgasaga we must above all keep in mind that originally Helgi was the only avenger and that his vengeance was originally no youthful exploit, but the deed of a mature man. We may venture to reconstruct the pre-Hamletian form of the vengeance story as follows. King Halfdanr and his sons Hróarr and Helgi are defeated in battle by king Fróði, and Halfdanr and Hróarr are killed. Helgi is severely wounded, but is saved and healed through the magic arts of the wizard Viðolfr, a retired retainer of Halfdanr. Helgi upon his recovery collects his friends about him and prepares to attack Fróði, but his plans are betrayed by a faithless retainer. In consequence Fróði does the attacking and seems to have won a victory. Helgi escapes, however, and kills Fróði the next night in a surprize attack. Here the exact course of events after the betrayal is uncertain. Fróði was perhaps egged on to his original attack by his wife.

The identification of Helgi and Amleth had a profound effect on this story. In the first place, the vengeance became a youthful exploit. Or, more accurately, the story became a story of Helgi's youth, with the actual vengeance at the end, just as in the Amleth saga. As a necessary accompaniment of this youth went the inability of the hero to defend himself by force of arms and his consequent use of simulated madness as a means of self-defense. In addition, a new interpretation was given to the faithless retainer Reginn. So far all the versions are in agreement. Other Hamletian motifs are to be found in the Helgasaga, but not in all the versions of it. Thus, pegs or nails are used in the vengeance scene in B, AB and H but not in HH. The murderer marries his victim's widow in H and AS but not in B, X or HH. The murderer is his victim's brother in HH, H and AS but not in B and AB; this last feature of the tale need not be derived from the Amleth saga, however, and in view of the first vísa of H (see above) the development must be held as comparatively late, whatever its derivation.

The problem of fitting all this new material into the original story was worked out differently and, it would seem, independently in the three main versions, viz., X, H and HH. In X, where the younger brother remained the sole avenger, the simulated madness motif gained the dominance, and eventually drove out the Viðolfr story, though Amlóði's wound may go back to that story. Reginn underwent the same metamorphosis as in the other versions but his change into a faithful retainer was carried out in a more thorough-going manner. However, as the simulated madness motif dominated the story, the faithful retainer was left with little real function. A similar development took place in version A, where the faithful retainer seems to be a survival from a more primitive form in which the motif played a more important part.

The feigned madness appears not only in X but also in H and HH. In the two latter, however, it manifests itself in such a way that it can be interpreted only as a survival from an earlier stage of the story in which it was made more of. The decline of the motif was undoubtedly due to the introduction of Hróarr as fellow-avenger. So long as Helgi was the only avenger feigned madness was suitable enough as a protection for him in his youth and helplessness, and faithful retainers, disguises etc. were not needed. Hence in HH Viðolfr was transferred to a later period of Haldan's (i. e., Helgi's) life, where he could serve the son of his lord to some purpose. Similarly, in version A the faithful retainer, who originally (as we shall see later) took charge of the exile and return, was almost completely ousted by the feigned madness motif and indeed probably would not have survived at all had he not been preserved in connexion with the gadfly joke. When, however, Hróarr was changed from victim to fellow-avenger, feigned madness became unsatisfactory as a working motif. In real life two brothers may conceivably go mad simultaneously, but such an event does not occur with great frequency, and such a device, when used in saga, lacks plausibility, especially when the madness is a simulated one. It strains one's credulity to believe that the villain could have been deceived by so exceptional a combination. The sagamen would therefore search for other devices, more plausible and so more satisfying esthetically. Here Reginn, the faithless retainer, offered a means of escape, and he was seized upon and utilized. Through contamination with the ostensibly faithless but really faithful retainer and foster-brother in the Amleth saga his character had improved, and to remodel him into a fóster-father was easy. As such he could of course put the children in hiding, and this would take the place of feigned madness in preserving their lives until they were grown and able to take vengeance on the king. Another motif which would serve the same purpose was the exile and return, a device so familiar in saga that I need not discuss it here, except to say that its presence in the

Amleth story itself probably antedated the development of Amleth's feigned madness.

In both H and HH the story of the brothers' youth is divisible into three stages. In the first stage they are hidden, by unnamed protectors in HH, by Vifill in H. In the second stage they are in exile, under the protection of Regno in HH, of Sevill and Signý in H. In the third stage they carry out their vengeance on Fróði at his hall. These stages correspond to the three stages of version A, for a discussion of which see below (cap. XIII). A peculiar feature of the first stage in the Helgasaga is the fact that the boys are treated as dogs, even being given dog's names, this for their greater security, of course. It is tempting to assume that this extraordinary method of concealment goes back to a more primitive form in which their feigned madness so expressed itself; cf. Amleth's bestial behavior in the first stage of A. In the second stage, in H, Helgi assumes the name Hamr, which according to Detter (HZ. XXXVI 16) means 'Hammel, Schöps.' Detter compares this to the Hamall of Helgakviða Hundingsbana II, a name having the same meaning and likewise applied to Helgi. Cf. also the name Hrút, used as a woman's name in Helgi's own family, that of the Scyldings. It seems clear that Helgi's nickname is an ancient one, antedating his connexion with the Amleth saga. Perhaps the ram was an animal held in special reverence by the Scylding family, a survival of a theriomorphic family god. At any rate, if Helgi were called a 'wether' in primitive story it is easy to see how his feigned madness might take the form of animal-like behavior and so give rise to the dog-story noted above. Hróarr, however, does not receive a nickname to correspond, but is known as Hrani 'blusterer.' Similarly, on the road to Fróði's hall Helgi acts like a fool but Hróarr does not follow suit, as we have seen. This distinction between the two brothers doubtless goes back to their difference of function in the early form of the story, in which only Helgi feigns madness, Hróarr being one of the victims. The survival of this distinction is of course important evidence in favor of my theory of the development of the story.

The first two stages mentioned above do not correspond with precision in the two versions concerned. In H the children are taken to an island in stage one; in HH (here the more primitive account) the island appears in its proper place, viz., in stage two. Again, the Regno of HH, who properly belongs only in stage two, is not kept altogether distinct from the "protectors" who are in charge of stage one. The first stage (that of concealment) originally belonged to Viðolfr, of course. When he was removed to a later period of the hero's life this was doubtless because of pressure from the feigned madness motif, which took the place of the concealment of the pre-Hamletian tale and rendered Viðolfr superfluous at his original station. Later, however, with the introduction of Hróarr as fellow-avenger, the feigned madness motif began to lose ground, as explained above, and an early form of the new development meets us in stage one of HH with its unnamed protectors, derived perhaps from the friends who in the original story helped Helgi after he had recovered from his wound. More complex was the development of the first stage of H. Here Viðolfr had managed to hold his ground. In consequence he was absorbed by the Hamletian retainer Vifill. This retainer however primarily belonged, in the original Amleth saga, to the second or exile stage (whence his identification with the Regno of HH and his influence on the development of the Reginn of H), although present, and of some assistance to his lord, in the first or feigned madness stage as well (whence his contact with Viðolfr in H). We might expect, then, to find the first stage in H contaminated more or less by material drawn from stage two, and in fact the island on which the boys ought to spend their period of exile is used in H simply as a place of concealment. Nevertheless, Vifill is Viðolfr's heir in more ways than one. Note particularly his wizardry, and the epithet *karl* 'old man' applied to him.

Reginn was from the beginning connected with the second or exile stage. In a more primitive form of HH he may have been instructed by Fróði to take the boys off with him and kill them secretly. When, however, in stage one the brothers came to be in hiding from Fróði rather than feigning madness at Fróði's court, Regno of course could no longer receive them from the king, who had lost all contact with them. It is clear, however, that the exile met with the king's approval, since even in the extant version he is represented as permitting it. In H, where the originally faithless retainer had been differentiated into two persons, Sevill attended to the exile and return while Reginn became the secret friend at court. For an explanation of this see above.

In both versions what is left of the feigned madness motif puts in its appearance at the beginning of the third stage. The reason for this is obvious: here and here only was the original contact with Fróði preserved, and of course the motif had no value except when the king was a witness to the capers. It is true that in H as we have it Fróði was not an actual witness to Helgi's follies, though he appears almost immediately after. In a more primitive form of the version, however, he must have been present, just as he is in HH. His elimination in H was due to the very isolation of the incident, an incident preserved because of its picturesque character but so much out of harmony with the disguise motif now dominant that the king's suspicions, instead of being allayed, as originally (and as still in HH), would have been aroused had he been permitted to see what was going on. The presence of such an incident in so inappropriate a setting is good evidence that originally the setting was different. For if we assume the present setting it is hard to see how any sagaman could have come to insert the episode where it stands. The parallel in HH, where there is no disguise and the madness serves a definite purpose, points in the same direction, of course.

We have now completed our analysis of the main features of the story of Helgi's youth. We have seen that this story came into being as a result of the identification of Amleth and Helgi, and that it contains elements derived from two main sources, viz., the Amleth saga and the pre-Hamletian story of Helgi's vengeance on Fróði. One task we have not yet essayed, however. We have left unexplained the names of the characters in HH. How did it happen that in that version the father came to be called Harald (for Halfdanr), and the sons Harald (for Hróarr) and Haldan (for Helgi)? Let us see.

From our study of the Beowulf and the Grottasöngr

we have already determined that Fróði was killed by the Halfdanir or Scyldings (led by Hróarr), and we have concluded that when the term Halfdanir ceased to be understood it was supposed to refer to Halfdanr and so changed from plural to singular. This change gave rise to a story to the effect that Halfdanr killed Fróði. In this form we find the tradition in Sweyn. Now there can be no doubt that such a story was known elsewhere also, for the reference in the Grottasöngr presupposes a situation out of which it could hardly have avoided developing. But if Halfdanr killed Fróði he must have had some reason for it, and the most plausible reason would be that he was avenging his father. In this way Fróði became the murderer of Halfdanr's father. This father appears in our story under the name Haraldr. Who was he? In Danish tradition the father of Halfdanr was the euhemerized vegetation deity Fróði, corresponding to the OE. Beow. The same ancestry appears in Norse accounts — in the Grottasöngr, for instance. It goes without saying, however, that Fróði could not have been Halfdanr's actual father. In reality, Halfdanr was the founder of the Scylding line, hence divine ancestors were given him. The only clue to his true ancestry lies in his name, which means half-Dane, i. e., either his father or his mother was a foreigner. Now since he was the founder of a new line it is plausible to assume that his father was the foreigner, and that he derived his title to the Danish throne through his mother. If so, it is possible enough that his father really was named Haraldr.

Turning now to Snorri's account in the Ynglingasaga (cap. 39) we read of a king Halfdanr of Skaane who was killed by his brother Guðrøðr at the instigation of Ása, a Swedish princess who was the wife of Guðrøðr. The father of the brothers was named Haraldr, as we know from other sources. As Olrik has pointed out (KS. II 84), this story is obviously parallel to HH. In it, however, Halfdanr is the victim, not his father. In this respect it is parallel to H. Evidently two variants of the same story were in existence; in one Halfdanr was the victim, in the other he was the avenger. The reasons for this uncertainty are clear enough, and have already been given (see above in the discussion of the Grottasöngr passage). As to the name Guðrøðr 'peace of God' one may conjecture that it stands for an earlier Friðfróði 'peace-Fróði' with the more general 'guð' substituted for the name of the vegetation deity. This would involve an identification of the euhemerized god with the Bardish king of the same name, of course, and we know that just this identification was made in the Skjöldunga, whence Snorri got his information.

However Guðrøðr came in, we can account for all the variants by assuming a father Haraldr and a son Halfdanr, the latter the founder of the Scylding line of Danish kings and the traditional (not the historical!) antagonist of the Bardish king Fróði. In its most primitive form this antagonism gave the formula: Halfdanr (historically the Halfdanir, i. e., the Scyldings) killed Fróði. This formula is the basis of HH. Later a misunderstanding and consequent 'correction' of the Grottasöngr gave the formula: Fróði killed Halfdanr. This is the basis of Snorri's story, and of version H of the Helgasaga. Where Halfdanr did the killing he was supposed to be avenging the death of his father Haraldr.

Where he was killed his death was avenged by his son (Helgi, Ívarr). Everywhere Fróði (Guðrøðr) was the villain. In HH and Snorri the villain was egged on by his wife, who was a Swedish princess. In HH her name is given as Úlfhildr; in Snorri, as Ása. The latter name also appears in Saxo (VI 194), though not in HH. Snorri's Ása was the daughter of the Swedish king Ingjaldr; Saxo's Ása was the sister of the Danish king Ingjaldr. If these two figures go back to the same person, Ása's connexion with the story is probably primitive and one would be inclined to set her as the original wife of Fróði. This though remains most uncertain, of course. In both Snorri and HH the wife of the villain pays the penalty for her egging on. In Snorri, Ása flees to her father Ingjaldr and along with him voluntarily burns herself alive in the flames of the king's hall in order to avoid falling into the hands of Halfdanr's son Ívarr (cf. queen Sigriðr's death in H). In HH, Úlfhildr is stoned to death by the avengers.

Snorri's version (hereafter called SS) was localized in Skaane. As HH was to all appearance a product of the same workshop, we may conjecture that it too arose in Skaane, though we have it in an Icelandic or Norwegian redaction, of course. Its East Scandinavian origin becomes more manifest in the second half of the saga, which deals with Haldan's adventures after he had taken vengeance on his father's murderer. The scene of these adventures is laid in Sweden, and, as Olrik puts it, the core of the story is Haldan's usurpation of the Swedish throne. Olrik goes on to point out (KS. II 83) that both AS and SS know a Halfdanr who is connected with Sweden, although, like the Haldan of HH, a Scylding.

According to AS his mother was Inga, the daughter of king Aun of Sweden; his father was the Scylding king Fróði. In SS we learn how he drove king Aun from Sweden and ruled that country for 20 years — until his death, indeed (Ynglingasaga cap. 25). Aun sought refuge in West Gautland. Now the Haldan of HH can hardly be separated from this son of Fróði. As Olrik says (loc. cit.), Olddigtningen har næppe oprindelig ladet to forskellige Skjoldunger af navnet Halvdan erobre den svenske trone, hvortil han havde en slags arveret paa mødrene side: Sverigserobringen maa fra först af tilhøre kun én Halvdan. As Snorri makes Halfdanr Haraldsson the victim of his brother he cannot have him usurp the Swedish throne, of course. That part of his career is therefore assigned to another Halfdanr, the son of the mythical Fróði. These two Halfdanrs were however in reality identical, as we have seen, the historical prototype of each being the Danish king of that name who founded the Scylding line.

How did Haldan become a usurping king of Sweden? We have seen that he became identified with the Helgi of H, evidently because each avenged his father's death by killing Fróði. But Helgi had been identified with Áli (Amleth). We might expect, then, to find some traces of Áli's history in this usurping king Halfdanr of Sweden, more especially since Áli became the subject of a special saga in Skaane, as we saw above (cap. III). Now a prominent feature of the Álasaga of Skaane was just this conception of Áli as a Scylding who usurped the throne of Sweden. And if we compare the usurpations of Áli and Halfdanr as told in the Ynglingasaga we find that they are essentially the same. Both

Halfdanr and Áli invade Sweden, defeat Aun in several battles and compel him to flee to West Gautland, where he remains as long as his antagonist lives. Furthermore, Halfdanr and Áli were both kings of Sweden for just 20 years, and each held the throne to the day of his death, undisturbed by rival claimants. The correspondence of the Swedish careers of the two kings is in fact complete in every detail, except for the manner of their death. Halfdanr died in his bed; Áli was assassinated. The discrepancy here certainly proves that Halfdanr was not a by-name of Áli, but our thesis does not contemplate more than a fusion product, of course. That Halfdanr should contribute to this product his name and nothing more would hardly be likely in any case. Here the manner of death certainly does not derive from either Áli or Helgi, and we have every reason to suppose that the original owner of the name contributed this ingredient to the story.

There are other features of the story of Haldan which support my connexion of him with Áli. Thus, he was known as Halfdanr *enn bjargrami* 'the mountain-strong,' an epithet to be compared with the statement in the Hyndluljóð that Áli was the strongest of men. Again, Saxo says that he was looked upon by the Swedes as a son of Þórr and worshipped accordingly. This curious development is exactly what you would expect of the strongest of men, who would be associated with the strongest of the gods. In connexion with the point a peculiar discrepancy in the stories relating to Þórr might be mentioned, as possibly it has some bearing here. In the Hervararsaga (FAS. I 413) and the Gautrekssaga (FAS. III 15) Þórr is represented as killing Starkaðr

Áludrengr; in the Víkarsbálkr, however (FAS. III 37), he seems to be represented as a friend of that monster, making him into a being more nearly human by tearing off his superfluous hands. Certainly this is Saxo's interpretation of the matter (VI 183). Is it possible that the slaying of Starkaðr had reference originally to Starkaðr enn gamli, and that Þórr slew him because he had assassinated Áli? This of course would fit in beautifully with the conception of Haldan-Áli as a son of Þórr. The evidence, however, is not sufficient to make us at all sure of our ground. — In general the later exploits of Haldan are of the same type as the exploits of Áli, but they differ considerably in detail. This difference has no bearing on our thesis, since the stories in question are late and of stock types such as might get attached to any hero. More important is the greater emphasis which sheer physical strength receives in the Haldan story; this finds expression in the use of such weapons as uprooted oaks. Ali's strength is manifested in less barbarous feats; the sword is his proper weapon. This difference reflects a difference in literary taste on the part of the sagamen who worked up the respective sagas, but it may also indicate a difference in character between Halfdanr and Áli.

On our interpretation, then, the Haldan of HH goes back to the historical Danish king Halfdanr, the founder of the Scylding line. His brother Harald, however, was of course not a historical person. His existence in saga is due to the fact that Halfdanr became identified with Helgi. As Helgi had an elder brother, Halfdanr had to be given one too. The very name Harald is clear evidence of the man's unhistoricity, as in the migration period no son would have borne the same name as his father.

There is another vengeance story in the Helgasaga, viz., Helgi's vengeance on the slayer of his brother. As this story has nothing directly to do with the Hamlet tale, however, and as its indirect effects on that tale have already been pointed out, we are justified in omitting it from our discussion and passing on to the second part of the Helgasaga, viz., Helgi's relations with Yrsa. These relations will be the subject of the chapter which follows.

Chapter XI.

Yrsa.

Our historical information on the subject of Yrsa is very scanty. Olrik's researches, together with the unanimous testimony of the Scandinavian monuments, have made it practically certain that she was a Frankish woman captured in a viking expedition and brought to Scandinavia, where she became the wife of the Danish prince Helgi and bore him a son, Hrólfr. From the Beowulf we know that Helgi died early, leaving one son, Hrólfr, who was brought up by Hróarr and his wife (1185 ff.). Evidently, then, Helgi's widow had either died or married again. Certainly she does not appear at court; in fact, the English poem has nothing at all to say about her, except in l. 62, where (if the emendation discussed in cap. V above be accepted) she is named as the wife of Onela. If this is the correct reading it is clear that the Beowulf poet thought her to be Halfdanr's daughter, and this is borne out by the fact that he gives the name Wealhþeow, an epithet which (on my interpretation) belongs properly to Yrsa, to the wife of Hróarr. The mistake was an easy one, of course. Yrsa was really only the daughter-in-law of Halfdanr, but when her husband died her status in the household became to all intents and purposes that of a true daughter. The most important likeness here was that she could be given in marriage by the ruling Scylding, quite as if she were a native princess.

And according to our emendation she was actually given in marriage to Onela. This would account for her absence from the Danish court as pictured in the Beowulf narrative, and for the relations between Hróarr and his wife and Hrólfr. If however we take the other tack and assume the correctness of the Beowulfian statement, assume, in other words, that Yrsa was a true daughter of Halfdanr, we are at once plunged into the most serious difficulties. In the first place, the name Yrsa becomes at once unaccountable, for it does not begin with H, and its foreign origin seems established (Olrik, DH. I 151 ff.). How could a daughter of Halfdanr be given a name appropriate enough for a Frankish woman but totally out of place in Scandinavia and more especially in the Scylding family. Secondly, if Yrsa was a true daughter of Halfdanr her marriage with Helgi would be incestuous, and the silence of the Beowulf on Helgi's married life would be strange in the extreme. It is true enough that the Grottasöngr and the later Scandian monuments represent Hrólfr as the product of an incestuous marriage, but Olrik has shown conclusively (DH. I 155 ff.) that this motif has a strong tendency to attach itself to great heroes who are the last of their race, and accordingly we are under no necessity of assuming that the incest was historical. Furthermore, in the sources containing the incest motif Helgi is always Yrsa's father, never her brother. Under the circumstances we can hardly avoid the conclusion that the author of the Beowulf was in error in calling Yrsa a daughter of Halfdanr; in reality she was his daughter-in-law. For a different interpretation see Miss M. G. Clarke (Sidelights on Teutonic History during the Migration Period pp. 82 ff.). For an excellent discussion of the limitations of the Beowulfian historical material see Olrik, Heroic Legends of Denmark pp. 26 ff.

The story of Yrsa as told in version H of the Helgasaga, though fantastic enough, certainly supports Olrik's theory of her foreign origin, a theory based solidly on the etymology and historical associations of her name. This story Olrik summarizes as follows (DH. I, 145; translation by Hollander): "Queen Oluf of Saxland was handsome of appearance, but haughty; she was a warrior queen who went about with shield and coat of mail, girt with a sword and wearing a helmet. She was the best match of those times in all the North but she would have no husband. Helgi conceived the desire to marry her, even against her own will. He arrived in Saxland with his fleet, and the queen, who did not have a sufficient force about her to make resistance, received him and his men as guests. In the evening, during the banquet, Helgi demanded that they should celebrate marriage at once. The queen was forced to consent; but Helgi was already dead drunk and when they went to bed she pricked him with the 'sleep-thorn,' shaved off his hair and tarred his head, put him in a sack and let his own men carry him to his ship. When he awoke next day and wanted to avenge the insult, the queen had already collected a superior army of Saxons, and Helgi had to sail away thus put to shame. Not long after he returned in disguise, hid two chests of gold in the ground, and, by the help of a thrall of the queen, lured her out alone to dig up the treasure. When she came to the place, she was seized by Helgi who kept her as his concubine. In due time she gave birth to a girl child whom she called Yrsa. She was given to cottagers to foster up, and passed as their child. When Yrsa was thirteen years old, Helgi came to the land 'to learn tidings;' he met the lovely girl tending the cattle, led her home with him, and married her, notwithstanding her anxious forebodings. Queen Olaf did nothing to hinder the wedding; but when Yrsa had given birth to a son, called Hrólfr, Oluf fared to Denmark and revealed to her daughter her origin and the incest she had committed. She took Yrsa home with her, and later married her to the Swedish king Athisl."

Olrik stops at this point; I will conclude the story in my own words. Helgi objected strongly to Yrsa's marriage to Aðils, and sailed away to Uppsala to take Yrsa away from her new husband. Aðils, not feeling strong enough to make a fight, received Helgi with seeming friendliness, and persuaded him to accept an invitation to a banquet at the king's hall. Helgi came, leaving most of his troops by his ships. In the meantime the berserkers in the service of Aðils arrived from abroad. Aðils set them in ambush on the road to the Danish ships, and as Helgi was returning to the anchorage after the banquet he and his men were set upon by the berserkers and the other forces of Aðils. In the battle that followed Helgi and all his men were killed. From this time on Aðils had undisturbed possession of Yrsa. Later on Hrólfr made an expedition to Uppsala, but in none of the monuments is this motivated as an attempt to avenge his father's death.

A similar story appears in the Skjöldunga. Here however the order of the husbands is different. In SS Yrsa is captured by Aðils and made his wife. Later Helgi in an expedition to Sweden takes Yrsa from Aðils and marries her. She bears him a son, Hrólfr. When he was three years old queen Álof comes to Denmark and reveals the parentage of Yrsa. Then Yrsa goes back to Sweden and again becomes the wife of Aðils. Helgi falls in an unspecified foray; his death is not brought into connexion with Aðils. In AS appears essentially the same story, but the detailed account of how Aðils happened to marry Yrsa is not given; we get only the bare statement that Yrsa was married to Aðils. This brevity is doubtless due to the fact that AS is only a synopsis (but see Olrik, DH. I 146 note).

Saxo's account is much shorter, and different in many ways. He says (II 51 f.), speaking of Helgi, Apud insulam Thoro uirgine Thora stuprum pati coacta, filiam suscepit, cui post modum Vrse uocabulum aptauit. . . . Cum ad insulam Thoro piraticam reflexisset, Thora, necdum amisse uirginitatis merore deposito, turpi commento nefariam stupri ulcionem excogitauit. Siquidem filiam nubilis etatis de industria littori immissam concubitu patrem maculare precepit. The product of this incestuous union was Hrólfr. After Helgi's death Hrólfr came to the throne, and gave his mother Yrsa in marriage to king Aðils of Sweden. In Saxo's account, then, there is no strife between Helgi and Aðils over Yrsa, as there is in the Icelandic sources.

Olrik (DH. I 147) summarizes as follows the elements common to the Danish and Icelandic versions (translation by Hollander): "Helgi in the course of his viking expeditions returns to a coast where he had in earlier times, now forgotten, ravished a woman. He beholds Yrsa (his daughter) and marries her. According to Saxo, it is the woman whom he had earlier ravished who, for the sake of revenge, brings about the new love; according to Icelandic tradition she knows of it early enough to have been able to prevent it, but fails to do so, for the incest is to be her revenge. She even waits three years so that the curse may fall also on the son who has been born." To this it may be added that Yrsa's mother is represented as a woman of the Þryð type both in Saxo and in the Icelandic sources. Everywhere her fundamental characteristic is her hatred of her mate. In H her Þryð-like qualities are given fullest expression, but greater fullness is in general characteristic of this version. The Skjöldunga, it is true, gives her a husband, but he plays no part whatever in the story, always being úr landinu when anything happens, the couple have no children, and the very name of the husband, Geirþjófr 'spear-thief,' has a late look. The other versions, according to which Yrsa's mother was unmarried and dangerous to her suitors, undoubtedly represent the primitive conception of the woman. In another respect too all the versions agree. Yrsa was married both to her father Helgi and to the Swedish king Aðils.

The historical course of events, on the present theory, may be reconstructed as follows. Yrsa was a Gaulish captive, taken by Helgi in some viking expedition to the Frankish coasts. Helgi married her, and she bore him a son, Hrólfr. While Hrólfr was still a child his father died, and his mother was given in marriage to the Swedish king Áli. Hrólfr himself remained in Denmark and was fostered by Hróarr, the Danish king. In the struggle between Áli and Aðils for the Swedish crown the latter was finally successful, defeating and slaying

Áli in a battle on the ice of lake Væni. Aðils now married Yrsa, the widow of his rival. In the meantime Hrólfr through the murder of Hróarr and Hrœrekr had gained possession of the Danish throne. When he learned of the defeat and death of his step-father Áli he undertook an expedition to Uppsala to avenge Áli and rescue his mother. This however he was unable to effect; indeed, he barely succeeded in escaping capture, and was compelled to return to Denmark empty-handed. Later the two kings came to terms, largely owing to their common hostility to the Geats. This led to the overthrow of Hrólfr by his cousin Hjörvarðr, aided by the Geats. Aðils's attempt to avenge the death of Hrólfr was unsuccessful. After the death of Beowulf, however, Aðils or some later Swedish king succeeded in overthrowing the Geatish kingdom. A good deal of this sketch of events rests on evidence slender enough, of course. The historicity of Beowulf in particular has frequently been called into question. So far as his name is concerned, these doubts are probably justified; at any rate, *Beowulf* is best interpreted as a by-name rather than as a true name. What was Beowulf's true name, then? Here we have little to go on, but more, nevertheless, than is generally supposed. In the first place, Beowulf's father, both in name and in career, gives the impression of a historical person. His son's name, then, would presumably begin with a vowel. Furthermore, we know that Beowulf was of the Wægmunding kin (2813 f.), but since no W-alliteration appears, his relationship must have been on the female side. Now we know that Wiglaf actually did have a kinsman on the female side, viz., Ælfhere (2604), and, curiously enough, this kinsman's name exhibits the very vowel-alliteration which we have a right to assume for Beowulf's true name. It is possible, then, that Ælfhere is an isolated survival of the hero's true name, which elsewhere had been completely driven out by the nickname. If so, we get more light on Onela's reasons for setting Beowulf on the Geatish throne after the death of Heardred. For Ælfhere seems to have been a Scylfing, and if Beowulf was of Swedish stock originally, the Swedish king would naturally regard him as the 'safest' man for the Geatish throne. For other possibilities as to Ælfhere see above (cap. III). In this connexion it is worth noting that the seeming ease with which Swedish kings were adopted by Geatish tradition may be partly due to the fact that both the Swedish kings and the Wægmundings were known as Scylfings and evidently sprang from the same original dynasty. All this, however, is very speculative matter, of course, and it is highly improbable that Beowulf's true name will ever be determined with certainty.

Let us now return to Yrsa. If the blood-taint motif has no historical basis, how can we account for the present form of the Yrsa story? Olrik has pointed out (DH. I 158) how the motif might have been brought in. Before its introduction the name Yrsa and the fact that Hrólfr was called Yrsuson as well as Helgason must have given rise to poetic speculation (DH. I 154 f.). Yrsa's romantic entrance into the Danish royal house and her chequered career as a wife must likewise have contributed to the development of tales concerning her. A woman with so strange a name and career must have had strange antecedents, the poet would argue, and curiosity about these antecedents eventually gave her a mother, made in Yrsa's image. We have seen that Yrsa originally was of the Þryð type, and that her original characteristics are well preserved as late as the account in Saxo (see above, cap. V). Her mother, then, became likewise a Þryð. Hence her virginity and her hatred of her suitors. But once the mother had come into existence a tendency would set in to differentiate between mother and daughter, to develop for each an individuality of her own. As the mother of Hrólfr, Yrsa would naturally be favored in this differentiation. The hero's mother must be blameless. Yrsa's objectionable qualities therefore became the exclusive property of her mother and Yrsa herself was represented as a victim of fate and circumstance. In Saxo this process has not gone so far but that we can determine Yrsa's original characteristics. In Iceland, however, she has become little more than a victim of fate.

We are now ready to consider Yrsa's career as a wife. In Saxo she marries Aðils after the death of Helgi and there is nothing to indicate any conflict between her two husbands. In Iceland on the other hand there is a very definite conflict, and Yrsa is the cause of it. The difference between Danish and Icelandic tradition corresponds very neatly to the fact that Áli and Helgi were not confused in Selund but were identified in Norway and Iceland. The Danes, who had forgotten Áli entirely, knew nothing of his war with Aðils. The Norsemen, on the contrary, who, as we have seen, fused into one story the youthful exploits of Amleth (Áli) and the father-vengeance of Helgi, did the same with the later history of the two heroes. In consequence we find Helgi at war with Aðils, and, in H, killed in battle with him. The resemblance here extends to an important detail like the berserkers come from abroad. It will be remembered that the Eadgils of the Beowulfian account was not strong enough to win the Swedish throne from Onela without help. He therefore sought and received aid from the Geatish king Beowulf. These Geatish auxiliaries appear in the Snorra Edda as berserkers led by Bjarki (i. e., Beowulf). In both accounts they are the decisive factor in Aðils's victory over Áli. Now the account in H of Helgi's death is strikingly parallel to the story of Áli's death in the Beowulf and the Snorra Edda. Aðils feels himself unable to cope with Helgi unaided, but when certain berserkers in his service arrive from abroad he through their aid is able to overthrow and kill Helgi. Later on these berserkers quarrel with Aðils and leave his service (FAS. I 39), just as in the Snorra Edda, though the break with Aðils is motivated differently in the two accounts. Note also Beowulf's break with Aðils (cap. III above). For Aðils's treacherous conduct towards Helgi compare the saga of Áli enn frœkni, where although the manner of death is different the idea of treachery plays a prominent part. The most important parallel of all, however, is Yrsa's marriage to her husband's murderer, a trait which version H shares with version A. We should expect this trait to be missing in the Danish tradition, since in Selund Helgi and Áli were not identified, and in fact no such trait appears there. Its appearance in H, then, is of the greatest significance in explaining the history of Helgi in West Scandinavia.

In the Skjöldunga Helgi does not die at the hands of Aðils; on the contrary, he is successful in his conflict with him and takes Yrsa from him. How can we explain this peculiar version of the tale? It is clear that we have here a blend of two distinct traditions concerning Helgi. In the one (found in H) Helgi captures and marries Yrsa, but has to give her up when he finds out that she is his daughter. Her mother then gives her in marriage to Aðils. This causes a war between the two kings, in which Helgi is killed. The other tradition (found, e. g., in Saxo) also represents Helgi as capturing and marrying Yrsa. When he found out that she was his daughter he was so cast down by his discovery of the incest which he had unwittingly committed that he left his native country and sought death (in battle) in the East. After his death his widow was given in marriage to Aðils. The Skjöldunga keeps both Helgi's conflict with Aðils over Yrsa and his death on a viking expedition. This is managed by utilizing a tradition according to which Aðils captured his wife by force on a military expedition (historically the expedition on which he slew Áli). Aðils is made the original captor of Yrsa, and Helgi defeats Aðils in battle, taking Yrsa from him. Later Helgi finds out that Yrsa is his daughter and lets her return to her former husband. Helgi goes off on a viking expedition and is killed. In this way the author of the Skjöldunga combines his sources into a consistent narrative. If we remember that the Skjöldunga is not so much a traditional saga as an attempt at historical writing by some learned priest or monk, who reconciled as best he could the discrepancies of his various sources, we can easily understand how the Skjöldunga version of the Helgasaga came to be shaped as it was. On any other hypothesis its account of events is inexplicable.

Both in H and in S the war between Helgi (i. e.,

Áli) and Aðils is motivated unhistorically. Instead of being a dispute over the succession to the Swedish crown it is a dispute over the possession of Yrsa. This romantic development nevertheless had its roots in history. The marriage of Yrsa to the murderer of her husband led to the growth of a love story in which her two husbands fought for her possession. The identification of Áli with Helgi facilitated this growth, as Helgi in his proper person had no claim to the Swedish throne. The true motive for the conflict was not lost, however; in the story of Haldan, where Helgi through his identification with his father became disconnected from Yrsa, the war with Eric, in part at least, is nothing more than a struggle for the crown of Sweden, and this appears even more clearly in SS, where Halfdanr fights with Aun, i. e., Eanmund. As Haldan was a Scylding, Saxo represents him as ruling both Denmark and Sweden after his overthrow of Eric. This is of course unhistorical, but corresponds to the account of Amleth in the Annales Ryenses, which represent him as king of Sweden as well as Denmark. The connexion with Sweden affords striking support of my main thesis, viz., the identity of Amleth and Áli (Onela).

In all its versions, then, the Helgasaga goes back to a clearly defined historical complex. In Denmark this remained the basis of the saga. In Norway and Iceland, however, it became fused with the story of Áli (Onela) and in consequence had a rich development in directions foreign to the tale in its native country.

Chapter XII.

Viglek.

We are now ready to take up the story of the death of Amleth as told in Saxo. The tale runs substantially thus. During Amleth's absence in England a certain Viglek had come to the throne in Denmark. Viglek had troubled Amleth's mother with ruthless demands and had taken from her the royal hoard. Amleth, upon his return, took all this quietly enough, and even sent to Viglek the best of his booty. Later, however, when a favorable opportunity presented itself, he made war on Viglek and defeated him. He drove Fjaller, the governor of Skaane, into exile; Fjaller retired to Undensakre (i. e., the other world) — in other words, he died. Viglek assembled new forces and defeated and killed Amleth in a final battle. Amleth's wife Ermuthrud thereupon gave herself to Viglek and shared his bed, in spite of previous protestations of undying loyalty to Amleth. Viglek had a long and peaceful reign and finally died of a sickness. He was succeeded by his son Vermund.

There are a number of observations to be made here. In the first place, Saxo evidently knows very little about Viglek, and can 't be said to make a villain of him; at any rate, his murder of Amleth is never avenged. We may be sure, then, that he had not long played the part of slayer. For the death of a great hero ought to be avenged, and in fact the death of Áli seems to have been avenged according to one story at least. As Snorri has it, Aðils (the historical slayer) was thrown from horseback and killed; the horse was apparently either Hrafn, the former steed of Áli, or a horse sired by Hrafn. Here then Áli was avenged by his horse — surely a vengeance poetical enough. The story may have developed, it is true, as a result of Aðils's hostility to the Týr cult (as we have seen, in Sweden the horse was originally an animal sacred to Týr). Nevertheless, it seems peculiar that no such story appears in version A, where Amleth is a hero of such dimensions as to call for an avenger. Compare the Hrólfr cycle, where the death of Hrólfr kraki was avenged in the later accounts, although the Bjarkamál itself by its silence as to the matter gives us good reason to believe that the vengeance story is unhistorical. The want of an avenger of Amleth is best explained by assuming that the true villain in some way or other got dissociated from the crime, his place being filled by another.

A very peculiar feature of the Saxonian account is the sudden introduction of Fjaller. I have already expressed the opinion that this mysterious person is simply a doublet of Feng. If one may judge from his localization, the villain of the tale went by the name Feng in Jutland, Fjaller in Skaane. On my theory he is to be identified with the Hæðcyn of the Beowulf, as we have seen. Now the earlier references to Viglek remind one strongly of the career of Hæðcyn, who, it will be remembered, captured Onela's mother and took from her the royal hoard (Beowulf 2930 ff.). He was later defeated and killed by Ongenþeow, but I have already shown that in the development of the story Onela took his father's place as slayer. We may then plausibly assign to Fjaller the earlier deeds which Saxo credits to Viglek, leaving to the latter only the final battle, and making intelligible the hostilities between Amleth and Fjaller, which Saxo altogether fails to motivate. Amleth's apparent acquiescence is a typical piece of Hamletian trickery which corresponds to his madness in the Feng story. The whole thing then becomes a Skaane version of the misdeeds and death of Hæðcyn, a version much closer to the historic facts than the version current in Jutland, and of course much less elaborated. It must be remembered, however, that we have only a fragment of the story, and even this in somewhat distorted form.

We have now stripped Viglek of everything except his final victory over Amleth and his marriage to Amleth's widow. Here he corresponds to Aðils, of course. Why was any substitution made? We have already seen that Aðils became the villain of the Eofor tale and fell at Eofor's hands. This development, which was strictly Jutish, prevented him from being further used as the villain of the likewise Jutish tale of the death of Amleth. A logical substitute for him would be Amleth's traditional successor on the throne. This successor was apparently Viglek, who, as we have seen, probably represents a fusion of the Geatish Wiglaf and the Anglian Wihtlæg. Historically Wiglaf was Beowulf's successor, but Beowulf, on account of his reduction to the rank of retainer (the reasons for which I have already explained) and his hostility to Onela, was early lost to Jutish tradition, though apparently longer preserved in Geatland proper, where Onela never became a full-fledged national hero, being eclipsed by his father. Amleth as Feng's successor would naturally follow Hæðcyn (crowding Hygelac out), and his historical associations with the Wægmundings would do the rest. The fusion of Wiglaf and Wihtlæg gave an appropriate place for the insertion of the Anglian line, which historically belonged to a much earlier period. Beowulf thus disappeared entirely from the scene. Hygelac, however, though crowded from his proper place, was not forgotten. Indeed, chronologically his position after the Anglian kings is more correct than it would have been had he maintained his place as successor of Hæðcyn, and perhaps it would be better to assume that he simply held his ground while his original associates, the other Hreðlings and the Wægmundings, were shifted back.

It certainly seems curious to find Viglek, who goes back, in part, to Wiglaf the son of Onela's faithful retainer Weohstan, taking the role of Eadgils, the slayer of Onela. No such development could well have taken place until the historical relationship had been forgotten. And it is clear that Viglek's assumption of the part was a comparatively late change, since though he plays the villain he does not get the villain's punishment and in general is about as colorless a person as one could well imagine. Evidently poetic tradition had not had time to make of him anything better than a mechanical device for ringing down the curtain. The loss of Aðils, the proper villain, took all the life out of the last scene. No wonder Olrik concludes that the latter part of the Amleth saga was a late addition to the tale. However in this conclusion he is in error, as we have seen. The figure of Ermuthrud, and Amleth with his passionate attachment to her, remain, and correspond with extraordinary accuracy to the Yrsa and Helgi of version H. Only the villain is changed, and the reasons for this have been explained in full above (cap. VI).

Beginnings of growth on the part of Viglek are to be seen in his encroachments on the material properly belonging to Fjaller. This growth was clearly in the direction of villainy; from a mere mechanical contrivance he was on the way toward becoming a true villain. The process had hardly more than begun, however, and in so ancient a tale as the Hamlet tale this is conclusive evidence that Viglek was not one of the primitive characters.

Chapter XIII.

The Primitive Plot.

We are now ready to attempt a determination of the primitive or pre-Saxonian form of the story. Closest to history is the Skaane version as preserved in Saxo. It appears, however, in such abbreviated or indeed fragmentary form that its complete reconstruction is impossible. As it stands this version may be divided into the following incidents: 1) Fjaller's mistreatment of Amleth's mother, 2) Amleth's apparent acquiescence and 3) Amleth's attack on Fjaller and the latter's defeat and death. Of these incidents the first two are attached to Viglek in the Saxonian text, for which see above. The first incident corresponds closely to the Beowulfian account, as we have seen. The second incident is typically Hamletian, especially as to the gifts; we may infer, then, that the Amleth of Skaane was not essentially different in character from the Amleth of Jutland. The third incident is told twice, first with reference to Viglek (who had taken Fjaller's place in the first and second incidents), then with reference to Fjaller (who luckily escaped complete elimination). Viglek is said to have been defeated; Fjaller was driven into exile. The representation of his death as an exile into the other world is a primitive trait. When this tradition took form, Fjaller still retained something of his supernatural character. The instrument of Freyr's vengeance might be killed, but the god himself, though embodied in this instrument, could at most be driven to retire to Undensakre. Hence there was something about Fjaller (i. e., Hæðcyn) which did not die, though rendered innocuous. Nothing of this supernatural element remains in the Jutland version, where Feng, in spite of his name, is in all respects a mere mortal.

The Skaane version, then, gives us a taste of the most primitive form of the Hamlet story. Its fragmentary character, however, disqualifies it for utilization as the basis of our reconstruction of the primitive plot. When we have completed this reconstruction we shall have a plot that is primitive but nevertheless somewhat later in form than the plot hinted at by the fragments of the Skaane version. Similarly, the story of Angantýr II in the Hervararsaga is both too primitive and too isolated an episode to be made the basis of our reconstruction, which must rest on the full accounts of the Jutland version of Saxo and the various variants of the Helgasaga, even though these versions give us the story in a somewhat later stage of its development.

Without further preliminary remarks let us now proceed with our reconstruction. We have already determined the following features of the primitive plot: 1) Feng slays Ørvendill; 2) he marries Geruth, his victim's widow; 3) victim and villain are brothers; 4) Feng succeeds to his brother's throne, Amleth, the son of Orvendill and rightful heir, being set aside; 5) Amleth remains at the king's court as a dependent; 6) in order to save himself from his father's fate he feigns madness, and his ruse is successful; 7) eventually he entraps and slays Feng, and succeeds to the throne; 8) he marries a foreign princess, a woman of the Þryð type; 9) he is finally defeated and killed in battle; 10) his widow marries her husband's murderer. In the above I have, for the sake of convenience, used the Jutland names of the characters. Of the traits enumerated, the first appears in all the versions except the Skaane fragment, and this fragment contains nothing in contradiction to the trait. The second trait, on the other hand, does not appear in the Hervararsaga and is directly contradicted by the Skaane fragment; it is therefore probably a later development, belonging indeed in our reconstruction but not in the most primitive form of the story. The origin of the trait has already been discussed above in cap. VIII. Its absence from versions X, B and HH of the Helgasaga is probably due to the influence of the historical complex of that saga rather than to that of the most primitive form of the Hamlet tale. The third trait appears in the Hervararsaga, and is therefore assured for our primitive plot; its failure to appear in versions X, B and AB of the Helgasaga is to be referred to the historical complex of that saga, also reflected in the first vísa of H. The fourth trait is fundamental both in the Jutland version of Saxo and in the Helgasaga; it is wanting only in B, where the hero and his father are of humble station. The fifth trait occurs in the Jutland version and in version X; for its loss in the other Helgasaga versions see above. The sixth trait dominates the story, and lends the hero his name, in the Jutland version and version X; in versions H and HH it also appears, though evidently in process of being eliminated, for which see above (cap. X). The seventh trait appears in all the versions. The eighth trait appears everywhere except in the folk-tales X and B, which acquired a conventional happy ending, and in version HH, where Haldan is represented as a bachelor (I ignore the story of Thorild and Asmund, which hardly fits in with the rest of Haldan's career). Similarly, traits nine and ten are confined to versions A, H and (with certain changes, for which see above) AS and SS.

In none of the versions, except AS, do we find our story narrated in skeletonized form as I have narrated it. On the contrary, it is told with a considerable degree of elaboration, either in part or in full, and it will be our next task to examine the various details given in the various versions and see which of them can with plausibility be assigned to the primitive plot. It will be convenient to begin with the details of trait one, viz., the slaying of Hamlet's father. As we have seen, this deed goes back to the accidental death of Herebeald at the hands of his brother Hæðcyn, told of in the Beowulf. The Swedish king Ongenþeow (Angantýr, Egill) later became identified with Herebeald. In the most primitive version showing this identification, viz., the Hervararsaga, the slaying is still represented as accidental, and is not followed by any taking of vengeance. Nevertheless, Hæðcyn profited by his deed, gaining the throne which otherwise his slain brother would have occupied. From the beginning, then, a cloud of suspicion, or at least of disapprobation, must have rested over the young prince; indeed, the Beowulf tells us (2441):

þæt wæs feoh-leas gefeoht, fyrenum gesyngad,

and further on (2467 b) we read that Hæðcyn was not dear to his father. As time went on, then, Hæðcyn, or Feng, as he came to be called, developed into a villain.

His original innocence, however, was not entirely lost, but was brought into connexion with another historical deed of his, viz., his capture of Ongenþeow's wife. Saxo's account of the matter runs as follows (translation by Elton): Such great good fortune stung Feng with jealousy, so that he resolved treacherously to waylay his brother, thus showing that goodness is not safe even from those of a man's house. And behold, when a chance came to murder him, his bloody hand sated the deadly passion of his soul. Then he took the wife of the brother he had butchered, capping unnatural murder with incest. . . . Also the man veiled the monstrosity of his deed with such hardihood of cunning, that he made up a mock pretence of goodwill to excuse his crime, and glossed over fratricide with a show of righteousness. Geruth, he said, though so gentle that she would do no man the slightest hurt, had been visited with her husband's extremest hate; and it was all to save her that he had slain his brother: for he thought it shameful that a lady so meek and unrancorous should suffer the heavy disdain of her husband. Nor did his smooth words fail in their intent: for at courts, where fools are sometimes favoured and backbiters preferred, a lie lacks not credit. So Saxo (III 87 f.). It would seem that after Herebeald and Ongenþeow had been identified Hæðcyn's manslaughter and his capture of Ongenþeow's wife were brought into connexion, and his original innocence of wrongdoing was reflected in a defense of his conduct which won wide acceptance. The version A account of the matter then has every claim to be considered as derived from the primitive plot. The corresponding incident in HH represents a different development. Here Fróði has his brother assassinated, out of jealousy of his greater glory. The crime was done secretly, however, and as a further precaution Fróði had the assassins put to death too. He even went so far as to institute an inquiry into the cause of his brother's sudden death. Nevertheless he was generally suspected of the crime. In this version Fróði's protestations of innocence reflect Hæðcyn's true innocence of wrongdoing, but the change in the manner of death does great violence to the original account, in which the slayer did not seek to deny his guilt, but rather attempted to explain the deed away, or, in version A, to justify it. HH, then, contains a dash of the original form of the episode, but only a dash. Version H has altered things still more; in it we get simply the standardized surprize attack and hall-burning. Similarly, in AB the father of Amlóði is defeated in battle and put to death. This failure of many of the versions to correspond to the details as given in the Beowulf and the Hervararsaga should not blind us, however, to the correspondence of all the versions in the central fact, viz., the slaying of Hamlet's father by the villain of the tale.

What was the primitive form of the incident? Obviously we need a form from which both A and HH can be derived. If we are to find such a form we must apply the old maxim, cherchez la femme. It will have been observed that behind the Saxonian account lies a fight between the brothers with Geruth as the prize. Indeed, Saxo explains Feng's jealousy of his brother as due to Ørvendill's success in obtaining Geruth for a wife. A rivalry story would indeed almost of necessity develop after Herebeald had been identified with Ongenþeow, for Hæðcyn actually took Ongenþeow's wife away from him. Cf. also the Höðr story above (cap. VII). In its pre-Saxonian form, then, the incident probably went somewhat as follows: Ørvendill and his brother Feng became estranged over Geruth, who had married Ørvendill. It finally came to blows and Feng killed his brother and married Geruth. This incident as it stood did not fit into the Helgasaga, where both Halfdanr (Harald) and Fróði were already equipped with wives. Nevertheless, in H its influence was sufficient to cause the elimination of Fróði's wife in favor of Halfdanr's widow. In HH Fróði's wife proved less amenable to expulsion, and the estrangement of the brothers was given the form of a falling out on account of the quarrels of their wives over precedence etc. But this development greatly weakened the motivation for the murder, and to make up for this weakening the villainy of Fróði had to be correspondingly strengthened. Hence the introduction of the hired assassin method. In H, the primitive form of the murder incident was later driven out by a conventional hall-burning story. Common to A, H and HH is the villain's jealousy of his brother's greater fame and good fortune; in H this jealousy has become the only motivation for the murder. To judge from version A, however, Feng's jealousy was primarily due to the fact that his brother rather than he himself had won the hand of Geruth. If then we add Feng's jealousy of his brother's fame to the primitive content of our incident we must make it secondary to the main motive, viz., the estrangement over Geruth.

Our discussion of trait one has necessarily involved trait two as well. We may therefore pass on to trait three, according to which the hero's father and the villain are brothers. Here there is little to be added to our previous discussion. It is worthy of note, however, that HH makes Fróði (the villain) the elder brother. This is not in specific contradiction to the other versions, which fail to specify the relative ages of the brothers. It is in contradiction to the Beowulf account, however, where Herebeald is the elder brother and heir to the throne, and the situation in both A und H seems to agree better with the Beowulfian account than with the HH account in this particular. Thus, king Røric presumably gave his daughter Geruth to the elder brother. The primogeniture of Fróði in HH, then, probably goes back to folk-tale influence (in folk-tales, as is well known, it is normally the younger brother who is the hero).

Passing over traits four and five, which need no further discussion, we come to Hamlet's feigned madness. In version A this madness expresses itself in a number of incidents, and in certain details which we shall consider presently. Of this material, just what belonged to the primitive plot? We shall not go far wrong if we include in the primitive form of the story the material to which we find parallels in versions independent of A, provided this material otherwise is of a primitive character. Let us begin with Saxo's account of the bestial habits of Amleth (translation by Elton): Every day he (Amleth) remained in his mother's house utterly listless and unclean, flinging himself on the ground and bespattering his person with foul and filthy dirt. His discolored face and visage smutched with slime denoted foolish and grotesque madness. All he said was of a piece with these follies; all he did savoured of utter lethargy. In a word, you would not have thought him a man at all, but some absurd abortion due to a mad fit of destiny (Saxo III 88). — This is certainly primitive enough. Are there any parallels to it? In AB we find the same sort of thing, much elaborated and with even grosser details, but the author of AB seems to have known Saxo and in consequence we cannot be sure that the bestialities which he describes are not merely an expansion of the version A account. This cannot be said of H and HH, however, and in both these versions we find the avengers living under bestial conditions. In HH they were hid in a hollow oak and fed as if they were dogs, even being called by dogs' names. Similarly, in H they were hid in a *jarðhús*, and given dogs' names. Parallel to the hollow oak and the *jarðhús* is the 'wretched hovel' of Ambales in AB (Gollancz 74, l. 30), which accordingly must be assigned to X (since it is wanting in A). Cf. also FAS. I 30. It seems clear that in the Helgasaga the hero lived in an outhouse of some sort, under more or less bestial conditions. This outhouse became a hiding-place when concealment took the place of madness as a means of protection against the usurper. In version A, on the other hand, no outhouse appears; Amleth lives with his mother. Now we have seen that Helgi went by a nickname meaning 'wether' and that this nickname probably antedates his identification with Amleth. Note in this connexion the passage in H (Jónsson 9) which reads: þat segja sumir menn, at þeir muni með geitum vera fæddir (the reference is to Hróarr and Helgi). It is probable, then, that version A has preserved the bestiality in its primitive form, and that the outhouse, with its human dog, goat or ram, is a variation of the bestiality theme suggested originally by Helgi's nickname and so found only in the various versions of the Helgasaga. For the ram or goat as a fetish of the Scyldings see above (cap. X).

Two specific details of this part of version A appear elsewhere as well and so are assured for our primitive plot. The first of these is the incident common to A and H, in which Amleth (Helgi) rides horseback so mounted as to face towards the horse's tail. The second detail is one of Amleth's clever sayings, which Saxo tells thus (translation by Elton): as they passed the sandhills, and bade him (Amleth) look at the meal, meaning the sand, he replied that it had been ground small by the hoary tempests of the ocean (Saxo III 89). Now the 10th century Icelandic poet Snæbjörn calls the sea Hamlet's quern (Skáldskaparmál 25). Obviously, then, he was familiar with Hamlet's reply to his companions in a form substantially the same as that given by Saxo.

Just as the courtiers told Amleth that the sand was meal, in order to hear what he would reply, so they called a wolf that crossed his path a colt, and when they found on the beach the rudder of a wrecked ship they told him they had discovered a huge knife. Each time Amleth rose to the occasion. This give and take evidently belongs together, and since one of the riddles (for that is what they amount to) is assured for the primitive plot by Snæbjörn's reference to it, we have a right to include the others as well, in spite of the fact that we know them only from version A. More difficult are the two incidents which from the Shaksperean names may be called the Ophelia and Polonius episodes, although in version A the characters in question go nameless. The Ophelia episode may be outlined as follows: 1) Amleth was suspected of feigning witlessness; 2) certain men were commissioned to test his intelligence by tempting him to sexual indulgence; 3) he was taken off and left alone in a remote spot, whither presently his foster-sister, the chosen temptress, came, ostensibly by chance; 4) his foster-brother warned him of his danger by driving towards him a gadfly with a straw fastened under its tail; 5) Amleth saw the gadfly and understood the danger signal; 6) he therefore, instead of lying with the woman on the spot, took her off to a safer place and there lay with her; 7) he exacted of her a promise not to reveal the fact of their intercourse; 8) upon his return home he admitted having ravished a woman; 9) in response to further questions he stated that his bed had been the hoof of a draught animal, the comb of a cock and the ceiling of a roof; 10) this answer, though right enough (as these are the names of three Jutish plants), was not understood by his hearers and so was greeted with shouts of laughter; 11) the maiden contradicted Amleth's statement that he had ravished her, and as there had been no witnesses of the act Amleth was not believed.

As it stands this episode is clearly the story of a test made to find out whether Amleth actually was a fool. If he ravished the woman, his deed would show that he at least knew what to do with a woman when he got her; if he failed to ravish her his folly would be manifest and would be accepted as genuine. There are certain features of the account however which do not fit in well with the extant motivation and lead us to suspect that this motivation was not the original one. In the first place, the choice of Amleth's foster-sister for a temptress is most extraordinary, if only for the reason that collusion on her part with the intended victim was to be feared. Again, the foster-brother's method of warning Amleth is odd in the extreme, and the facility with which the warning was understood and acted upon can be described only as miraculous. Thirdly, the elaborate apparatus by virtue of which Amleth was able to confound his enemies seems unnatural; a much simpler and more obvious solution would have been to heed the warning by letting the maiden alone. Certainly the finale as we have it is too complex in structure and too clumsily conceived to be truly primitive. Finally, the total lack of parallels in the other versions gives us negative evidence against the episode, though this point is of no great weight.

If however we reject the extant motivation we must offer something better in its place. What have we to go on? Apart from the motivation itself, the chief difficulty in the episode as it stands is the actual rape of the foster-sister. The presence of this feature made necessary all that elaborate scheming which protected Amleth from the consequences of his deed but gave to the episode its clumsy and unprimitive look. We may conclude, then, that the rape of Ophelia was the central incident of the episode in its primitive form, as otherwise an incident so inconvenient to the test motivation would hardly have arisen or, if already present, would have been discarded. Let us throw the extant motivation overboard, then, and reduce the episode to the single incident of the rape of the foster-sister. At once the bestiality of the deed stands out, and its relation to the rest of the tale becomes obvious. The considerations advanced in cap. IX have already led us to assume that Hamlet's folly was genuine at first, and that the conception of it as feigned was a later (though still a very early) development. And in the most primitive form of the tale the youthful (as distinguished from the mature) Hamlet must have been little better than a brute. Indeed, even as late as the 12th century version A he wallows in filth like a beast of the field. There is thus no difficulty in assuming that sexually too he behaved like a lower animal; in Hamlet's own words (to his mother), "brute beasts are naturally incited to pair indiscriminately," and what better explanation could we wish for his rape of his foster-sister? I look upon this rape, then, simply as another expression of the bestiality otherwise so manifest. When the times became less primitive, however, and especially when Hamlet's folly came to be thought of as feigned, the rape in all its crudeness would naturally become offensive, and various devices might be employed to tone it down. The need for toning down would certainly be imperative if (as it is tempting to assume) the foster-sister was originally a true sister — and the Saxonian text itself is not irreconcilable with this assumption. However that may be, the test motivation which we actually find can most readily be explained as an attempt at extenuation; if the maiden were a temptress, deliberately thrown at Amleth by his uncle, our hero could hardly be blamed overmuch for taking advantage of the situation, especially since it gave him another opportunity of indulging in some characteristic trickery, by virtue of which, as so often, he was able to eat his cake and have it too. For the introduction of the feigned madness motif had changed Amleth from a strong fool to a trickster of the first water, both in word and in deed. Hence our episode, though far from primitive as it stands, is a thoroughly Hamletian growth and cannot be explained by outside influence of any sort.

But where did the test motivation come from? Just as the feigned madness motif grew out of Amleth's youthful follies (see cap. IX above), so the various tests to which Amleth was subjected grew, inevitably enough, out of the conception that his folly was feigned. The reasons for this growth are so obvious, and so compelling, that we need not go into the matter, but may turn our attention at once to the tests which actually occur. We have already seen that the Ophelia episode was not originally a test, but acquired its present motivation by a process of remodeling. The riddles likewise need not originally have been tests, although they are so interpreted in version A. The Polonius episode, however, was undoubtedly a test from the beginning; before its introduction into the tale the other tests probably lacked the test motivation, and their present motivation they apparently owe to their contact with the Polonius episode. The episode itself employs the universally familiar motif of the eavesdropper who is caught, and it would be folly to spend time searching for the "sources" of such a theme. Nevertheless there are certain features worth noting. As Feng ostentatiously absents himself from the court one would expect him to do the spying, either alone or in the company of Polonius. His departure probably derives from some orthodox form of the motif, but inasmuch as the Hamlet tale already included an account of his death irreconcilable with the eavesdropping motif he could not be utilized as a fellow-spy. The account of Polonius's death and the disposal of his body combines primitiveness and Hamletian trickery in a most striking manner. The whole episode is clearly of native growth, and any search for parallels would be a waste of time. Hamlet's long harangue to his mother, however, does not belong to the primitive plot but was added by Saxo himself (for such additions see te next volume of this work).

It will have been observed that in the discussion of the Ophelia episode no account was taken of the foster-brother. He is in fact quite superfluous here and, as we saw in cap. X, his warning is not primitive, but grew out of a misunderstood pun. His place in the primitive plot will be discussed below. When the Ophelia episode was given its present motivation the foster-brother was of course available for use in giving the hero help, and the form of the pun dictated the form in which this help should be given.

The Ophelia and Polonius episodes appear only in version A (the Addomolus of AB is evidently based on Saxo). Both should be assigned to the primitive plot, however; their antiquity is manifest, and their failure to hold a place in the Helgasaga (if they ever made their way into it) is explicable enough — with the substitution of concealment for feigned madness any episodes used as intelligence tests would have to go.

The next stage both in A and in the Helgasaga is the exile and return, and in view of the agreement of the versions here this motif must be given a place in the primitive plot. Nevertheless the episode as it stands in A is clearly late, and so does not fall within the scope of this chapter. The reconstruction under these conditions becomes difficult enough. We had best begin by trying to find the primitive function of the foster-brother in the tale. His namesake the Vifill of H ought to help us here, but unfortunately this Vifill by his identification with Viðolfr largely lost his proper part and took over that of another. We do find him sending the princes to Sevill, however, and this activity, which certainly never belonged to Viðolfr, gives us a hint as to the nature of his activities in the primitive story. His home on an island, too, points to an intimate connexion with the exile and return. One may offer, then, the following reconstruction. The faithful follower (foster-brother in A, foster-father in the Helgasaga) is directed by Feng to put Amleth to death secretly, but lets him escape. Feng is given false proof of Amleth's death (compare HH, where the mangled bodies of a bond-woman's sons are offered in evidence). Amleth's funeral obsequies are accordingly performed, but while they are in progress he reappears and executes his vengeance. This reconstruction is supported by certain features of the HH account, more particularly Fróði's consent to the exile, which would indicate an earlier form in which he directed that the boys be led away (to be killed). Again, the reconstruction makes more natural and intelligible the passage in A where Amleth instructs his mother to perform pretended obsequies for him a year after his departure. The history of the Reginn-Regno of the Helgasaga also becomes more intelligible on this hypothesis. In spite of all this, however, our reconstruction has a basis insufficient to give it more than plausibility.

We now come to the vengeance scene itself. Here we will first consider the wooden hooks or nails, the instruments of Amleth's vengeance. Saxo's account of these in version A reads as follows (translation by Elton): He (Amleth) used at times to sit over the fire, and, raking up the embers with his hands, to fashion wooden crooks, and harden them in the fire, shaping at their tips certain barbs, to make them hold more tightly to their fastenings. When asked what he was about, he said that he was preparing sharp javelins to avenge his father. This answer was not a little scoffed at, all men deriding his idle and ridiculous pursuit; but the thing helped his purpose afterwards (Saxo III 88). Substantially the same thing appears in B and AB and so may be assumed for X. The same instruments of vengeance also appear in H at the vengeance scene itself, although we get no preliminary information about them as we do in A, B and AB. So far as I am aware the motif is peculiar to the Hamlet tale and so, like the feigned madness motif, probably grew out of the saga-stuff itself. How can we explain such a development? In the first place, as we have seen, it is clear that Hamlet could take vengeance on his father's murderer only by resorting to a trick or device of some sort. Indeed, he had to pretend to be mad in order to save his own life. This peculiar situation put all the emphasis on his cleverness rather than on his doughtiness, of course. Now the word *krókr* might mean both 'trick, wile' and 'hook.' If Hamlet vanquished the villain by trickery, then, it is easy to see how, more concretely and naively, he might come to vanquish him by the use of hooks. We have, it is true, no direct evidence that *krókr* was used in the native version of the tale: B and AB use *spýta*; H has *nagli*. It seems unlikely, though, that Saxo's *uncus* translates anything else than *krókr* (Danish *krog*). Furthermore, as Detter has pointed out, *nagli* is misunderstood by the retainers of Fróði in H, and this seems to correspond to the incident in A quoted above, where the retainers of Feng (to their sorrow, as it turned out) refused to take seriously Amleth's statement that he was making the hooks to avenge his father with.

In all the versions noted above the hooks (pegs, nails) are used to prevent the king's retainers from leaving the hall. In H the doors of the hall are nailed up; in B and AB the retainers are fastened by their clothes to the benches; in A the hooks serve to fasten the hangings which Amleth spreads like a fishing-net over the drunken retainers. Thereupon in all the versions except B the hall is set on fire and the retainers perish miserably in the flames. In B the retainers, when they find themselves fastened to the benches, get to fighting among themselves and kill each other off. For the king himself a special fate is reserved in A; he is slain by Amleth, who for the purpose makes use of his uncle's own sword. Traces of this special treatment appear in H and HH. From the evidence it is clear that in the primitive plot Hamlet 'burnt in' the king and his followers. This motif is one of the most familiar in Scandian literature, and it undoubtedly reflects a common method of attack. Our tale differs from an ordinary hall-burning, however, in that Hamlet accomplished the whole thing unassisted. His use of brain instead of brawn is characteristic, of course. In H, however, the faithful retainer Reginn assists the brothers.

As to the queen, she is saved in B and AB, and presumably in A. In H and HH she perishes with her husband. In B and AB there would be no point in her death, of course. In HH she is not the mother of the brothers, and is killed because she had egged on her husband to enmity towards his brother. In H she dies voluntarily. In the primitive plot she was probably saved; the Skaane version, at any rate, points in that direction.

Amleth now takes possession of the throne. The long harangue which Saxo puts into his mouth at this point forms no part of the primitive plot, of course. The rest of the tale, as given in version A, is for the most part late, and need not be considered here. The Skaane fragment we have already discussed. The story of Ermuthrud, however, and of Amleth's final death and his widow's marriage to her husband's murderer, does belong to the primitive plot. What was its primitive form? The Helgasaga makes Helgi capture Yrsa on a viking expedition, and we have no reason to doubt the essential historicity of this account. The Ermuthrud story in versoin A probably goes back to the Anglian tale of Þryð, the wife of Offa, however, as we have seen, and according to this tale Þryð came to Offa from overseas (Beowulf 1949 ff.). Version A seems to have combined the two traditions, retaining or rather emphasizing Ermuthrud's initiative but making Amleth meet her abroad. Her location in Scotland (i. e., Ireland?) rather than in

France breaks with both traditions and cannot belong to our primitive plot, which probably ran thus: Amleth makes a viking expedition to the Frankish coast and there encounters a virgin queen or princess named Yrsa or Thruth. She has hitherto been grim to all suitors, but Amleth meets with her favor and she wooes and wins him. The pair then return to Jutland. Finally Amleth falls in battle against his enemy Aðils (later Viglek), and his widow thereupon marries the victor. The first two husbands of Yrsa were thus rolled together in Jutland just as in Norway. The process was not the same in each case, however. The only deed of Helgi's which can lay claim to historicity is that expedition of his on which he captured Yrsa. And this is the only deed properly belonging to the Scyldings of which any trace appears in A. In other words, Helgi and Áli became identified in Jutland before Helgi began to grow as a saga hero. In Norway, on the other hand, the two heroes were not identified until Helgi had attracted to himself deeds properly belonging to other Scyldings and had become a full-fledged saga hero. Hence in Jutland Helgi was absorbed by Áli; in Norway, Áli was absorbed by Helgi, and this absorption must be considered as only another stage of the process by virtue of which Helgi had already drawn to himself much saga-stuff not originally connected with his name.

We may fittingly conclude this chapter and Part I of this work by giving, in abbreviated form, our reconstruction of the primitive plot of the Hamlet tale, assembled, as it were, from the various portions of the analysis above: Kind Ørvendill of Jutland and his younger brother Feng become estranged over Geruth, the elder brother's wife. It finally comes to blows and Feng kills his brother and marries Geruth. He also succeeds to his brother's throne, the rightful heir, Amleth, the son of Ørvendill, being set aside. Amleth fears for his own life and seeks safety in feigned madness. This madness takes the form of brutish, witless behavior together with talk apparently senseless but in reality full of meaning, if one is able to see through it. Amleth's bestial behavior is exemplified in his filthiness and in his rape of his sister (?) or foster-sister. His witlessness further appears in such details as his horseback ride, where he sits facing toward the tail of his mount. The so-called riddles illustrate his practice of giving answers which are both nonsensical and to the point. This is further illustrated by his reply to his faithful retainer Vifill. Amleth spends much of his time in whittling out wooden hooks. When asked why he busies himself thus he replies that he is preparing the hooks to avenge his father with. This reply is not taken seriously, but his skill in making the hooks leads some to suspect that he is not so witless as he appears to be. Feng therefore arranges for Amleth an ostensibly private interview with Geruth, but conceals in the room a spy, viz., the man who had suggested the plan. Amleth, however, suspects something and before unbosoming himself to his mother he finds and kills the spy. Feng now fears the worst and so commissions Vifill to put Amleth to death secretly. Vifill, however, allows him to escape, satisfying Feng of Amleth's death by producing a mangled body (?) which he represents as that of Amleth. Amleth's funeral obsequies are now celebrated, but toward the close of the celebration, when the company is well drunk, Amleth returns, with his hooks renders the retainers helpless and sets fire to the hall. He then proceeds to the king's bower, and kills him there with his own sword. Amleth now assumes the throne. Later he makes a viking expedition to France (later to the British Isles). In the course of this expedition he encounters a virgin queen or princess named Yrsa or Thruth (later Ermuthrud). She had hitherto been grim to her suitors. Amleth, however, meets with her favor, and she wooes and wins him. The pair now return to Jutland. Finally Amleth is killed in battle with his enemy Aðils king of Sweden (later Viglek). Amleth's widow thereupon gives herself to Aðils.